THE BOOK OF
BURNHAM-ON-SEA

(it wasn't 'on Sea' until 1919)
The Ebb and Flow of a Somerset Seaside Town

by Winston H. Thomas

Edited, with additional material by Robert F. Thomas

HALSGROVE

First published in Great Britain in 2011

British Library Cataloguing-in-Publication Data
A CIP record for this title is available from the British Library

ISBN 978 0 85704 099 2

HALSGROVE
Halsgrove House,
Ryelands Business Park,
Bagley Road, Wellington, Somerset TA21 9PZ
Tel: 01823 653777   Fax: 01823 216796
email: sales@halsgrove.com

Part of the Halsgrove group of companies.
Information on all Halsgrove titles is available at: www.halsgrove.com

Printed and bound in the UK by the MPG Books Group

CONTENTS

Acknowledgements

(In no particular order)

Somerset County Library, Burnham on Sea branch; for checking items with the enquiry desk and saving me many trips to Taunton.

Somerset County Library, Local Studies library, Taunton (now part of Somerset Heritage Centre); for excerpts from local newspapers, their extensive collection of books and papers on local topics and large scale local maps.

Cornish Studies Library, Redruth; for excerpts from local newspapers.

Weston Library; for excerpts from local newspapers.

Somerset County Record Office, Taunton (now part of Somerset Heritage Centre); for access to old maps, documents and other papers.

The Environment Agency; for maps and information on past floods in the area.

To the friends, relatives and the many other people, who have all helped with nuggets of information, advice, and encouragement over the years that this book has been in preparation and without which it would be a much poorer offering. I ask that you forgive me for not mentioning your name here. It is not because I am too lazy to make a list of names, rather that I would hate to hurt anyone's feelings by inadvertently omitting one single person from such an inevitably long list.

Preface

Whilst, understandably, fairly continuous records relating to our national, political and social history have survived for centuries, unfortunately there is much less written evidence remaining available to anyone attempting to write the history of a small provincial town. It is therefore a matter of great importance that records such as old documents, books, manuscripts, photographs and artefacts relating to the locality, including any that may be in private ownership, be preserved. With that object in view Somerset Heritage Centre and the County Museum Service are usually pleased to accept any suitable historical material offered to them, and have the necessary facilities available for the repair, and preservation in ideal conditions of any such items.

The study of local history has become a matter of keen interest to many people wanting to learn more about where they are living, or were born. Evidence of this is to be found in the number of archaeological and local history societies as well as genealogical groups that now exist in communities of all sizes.

As a native of Burnham I have from my school days been intensely interested in the history of this locality and while having no pretensions to being either a writer or historian I have endeavoured within the following pages to set forth as much information as I can of the story of Burnham as I have known it.

When a book is concerned with local history, its purpose is better served by setting forth the facts in some detail than in general terms, and I make no apology for doing this as the reader is often enabled thereby to relate the written word with other facts as he or she knows them and so obtain a more complete picture. My family, although by no means claiming to be the one longest resident here, has had however, an unbroken period of residence in Burnham for over 135 years[1]. I recall many occasions when my parents, grandparents and many old inhabitants long since departed spoke to me of what the town looked like and what characters and events made up the local scene from the early part of Queen Victoria's reign down to the earliest years of my own recollection, before the First World War.

Many families, including my own, possessed picture post-card albums, some of which with constant use eventually disintegrated making it necessary in the absence of replacements to store them elsewhere. Regretfully, this caused the loss of many, but among those surviving cards and photographs are a number of old photographs dating from the mid 1880s showing views of Burnham greatly different in appearance from the town we are familiar with today.

My search for all such material concerning Burnham's past has been widespread and involved a great deal of travelling, calling on people who had either themselves at one time lived locally here, or who had relatives who had done so; as well as considerable correspondence with one time residents at home and abroad. Generally speaking requests for information, help in loan of old photographs for copying, and access to old documents in private ownership have been sympathetically received, although sadly in the course of this research it has become evident that over the years a great deal of valuable material has been destroyed, mainly due to a lack if interest or awareness of its historical value by the current owners.

Although every effort has been made to ensure factual accuracy which is the keystone of such a work as this, it is perhaps inevitable that an occasional error will occur particularly when my own recollection of events in my lifetime may, at times, be at variance with those of my contemporaries. I therefore ask all readers to accept this history of Burnham as a sincere attempt to set out as comprehensively as possible for the present and the future inhabitants of this town its story and ask for their indulgence for any errors and omissions of which I may unwittingly be guilty.

Winston H. Thomas

---

1 This was written some time before 1980.

Foreword

Not long before my father's death during the 1980s it became apparent that he would never be able to complete the book about Burnham that he had laboured so long over. It has therefore fallen to me to take up the pen where he laid it down. I have endeavoured to use his own words where possible and have only altered them or added my own when I considered it necessary from a point of clarification or to add something which only came to light or happened since his death.

(A small but significant point, is that although this is *The Book of Burnham on Sea*, it is more acurately 'The Book of Burnham', as on the Sea was not added until 1919/20.)

One of the problems encountered when attempting to write a book on local history, regardless of whether it is about Burnham or Birmingham, is changing boundaries. Unlike Birmingham where nearby villages have been absorbed and become suburbs as the boundaries have been pushed ever outward, the shape of Burnham has changed radically as for various reasons the boundaries have been moved. One has to consider, also, the boundaries as perceived by those living in the area, especially those with families which have lived in the locality for several generations. For example, many older people in Highbridge feel wronged by the town being incorporated with Burnham in 1933 in spite of the fact that until 1860 after the building of Saint John's church it had been part of the parish of Burnham for several centuries, not the few relatively brief decades that they had been separated. For this reason, people,

places and events in Highbridge have been included where considered appropriate but without any intention of usurping the function of any current or future book specifically about that town.

It seems foolish not to bring the work as up to date as possible on the basis of what happens today will be history tomorrow, and contemporary reports are preferable to hearsay or supposition. I, therefore, make no apology for bringing this work as up to date as is practicably possible, and 2010 is a nice tidy date to finish on, although history continues to be created every day.

Although any book on local history requires to be illustrated, care has been taken in this instance to avoid producing yet another book of pretty pictures. Illustrations, as the word implies, should complement and enhance one's understanding of the text, and that is the reason for which they have been used although I must admit that one or two have been included solely on the basis of my liking for them – the matriarchal figure of Fanny Dowes and the fishmonger with 'a fag in his gob' being two of my special favourites.

One of the greatest problems that my father and I encountered in the compilation of this book was 'What do we include, and what do we leave out?' – always a problem in a work of this nature. I hope that this book will answer many of your questions about our town, but not all of them, so that you may be stimulated to carry out further research of your own

Robert F. Thomas.
August 2010

Chapter 1

In the Beginning

Although Burnham as a defined area on the west coast of Somerset standing at the mouth of the River Parret is known to have existed from the earliest days of recorded English history, comparatively little written material has survived covering the period of about nine hundred years from the reign of Alfred The Great **871-901** to the closing years of the eighteenth century. Most of that which has, is to be found in the Cathedral archives at Wells and the new Somerset Heritage Centre, which also holds the older Burnham parish church records. In addition to such records as these, others were also to be found in private collections, one of the largest and most interesting of which was that of Mr William Stoate of Burnham who had long been interested in both national and local history. His collection consisted of numerous ancient documents, old books, maps, and drawings many of them concerned with some aspect or other of Burnham past[2].

Remains of Roman flooring, cobbled paving and pieces of pottery found when excavating for factory foundations in the Worston Road area during the early **1950s**, together with the discovery of the foundations of a Romano-British temple on the south eastern part of Brean Down overlooking the River Axe, and the large number of coins, pottery and artefacts found in the surrounding area provide fairly conclusive evidence that a settlement of some sort existed here during the Roman occupation.

The proximity of the lead mines on the Mendip Hills, made this part of the coast, between the mouth of the River Brue and Brean Down, a convenient place not just for sea fishing but for beaching trading ships for loading and off-loading their cargoes. The suitability of the beach for this purpose is borne out by the fact that between **1861** and **1906** colliers were regularly run ashore just south of the low lighthouse where they were unloaded into wagons on a temporary railway track specially laid through the sand dunes for the purpose by a local family of coal and salt merchants named Hodges who lived at 'Wharf Cottage' which stood on land between 'Ellen's Cottages' and the drive to Saint Anne's Villa, part of which is now Gore Road.

The effect of the Roman withdrawal on the native population after over 400 years of occupation would have been no less catastrophic here than in any other part of the country. With the absence of Roman administration, laws, manners, and customs the Dark Ages had arrived. This was the time when fact became inextricably mixed with fiction, when the legends with which we are familiar first became part of our local and then national folklore; the time of King Arthur and of Merlin, both of whom have particularly strong local associations.

The story of the visits of St Joseph of Arimathea to the West Country, supposedly bearing the Chalice used at the Last Supper and for the recovery of which many of the Knights of the Round Table dedicated their lives is perpetuated in some of the place names in the area. Local tradition and usage gives Paradise as the land between Stoddens Road and Brent Broad and stretching from Middle Burnham to that part of the coast upon which it is popularly supposed that St Joseph made his landfall and with his small band of supporters walked across the fields to the Mendips passing through the ancient villages of Priddy and Charterhouse before descending to the plain and so on to Glastonbury and Weary all Hill (corrupted to Wirrall Hill) in a part of Glastonbury also known as Paradise. Here grows the Holy Thorn which reputedly sprang from St Joseph's staff which took root there. Logic dictates that although there may be some justification for 'Paradise' being a part of Glastonbury there can be none for the Burnham one which is based on its being the nearest point to the coast to Glastonbury; a route that would have been virtually impossible in those days when most of the land, that was not flooded, was dangerous bog. The suggested route along the Mendips to Glastonbury is only

---

2   After the death of William Stoate some of his papers passed into the collection of Mr E.A. Baker of Weston super Mare.

tenable if the journey to Glastonbury was secondary to trading visits to the mines at Priddy and Charterhouse. Even so, such a route would be much more likely to have started nearer Brean Down. This supposition is supported by the fact that many experts, including Dutch engineers with long experience of land drainage problems in their own country, expressed the view that at one time the waters of the River Brue made their outlet into the Bristol Channel between Burnham and Brean Down, at more than one point via much smaller streams. The existence of these several streams resulted in the formation of what could only be described as a delta. The way in which the river meanders between the Highbridge and Huntspill banks between the Clyce Bridge and its confluence with the River Parret, even today, gives us some idea of how it might have been in those earlier times. In the absence of artificial barriers of sufficient size and substance to prevent tidal water from reversing the flow of these streams, the whole of this area was subject to almost continuous flooding which led ultimately to the creation of the Brent Marsh. Not the ideal place to make landfall. In this unstable condition, although covering many thousands of acres this vast area was quite unproductive which no doubt explains why no reference was made to it when a great land survey was made about **900**.

There are some who believe that St Joseph of Arimathea who was, supposedly a merchant, on an earlier trading visit, was accompanied by Christ Himself[3] who, taking the Mendip route to Glastonbury, inspired Blake to compose the verses of that well known hymn Jerusalem:-

And did those feet in ancient time
Walk upon England's mountains green,
And was the holy Lamb of God
On England's pleasant pastures seen.

And did the countenance divine
Shine forth upon our clouded hills
And was Jerusalem builded here
Among those dark satanic mills.

The clouded hills referred to by Blake in this hymn are considered by many to be an allusion to the Mendips which extend eastward across Somerset from Brean Down, with the Satanic Mills, being the lead mines which were already well known to the Romans and Levantine traders of the time. This is by no means a purely local legend. Some years ago two American ladies while on a visit to Burnham asked to be directed to Paradise explaining that as members of a religious organization in the United States they had been asked by fellow members to follow the ancient Mendip route taken by St Joseph and, on their return, give an accurate and detailed account of their experience.

During the occupation of Britain by the Romans all the country south of the Mendips and the Bristol Channel coast was called the Britannia Prima and it was not until some three hundred years after they had left in **410** that this part of the country became known as Somerset.

The inhabitants of these parts were compelled by the nature of the terrain and climatic conditions to live in dwellings constructed around these meres and marshes on ground well above the average water level. Because of the manner and nature of their existence they became known as the Seomersaetons (Seo-Mer-Saeton) i.e. dwellers by the sea and meres (lakes)[4]. So marshy was the land around Brent Knoll that the monks of Glastonbury in an ancient grant of theirs dubbed it Mons Ranarum (Frogs' Mount, or Island of Frogs).

A further link with that distant past is also to be found in the name Mark Causeway which was the main track way through the marsh lands to the higher ground at

Blackford and Wedmore. It was the Danish invaders ignorance of the whereabouts of these devious trackways through the Somerset marshlands that made King Alfred's fortified camp at Athelney well nigh impregnable. Similarly, some eighteen miles or so to the south west of Burnham, protected by the encompassing sedge meres lay King Arthur's supposed retreat the mystic Isle of Avalon immortalized by Mallory in his *Mort D'Arthur*.

Wedmore, later to become famous on account of its association with Alfred the Great, together with Brent Knoll and Glastonbury Tor, represented the only permanently dry land between the Mendip and the Polden Hills, and really were islands in the wetlands. Burnham, Brean (Berrow, as such, did not exist then) and many other small settlements were situated in an area largely below sea level, which at one time, in the absence of any system of land drainage remained waterlogged most of the time, and with some parts permanently covered by large stretches of water formed what was in effect a large lagoon.

---

3 *Did our Lord visit Britain*, by Rev. C.C. Dobson M.A. 1936.

4 Another suggested origin for the name Somerset is that because of the marshy nature of the landscape the people lived on higher (drier) land during the winter and only came down to the lowlands in the summer, hence the Land of the Summer People.

The Romans' departure from Britain was noted in the Anglo Saxon Chronicle, "Before leaving the Romans collected all the treasure that were in Britain and hid them in the ground so that no-one could find them afterwards, and took some with them into Gaul"; a statement supported by the number of Roman ruins and hoards that are still being, literally, turned up.

The Dark Ages which followed their lengthy occupation had by now all but passed into limbo. The country from north to south was being attacked in a most ferocious manner by, at one time or another, the Picts and the Scots and, from the Continental mainland, by the Angles, the Jutes and the Danes, and it was in the area around Burnham that King Alfred was to achieve his most outstanding victory over the Danish invaders which resulted in the signing of the Treaty of Peace with Guthrum (Godrum), at Wedmore in **878**.

The account of this victory in the Anglo Saxon Chronicle states that after their defeat "the enemy gave Alfred preliminary hostages and great oaths that they would leave his kingdom and promised that their King Guthrum should receive baptism, and they kept their promises". Three weeks later Guthrum with thirty of the most important men in his army came to him at Aller which is near to Athelney and the King stood sponsor to him at his baptism there, and the unbinding of the Chrism[5] took place at Wedmore. He was twelve days with Alfred and honoured him and his companions greatly with gifts.

Ninth century residents of Burnham would have had a grandstand view of the naval battle fought so successfully against the Danes by Alfred out in Bridgwater Bay and covering the area of sea between Watchet and Combwich (at that time occupied by the Dane Odda who had greatly fortified it) "the Danes had a fleet in the Severn Sea under Hubba[6] and Inguar. These landed at some place on the north coast of Dumnonia (Devon) which at that time extended as far as the River Parret". Both Hubba and Inguar were killed, together with some twelve hundred of their men.

The Anglo Saxon Chronicle states that "the Danes used warships which they had built many years before. King Alfred had Along ships" built, to oppose these Danish warships. "Many were almost twice as long as those of the enemy. Some had sixty oars; some, more,

and were both swifter and steadier, also higher than the enemy's. They were built neither on the Friesian nor Danish patterns but as Alfred, in his wisdom, considered would be most useful in these waters".

There can be no doubt that Alfred was the first King to appreciate the importance of a strong navy. It must be remembered, though, that "The winning side writes the history books" and that as a newcomer to naval warfare, the reports of his victories at sea are perhaps, to some extent self congratulatory and therefore not as accurate as they might have been although without in any way detracting from his achievement.

Place names in this region of Somerset serve as constant reminders of those times. Those mid channel outliers of the Mendip hills, the islands of Steep and Flat Holm[7] together with Botestal Rocks by Stolford and nearby Danesboro with Battleborough on the southeast shoulder of Brent Knoll all have Danish origins.

That it was much about the same time that the Saxon kingdom of Wessex was established by Berdic in **495** that Burnham became so named is not an unreasonable assumption to make. The definition of the name is of Saxon origin: 'Ham' a settlement 'Burne' a stream or river or as J. R. Churchill more widely interpreted its meaning 'the haunt of man beside a flowing stream'.

The use of the word Hams in the same context is again to be found in the place name of that area a few miles south of Burnham known as Pawlett Hams whose lush fields lie along the east bank of the great bend in the River Parrett after it has passed Dunball. Similarly, the name of Keynsham near Bristol derives from the original 'Keynes Hams'. This is not a particularly local usage as there are also the South Hams in Devon.

King Alfred was certainly Lord of the Manor of Burnham and makes mention in his will, of it being part of his demesne. This fits with the claim that, in common with other land between Glastonbury and the sea being at one time monastic property, most of which was returned to the control of the abbey after the defeat of the Danes; Burnham was excepted and retained by the King, because of its perceived strategic importance.

Alfred was succeeded by his son Edward the Elder **(901-925)** in whose reign the manor of Burnham

---

5 Unbinding or loosing the Chrism (depending on which translation from the Saxon is used) refers to the opening, or unsealing, of the flask in which the Chrism (the holy oil used for baptismal and other religious purposes) was transported. Nowadays a cork or screw stoppered bottle would be more likely, but in Alfred's day a leather cap or bung of some type secured with cord or thong would have been the norm hence unbinding.

6 Hubba is still remembered in the name Uphill, corrupted from Hubba's Pill, or river, and Hobb's Boat (Hubba's Boat) Inn at Lympsham near Weston super Mare.

7 Holm being Danish for island.

was held by Brixi a Saxon thegn who "gelded for four hides", that is to say he paid a tax levied on it by way of Danegeld, the defence of the realm contribution exacted from all land owners in those troubled times and although used originally for making war against the Danes it later devolved into becoming a permanent source of revenue; in much the same way as Motor Tax has developed in modern times.

It was about this time that the system of dividing the country into groups of families varying from one hundred to one hundred and twenty to form one corporate body to be known as a Hundred was set up. A hide describes an area of land considered to be sufficiently large to adequately maintain one family and a hundred hides became the Hundred. The terms Hide and Hundred may sound strange to our ears but the principal was sound in that it has only been modified slightly to give us the Local Government districts and post codes that we are using over a thousand years later, although as families varied somewhat in size the term Hide of necessity was not an exact measurement of land area, especially as no two plots of land were equally productive.

One such Hundred was that of Bempstone in which the Manor of Burnham was situated. Bempstone Hundred embraced an area extending from the sea in the west to the Hundred of Glaston in the east and from Brent and Wrington Hundred in the north to the Hundred of Huntspill in the south. Although modified at a later date this was therefore mainly a system of land division according to its population and not of area, a fact which accounts for

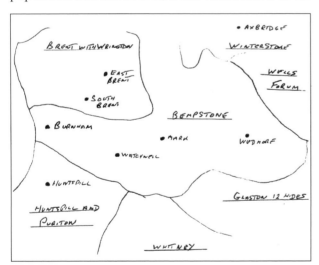

Sketch map showing Bempstone and the surrounding hundreds of Brent with Wrington, Winterstoke, Wells Forum, Huntspill and Puriton, Whitney, and Glaston 12 Hides.

the variation in size between the forty three Hundreds which make up the county of Somerset[8].

In **1286**, in a matter concerning the settlement of a dispute between Johannes Tregoz and Johanne Coggan Burnham is mentioned as being in the Hundred of Bempstone[9] and that Johannes Tregoz holds East Burnham and West Burnham from the aforesaid Johanne Coggan for the service of one Knight and the same Johanne holds them from the king and this same John Tregoz in **1285** was given the right to hold a fair annually at Burnham of which he was for some years Lord of the Manor. The Tregoz family came over to England with the Conqueror from Tessy-Sur-Vire.

The 'Description of England', better known by its nickname 'Domesday Book', that comprehensive record of all lands and occupiers thereof together with inventories of all manner of things therein, compiled in **1086** by order of William the Conqueror states that "Walter himself holds Burnham". This Walter-de-Dowai, an acquisitive Norman baron had loyally supported William in his subjugation of the English and was in consequence, richly rewarded by being given the Manor of Burnham together with many others between Bampton and Worle.

Striking evidence is to be found in the Domesday record of the ravages which were committed in this process of subjugation; the number of houses in the towns being reduced on average to around one half of the number existing in the days of Edward the Confessor. This harsh treatment meted out to those living in the more populated areas might have been hardly worth the effort involved in such a remote area as Burnham where until well into the nineteenth century no properly made up approach roads existed but this was not so. Notwithstanding its remoteness, Burnham did not escape the arbitrary manner in which land in general had been confiscated since the Conquest by those in a position to do so, which, understandably gave rise eventually to numerous situations where rightful ownership and boundary limits were matters very much in dispute before the courts. There are also, of course, individuals, contentious by nature, who will, regardless of the outcome, resort to litigation, given the opportunity to do so, and it appears that even during the middle ages Burnham folk were prone to indulge themselves of this luxury, not infrequently having recourse to action in the high court to settle such issues that in this present age would commonly be dealt with by the county courts.

8   We see the same thing with District Councils and post codes, both of which are based on the number of dwellings they serve.

9   Kirby's Quest for Somerset.

10

Among such litigants there appeared from time to time members of the De Marisco family whose names occur frequently in the records covering Burnham and the surrounding district for a period of almost two hundred years from the middle of the twelfth century onward. The De Mariscos were owners of Lundy Island from **1150** until **1289** with a gap of forty years from **1242** until **1281** when because of the piratical activities of some of them, William De Marisco[10] in particular, it became forfeit to the crown. This royal encumbrance might well have been the aftermath of an earlier dispute for an entry in the Pedes Finium[11] **1196-1307** (Somerset Record Society pp. 9/10 no 66) states **1202** King John): "An action tried at Westminster between Nicholas De Hioilly claimant and Henneri Seinte More tenant for all the land of William De Marisco in Hunespill and all the village of Cameleg and with all appurtenances which the said Nicholas claimed from William De Marisco and by confirmation of the King. Plea being brought between them then Henneri conceded to Nicholas and his heirs the said land in Hunespill and Cameleg to be held by himself by the farm of £10 per annum payable 100/- at Easter and 100/- at Michaelmas until the brothers of the Knights Templar or their successors shall recover the Isle of Lundy which William De Marisco holds. When the said Knights Templar shall recover the said Island the said Nicholas and his heirs shall be quit of the said farm and the land at Hunespill."

Again in Pedes Finium (ibid. no 156 p 340 Edward 1305/61.): in an action at Westminster on the morrow of the Purification between Nicholas De Langbard querant and John De Marisco of Burnham deforciant for a messuage and a virgate[12] of land at Burnham juxta South Brent, plea of covenant was summoned. John acknowledged the right of Nicholas to hold of the chief lords of that fee; and he warranted the same. Fordus John was given £20 sterling by Nicholas.

There were from time to time, however other actions between members of local families which were brought before the courts less as matters of dispute but oft times mainly for the purpose of getting an established title to the land in question entered in the court records solely for the benefit of any successors. Such a case was one tried at Shirebourn (Sherbourne) (Pedes Finium S.R.S. p146 No 67) Henry III **1248** . In the three weeks of John the Baptist between Thomas De Rammesden and his wife Isabella as queriants against Nicholas De Stawell defendant for two parts of a virgate of land at Bergh (Berrow) two parts of thirty acres of arable land and thirty acres of meadow at Burnham, and half a virgate of land at Brene (Brean). The outcome of this action was that De Stawell acknowledged the right of Thomas and Isabella to hold the land as a gift from him, subject to the payment by them to him of a half pound of pepper annually at Michaelmas, and also as the feudal system was then in operation to discharge on behalf of Nicholas his liability of service to his chief lord in respect of that land; which service was to be given in perpetuity and for which Nicholas gave them 40 marks.[13] The names of the parties to this action again appear with others similar in the records of cases tried at the Great Assize held at Ioelcester (Ilchester) and subsequently during the reign of Henry III and vary but little in substance between one another, and no doubt because of the many new laws relating to the ownership and tenure of land, which were passed during the reign of his son Edward I there appears to be little abatement in the number of lawsuits concerning ownership of land at Burnham which the courts were called to adjudicate upon throughout his and the ensuing reign of Edward II. Land and other property at Worthestone (Worston) and Honespille (Huntspill) often being the subject of such actions, In fact during the latter's reign even the actual ownership of the manor of Burnham was several times in dispute.

In these times even such an isolated area as this was not devoid of crime, as the rolls of the itinerant judges (the forerunners of our circuit judges) record. The following two cases[14] are of some interest. Richard Brente, son of Adam Murbein was arraigned on a charge of theft. He wisely elected to be tried by a jury of Burnham men[15] in preference to trial by ordeal and they after due deliberation found him not guilty. On a much more serious charge, that of horse stealing, the same jury found him unfit to plead as he was considered to be suffering from madness at the time of the offence and therefore lunatic. He was in conse-

---

10 William De Marisco was a son of Geoffrey De Marisco, Chief Justice of Ireland in the reign of Henry III. *The History of Lundy*, L.R.W.Lloyd. Retribution eventually overtook him when a hastily recruited lynch mob pursued and caught him, after which he was hanged, drawn and quartered.

11 Literally foot of fines. Fines in this context are not a punishment for wrong doing , but a legal. charge on property.

12 An imprecisely defined area of land in much the same way that a close is an unspecified area that is enclosed.

13 Unlike the mark which was the currency of Germany and other countries until the late twentieth century, the mark in this context is a unit of accounting which was universally recognized among most trading nations, in the same way that the dollar is used today.

14 Somerset Pleas vol. 2 Henry III, pp 58 & 248.

15 Maybe this is why the Old Court House and Court Farm were so named. Certainly the building was old enough.

quence put in bond to be of good behaviour for an indefinite period.

A matter of a far more serious nature was that concerning a burglary at the home of Matthew the Chaplain when thieves broke into his house at Burnham, for in addition to ransacking the place they also assaulted and bound Walter his clerk and murdered the chaplain's brother Thomas when he attempted to prevent their getaway. Sadly there is no indication in the records that the miscreants were ever caught and brought to justice.

Moving forward 100 years records show that some Burnham folk had still not lost their appetite for litigation and by reason of the information it provides in just one instance regarding the origin of local place names the following brief details are of interest. At the Hilary Term in the Queen's Court at Westminster in **1579**, before Her Majesty's justices James Dyer, Roger Manwood, Robert Morrison and Thomas Mead an agreement was reached between Christopher Kenn plaintiff and John Grimes and his wife Joan defendants concerning two messuages, two curtilages, two gardens, two orchards, six acres of land, twenty acres of meadows, 50 acres of pasture, sixty acres of furze and heath and forty acres of moor all within Loveland[16] at Burnham and also at Huntspill and Pawlett, the terms agreed finally between the parties and approved by the court were that the said Christopher Kenn should pay to the said John and Joan Griggs the sum of £40 sterling in complete and absolute settlement of their claim against him.

---

16 Loveland, an area to the East of Burnham, lives on in Love Lane, which is known to have been so called for something in the region of two hundred years.

Chapter 2

Early Years

Until Queen Victoria's reign the lines of communication by land between Burnham and the outside world were the ancient sandy track called Stoaten Lane[17] which roughly followed the line of the present Stoddens Road to Middle Burnham where it was joined by Love Lane, before continuing, via Edymede (Edithmead) to the Bridgwater turnpike (A38) with a similar track running from Burnham church to Highbridge which provided a second link with the turnpike. A visitor to Burnham in the eighteenth century described these two tracks as being sandy lanes so full of holes as to make it well nigh impossible for a wheeled conveyance to pass that way, and added that two miles of this was more than enough to deter all but the most determined traveller and that until some marked improvement was effected Burnham would remain isolated and remote from other parts of Somerset. Sandy Way (Burnham Road) was still very much a sandy way when the Rev. Dupuis walked along it from Highbridge railway station in **1865**.

In spite of such criticism nothing much was done to improve the situation and in the **1830s** Paradise Road (Berrow Road), still but a sandy track bordering the dunes was in so bad a state that it brought forth the comment that 'two horses are insufficient to pull a coach over it' which probably accounts for Dr Walker King's[18] use of a four-in-hand when travelling around the neighbourhood on his parochial duties. Although some improvement in the state of the local highways was effected toward the end of the nineteenth century by rolling in crushed limestone to provide a more durable metalled surface even up to as late a date as **1900**. Photographs clearly show that the condition of the local approach roads left much to be desired. In fact the streets in all parts of the town, while in the main devoid of pot holes lacked even a basic tarred surface making it impossible to keep them properly clean for any length of time. It was not to be wondered at that in those early days of motoring the tremendous clouds of dust rising from un-tarred roads as cars 'scorched'[19] past made the wearing of goggles and veils an absolute necessity and left local hedgerows covered with a thick white deposit.

Writing to a Mr Billingsley[20], a friend of his, in **1794** Richard Locke[21] commented that, "£20 is sufficient to build a cottage of ye scrapings of ye roads and planting an half acre to orchard surrounded thick with willow much wanted by our fisheries." (Presumably for fish baskets and salmon butts). These road scrapings together with clay removed when ditches were thrown and suitably re-enforced with straw became the cob[22] with which many of the cottages were constructed. Their walls were very thick which made them cool in summer and warm in winter. Until they were pulled down in **1898** a number of such cottages stood on the north side of Love Lane between the present council houses and the roundabout, their internal walls were of wood frame, covered with reeds and plaster.

Apart from the old buildings that front the east side of Victoria Street, in general terms it was not until **1837** the year of Queen Victoria's accession that the

---

17 Stoddens is a corruption of Stoatens Lane = The lane of the stoats. The en suffix serving to create an adjectival form of a noun or verb, as in wooden or boughten.

18 See Chapter 9.

19 The Motor Car Act 1903 raised the speed limit from 14 to 20 MPH.

20 Almost certainly John Billingsley, who was engaged at the time in producing a survey of the drainage of the surrounding moors.

21 See Chapter 9.

22 Cob is a mixture of clay, sand or gravel and straw combined in much the same way as the Egyptians made (and still make) mud bricks. Because the nature of the clay has not been changed by firing in a kiln it retains its hygroscopic properties and acts like a wick allowing moisture from the ground to soak up through and evaporate through the wall surfaces. Buildings made of cob can last for centuries as long as this process continues uninterrupted, even when the structure is close to water. If however the surface of the wall becomes impervious either by plastering or painting then the clay resumes its semi-liquid state and the structure collapses.

first of a succession of individual buildings and terraces were created that over the following sixty years or so were to become the 'Old Burnham', as it was and as it remained for so many years until the tremendous expansion occurred when the outlying areas of the amalgamated urban districts of Burnham and Highbridge were developed in the years following the war of **1939-45**. A very clear picture of the layout of the two towns in the early nineteenth century is provided by the survey carried out by James Peachy Williams a land surveyor of Bridgwater on behalf of the Tithe Commissioners in **1838**. Comparing this with the O. S. map surveyed in **1884** shows clearly how Burnham developed during the first fifty years of Victoria's reign. The map produced from this earlier survey covering the Burnham and Highbridge area is of a similar scale, which makes direct comparison fairly easy. Used in conjunction with the register to which it relates it is possible to determine in some detail the appearance of Burnham at that time and the names of the principal inhabitants.

Victoria Street, together with Oxford Street and Manor Road[23] are the oldest streets in the town with the back to backs of George Street and Chapel Street following close behind. There can be little doubt after inspection of the deeds appertaining to several of the properties on the east side of Victoria Street that nothing now remains of the few isolated dwellings that stood near the church at the end of the eighteenth century referred to by Richard Locke in his writings about the area, although there is no doubt that some of these old buildings did survive for many years. Evidence of this being in the interview given on his retirement in **1918** by George Miles[24] a master butcher of Burnham, then over eighty years old who spoke of seeing thatched fisherman's cottages in Victoria Street opposite where the Ritz cinema now stands. In addition to these there was, until quite recently, a building at the back of what is now (**2010**) Barclays Bank that had all the appearances of having been a pair of small brick built cottages with sloping upstairs ceilings.

Until they were pulled down during the first decade of the twentieth century to provide a site for Mr Sherrell's new bakery[25] and confectionery shop at 53 Victoria Street and the small house adjoining it, there stood some very old cottages which were built entirely of cob. There can be little doubt that these were stand-

Portion of Tithe map showing central Burnham.

ing there in Locke's time. Further evidence indicating the considerable age of these cottages was provided by some ancient oak panelling which had been plastered over and which literally came to light at the time of the demolition. Most of the remaining buildings on the east side of Victoria Street were built during the first thirty or so years of the nineteenth century with the exception of the two one time cottages opposite the Ritz which appear to be much older.

The *Kelly's Directory of Somerset* for **1939** shows Messrs Tuckers Garages as occupying their new premises at 47 Victoria Street[26] which was built on the site of Ivy Lodge, a regency period house which for some ten years previously had been the house and surgery of Mr J. Clement Shuffrey the local dentist.

Apart from being converted into business premises by the installation of a variety of shop fronts over the years and the removal of all the front gardens bar two,[27] the building line southward from number 45 remains as it was originally, excepting that it became

---

23 Manor Road was at one time considered as part of Oxford Street. Even earlier, together with Highbridge Road, they were known as Church Street.

24 *Burnham Gazette* 02/02/1918.

25 Although the property has had several new shop fronts since Mr Sherrell's day it can still be easily identified by its balustraded parapet.

26 2009 and this property has been demolished and the site cleared for redevelopment.

27 The gardens of the properties referred to, Nos. 31 and 29 have since been concreted over but their side walls still remain (2009).

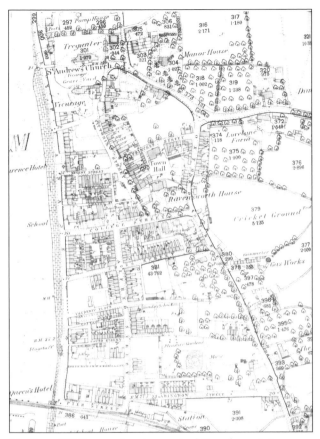

Court Farm (The Old Court House).

Portion of O S map showing central Burnham. 1st edition, surveyed 1884. Note railway track running down the jetty with a branch off to the lifeboat house. The rectangular shape bottom left is the reservoir which held the water used for flushing out the gut – its remains are still visible when the beach level is low enough.

necessary in **1859** to demolish two or three houses to provide an entrance into the new roadway then being laid down and which was opened up in **1863** and called Princess Street, no doubt as a compliment to the Princess Alexandra of Denmark who in that year married the Prince of Wales, later Edward VII.

Other than St Andrew's church the oldest building in twentieth century Burnham was the old Court House[28] which when advertised for sale was described as a thirteenth century Building. It stood in extensive grounds on the west side of the Berrow Road. Constructed of stone, with mullioned windows, flagstones on the ground floor and a Jacobean staircase giving access to the upper rooms, it was said to have at one time been used by the monks from Glastonbury as a fishing lodge which seems more than likely as records show that the abbey had estates in this area. Regardless of whether the building was a court house during its early years there is no doubt that it was officially known as Court Farm from **1884**

up until the time of its sale in **1929** when it was bought by a local builder who pulled it down and erected a row of semi-detached houses on the site.

Houses built on site of Court Farm. Viewed from similar viewpoint to 4 (Blytheway).

At the time of the survey, anyone walking to Burnham from Berrow, having passed the Wellington Hotel on their right would have continued past London House, then Court Farm, with Ivy Farm almost opposite. Next came Paradise Farm on the left and Laburnum (more recently La Burnham) Cottage on the right with the high Lighthouse now not far off, after passing which St Ann's Villa away on the right amid the sand dunes with its long drive reaching down to Berrow Road (Paradise Road as it was then known) and to which massive wrought iron gates gave entrance with the gate keeper's lodge just inside. The lower part of that driveway is now (minus its gates and much widened) Gore Road, the gates having been removed, on the development of the Glen Hilda Estate in **1909**, to Rosewood Farm where they remained until that part of Love Lane was widened in **1974/5**.

Opposite the drive to St Ann's was, as now, the top end of Stoddens Road (then Stoaten Lane). There were only three houses in the lane at the time of the **1838** survey, two of them standing opposite each other midway between the present junction with Rectory

---

28   At that time The Old Court House, officially known as Court Farm, was in the parish of Berrow which extended to Brent Broad, just north of the Lighthouse.

High Light with chimney for original oil lamp – viewed from the Berrow Road.

Road and Middle Burnham; the third being Stoddens Farm, the only one now remaining. Neighbouring Middle Burnham Farm dates from much the same period, as do most of the older farmhouses between Middle Burnham and the Turnpike (now the A38 Bristol Road). There is physical evidence that some, if not all, of these farms were largely committed to dairying, in the existence of a grove of Conker[29] trees at the eastern foot of the bridge over the railway line.

Continuing southward from St Ann's Villa and

Another group of happy hay-makers on another farm – note the barrel of cider. In those days a cider allowance was often part of a labourer's wages.

Hay making, using real horse power at Middle Burnham Farm.

the top of Stoddens Road the next building of any consequence is the unusually shaped building known now as the Colony, but known at the time as Dod's Cottages,[30] and identified as such on the **1838** map. Although the entrance gates are long gone, the oddly shaped gate keeper's lodge, vaguely suggestive of a turnpike toll house still stands at the foot of the long drive which winds up between the trees from the Berrow Road to the houses on top of the dunes.

29 Horse Chestnut wood is very white and straight grained which made it ideal for the manufacture of milking pails in the days before stainless steel.

30 *On Mineral Springs at Daviesville Burnham* written in 1886 Dr G. Herring M.D. makes reference to Dodd's Cottages being recently built. Among a series of drawings made in 1845-6 of views from the upper windows some show the gardens which at that time extended to the Berrow Road and upon part of which the present Treasure Court flats now stand. When first laid out the semi-circular drive went right up to these houses with no small gardens intervening as is now the case.

When the property was re-roofed in the nineteenth century, the tiles came from the yard that was at the bottom of what is now Westfield Road. During the mid nineteenth century the Estlin family who owned the yard also occupied the Colony. Their long disused clay pit, for many years known as Hunt's Pond, is now the lake from which Lakeside Holiday Park (**2010**) takes its name and is backed onto by some of the homes in Rectory Drive.

Opposite the Colony drive was that of Paradise House, also with its lodge (long since gone). The estate was bounded on the west by Paradise (Berrow) Road and on the north by Stoddens Road and extended eastward beyond the double bend in Stoddens Road. At that time it was owned and occupied by Sophia Anne Blake and comprised two houses with gardens, two orchards and several fields and areas of parkland. Unlike the Colony which only had the one name change, Paradise House had four or five of which 'The Grove' was the most enduring. Long after the estate was broken up and the buildings demolished, the name lives on in the name of the road which follows the line of the original driveway from the Berrow Road for around a hundred metres before turning northwards to Stoddens Road across the western part of the estate which was developed during the early part of the twentieth century after some of the land was sold off by the Rev. Ker-Thompson.

Lodge at entrance to the Colony drive – very little altered.

Lodge at the entrance to the Grove – demolished when the road was laid out.

After the Colony came a small estate extending from the roadway to the beach on which stood Poplar Villa or Cottage which name was later given to that particular road when development of the estate began in the closing years of the nineteenth century. The last occupier of Poplar Cottage was a Mrs Longman who was there until **1906** according to Kelly, by which time the Berrow Road frontage and much of the north sides of Poplar Road and Grove Road were built on and occupied. A little further south on land leased from the diocese by Reverent David Davies are two groups of buildings described as 'house and stables and outhouses' These buildings were in the vicinity of where Hall Terrace is currently located at the rear of Seaview Road and may well have been the stabling for that property; although Mrs King, for whom the Hall was built is listed as the owner of a stabling facility adjoining the Vicarage where Vicarage Chambers and the public shelter now stand (**2010**).

Until George Reed commenced the building of Catherine and Julia Terraces during the **1850s** there was a fairly large area of sand dune and warren extending southward along Paradise Road parallel with the beach from the Poplar estate to St Andrew's church in the vicinity of which were the few substantial buildings which still remain. They were North and South Myrtles, the Daviesville Spa and adjoining houses and eastward of them The Hall and Tregunter close to and facing Berrow Road and Victoria Street respectively.

Opposite Tregunter was the partly completed terrace of two houses (now four) known as Brunswick Place[31] with a small residence Brunswick Cottage close by. John Gunter, who lived at Tregunter was for many years chef to George III and it was this association with the Royal House of Brunswick that the name of

31 See Appendix 2.

this terrace derives. A short distance eastward of this cottage stood an attractive residence known as The Elms standing on what is now the largest of the Manor Garden lawns. The house was demolished when the estate was taken over and developed by the Burnham Urban District Council in **1905**. The residence built by George Reed and known as Manor House (later to become the Local Council Offices) and the established gardens surrounding it were already in existence sometime before the **1838** survey was made.

Continuing down what is now Manor Road, but was around that time, known as Church Street or Crosshill, one passed Homebush, parts of which are extremely old, then owned and occupied by John Buncombe a professional land surveyor who for many years carried out at one and the same time the duties of Clerk, Collector, and Inspector of Nuisances to the Local Board of Health.

Attached to and extending westward from Homebush at this time was an annexe (Locke's Room) and other ancillary buildings including stables and coach houses, believed to have been used by George Reed, then in occupation of the Manor House opposite – certainly there is only one building shown on the Manor House site that might have been suitable in size and location for the purpose but this had been demolished by the time of the **1884** survey which shows no other buildings of a suitable size within a close proximity. For a few years, Burnham children attended a day school at these premises at the time that George Reed was residing at his Manor House, close by. Whether the noise which inevitable occurs when children are at play in any way influenced him in his decision to build a new school on the sea front and thereby effectively putting their shouting out of earshot is not recorded.

The grounds of Homebush, on part of which the Parish Hall was later to be built, at this period in time, extended to the rear of the properties in Victoria Street opposite the church.

Fifty yards eastward of Homebush was the three way junction of Crosshill, Tags Tail Lane[32] and Church Street. This became four ways with the creation of St Andrew's Road in the first half of the twentieth century. Somewhere near this junction was a fenced area, much frequented by local farmers who, whilst concluding deals of one sort or another between themselves, were entertained by the spectacle of bull baiting.

Continuing Eastward along Love Lane, Dunstan House was at this time a farmhouse owned and occu-pied by John Board, and it was on the surrounding fields later to become known as the Board estate that nearly a hundred years later 'The Saints Area' of Burnham was laid out as a residential development. Love Lane Farm opposite Dunstan House also with extensive grounds was then owned and occupied by Ferdinando Board another landowner of some importance in the locality. Love Lane Farmhouse was demolished on 10 February **1979** with the outbuildings and barn giving way later to 15/17 Love Lane, the Medical Centre and the Ambulance Station.

Of the older cottages standing on the south side of Love Lane that were there in **1838**, one was the home of an old woman, Winter by name, the last of her kind in Burnham, who was considered by the superstitious locals to be a witch and to 'overlook' people or in the vernacular 'to put toads on 'em'.

At the end of Love Lane before turning north for Middle Burnham there stood, opposite each other, on the left Manor Farm then owned by John Dod and John Dod (father & son?) on the right Rosewood Farm, also owned by the pair. Both of these farmhouses were subsequently pulled down and modern buildings erected on the sites but in December **1974** when the approach road to Burnham from the M5 was under construction Manor Farm was demolished and the site cleared for future development. Rosewood Farm lives on as Rosewood Drive etc., with the farm house becoming the Rosewood Public House.

The only buildings standing in **1838** along what is now the Esplanade and which, with two exceptions, remain today are the buildings comprising the Daviesville Complex i.e. North and South Myrtles, Steart House, wherein were the mineral water baths and assembly rooms, The Round Tower (originally Rev. Davies's Lighthouse) Marina House and Beverly Cottage; the Royal Clarence Hotel some two hundred metres to the south, and a short distance further on Sea View Cottage which was subsequently pulled down to make way for Paxton House at the seaward end of the foot path leading down into what is now Chapel Street. A further two hundred metres walk over the dunes would have brought our traveller to another house, also demolished; on the site of which the building that has been known for many years as The Fernery or Fernery House, was built where Adam Street now joins the Esplanade. A few metres further on was the property later to become known as the Steam Packet Inn and subsequently York House. Beyond this point there was nothing but sand dunes as far as Pillsmouth where the River Brue joins the Parrett.

---

32 See Appendix 3.

Chapter 3

Growth and Expansion

Up to the time of the Tithe Apportionment Survey the parish of Burnham, like many other rural parishes, had changed little since mediaeval times; various Lords of the Manor and lesser landowners had come and gone but, like 'Old Man River', Burnham had 'just kept going' and stayed much the same. Of the 260 non-agricultural buildings listed in the survey, with the exception of one hotel, one shop, and one cottage, they are otherwise described as houses, regardless of their size. After **1838**, following the Reverend David Davies's spa complex a decade or so earlier, development followed an exponential curve until the latter part of the twentieth century with time out only for the First and Second World Wars.

Prew's Terrace was one of the first post survey developments. It was built in **1843** followed by the Custom House. With few exceptions the remaining properties were built between then and the end of the century, with Vicarage Terrace, Royal Parade, the National School, and Beach Terrace being completed by **1865/66**, as were Catherine and Julia Terraces, although the interior of Julia Terrace was not finished until several years later[33] with Victoria buildings coming in 1897. The building currently (**2010**) known as York House has been so known since about **1870**, having previously been the Steam Packet Inn.

When the Reed's Arms Hotel with its tap, the Pier Hotel, were first built the nearest building was the Custom House; the Burnham College building at the other end of Pier Street came a few years later. Coinciding with the building of these hotels George Reed for whom they were built, had the present Pier Street[34] laid down as a metalled roadway together with a short section along the west elevation of the

Reed's Arms, mid to end of nineteenth century; viewed from dunes near location of present holiday village. Note absence of Victoria buildings between Adam Street and Cross Street, as well as between hotel and custom house.

33 See Chapter 7.

34 Pier Street was at that time known as Sunnyside; the Reed's Arms being Number One.

hotel and another short section at the south end of what is now High Street and adjoining the newly built railway station.

In those early days there was no Esplanade as we know it. That came, between **1840** and **1860**, when Prew's and the other terraces were constructed fronting seawards. Until then all the existing buildings were accessed from the Berrow Road or Victoria Street. Myrtle Drive was originally the carriage sweep for the Rev. Davies's spa complex and the purpose of Regent Street as it is now known was little more than to service the Clarence Hotel.

Some short distance from the Clarence and extending northward to the seaward entrance of the churchyard the sand hills on their west elevation had been buttressed and contained within a slightly inclined stone wall along the top of which iron railings had been placed. The whole of this area of sand hills had been levelled and grassed over by Rev. David Davies to provide an elevated walk some ten feet or so above the public footpath below. By courtesy of that reverend gentleman it became the practice of residents and visitors alike, when the weather was suitable, to parade or otherwise take their ease at this pleasant spot. This privilege was evidently abused because in **1846** he found it necessary to close it to the public. Because of this action several indignant letters appeared in the *Bridgwater Times* for July of that year, from various people who were under the mistaken

An original photograph taken from the church tower in 1903. Showing Vicarage roof, bottom L; beyond is the Lifeboat Pavilion. Further on is the Burnham Institute building on the N side of Regent Street with the shops opposite. Top R is Vicarage Terrace with Rev. Davies's fenced promenade, bottom R.

impression that it was public property. Following its closure as a place of public resort part of it was built on when Vicarage Terrace[35] was erected at its southward end (corner of Vicarage Street[36]). As for the remaining area, for many years it was left unused until purchased in **1925** by the Burnham Attractions Association Ltd and presented by them to the Town Council who in **1927** had all the sand removed to road level and the site laid out by the En-tout-Cas Company to create the Marine Cove which was opened in June of that year by Mr J.B. Braithwaite[37]. Contrary to some opinions expressed at the time, this

Vicarage Terrace – part of Rev. Davies's fenced-off promenade may be seen on the left.

35   Vicarage Court now stands on the site

36   Once known as Saint Andrew's Street.

37   See chapter 9.

Marine Cove opening ceremony – June 1927.

Marine Cove, shortly after it was opened – note the tall sundial L of centre; anything shorter would have been useless for much of the time because of the high boundary wall.

land did not appear to have ever formed part of the churchyard as no evidence of any burials having been made there was found when the excavation work was carried out.

Among other Burnham buildings in **1838** was an old inn called the Mason's Arms which stood at what later became the junction of Regent Street and Victoria

Mason's Arms – note the narrow gap between it and the building to the R.

Street. It was later pulled down and the Lifeboat Coffee Tavern, Restaurant and Temperance Hotel was built on the site. The table of charges of that time makes interesting reading:- hot dinners were either 6d or 1/- while afternoon tea, consisting of a pot of tea, bread and butter, jam, cake and local shrimps cost all of 6d. The charge for a single bedroom was 1/6d per night while that for a double room was 2/-. Hot baths at 6d a time were also available to local people who lacked this facility in their own homes. Shortly after its opening the management inaugurated a passenger and carrier service between Burnham, Bridgwater and Weston super Mare. The vehicle used for this service was described at the time as a horse drawn

Lifeboat Coffee Tavern tariff.

char-a-banc, affectionately known over a wide area as the Somerset Lass this vehicle was often chartered to convey parties of people on tours about the county, and on such occasions was variously drawn by two, three or four horses according to the distance and number of passengers to be carried. One of the most notable of these excursions was that of 21 August **1901** when, to celebrate the millenary of King Alfred the Great, a grand circular tour was made with a full complement of passengers during which Sedgemoor, Athelney, Glastonbury and Wedmore were visited.

Lifeboat Coffee Tavern. Built on the site of the Mason's Arms – note the larger gap to the R of the building

Somerset Lass outside the Lifeboat Restaurant waiting to depart.

The cost of the round trip for adults was 5/- and 3/6d for children. Both luncheon at Athelney and tea at Wedmore being provided at a combined charge of 2/- per person.

Following the construction of the Lifeboat Restaurant a temporary structure was erected on land a little further along Victoria Street where the double-fronted gable-roofed property (No. 7) currently (**2010**) stands. The main purpose of this structure was to accommodate overflow parties from the main restaurant opposite, and continued to be so used until the Lifeboat Pavilion was built and opened in **1901/02** after which time the temporary pavilion was demolished.

What later became lower College Street is shown on the **1838** Tithe map as a continuation of Victoria Street turning eastward to join Oxford Street. On the north side of this rough roadway standing in spacious grounds surrounded by trees, lawns and shrubberies stood Ravensworth House, an imposing mansion which later became known as Ravensworth House School for Boys, upon the approximate site of which the present Ravensworth Terrace now stands. After the building of Ravensworth Terrace the development of this small estate was completed by the erection of the terrace of houses on the north side of lower College Street in **1903/04**, the last house being number 38, on the corner with Oxford Street.

Close to the junction of Manor Road with Oxford Street stood a row of old cottages, at the bottom of Princess Street. In one of these, for many years, had lived one Henry Sweet, who like his father before him was the local chimney sweep. Above his door was a signboard inscribed in bold letters which proclaimed to the reader the following message:-

'Henry Sweet, he does live here
He will attend your orders far and near
With his brush, scraper and machine
He will sweep your chimney neat and clean.
And should your chimney be on fire
He will put it out if you require
For through neglect and want of care
There's many a house been destroyed by fire.'

This useful advice was not always taken heed of, as many people cleared the soot from their flues by deliberately allowing their chimneys to catch fire in order to avoid paying the moderate basic charge of nine pence for this service. Although effective this sometimes proved to be a false economy, a major fire, on occasions resulting from the dubious practice as was the case when around **1801** the Fox and Goose Inn at Brent Knoll was destroyed as a result of a servant maid 'adden fewel to the furnis'.

Extending southward, from near the junction with Love Lane to a point opposite the Crown stood a row of cottages most of which, although since modified still stand today (**2010**). Several have had shop fronts added and some, subsequently, had them removed. These cottages and lower College Street (Victoria Street, as it was then), marked the eastern and s outhern limits of what might loosely be described as the built up area of Burnham. Such other buildings as there were, were relatively few and definitely far between.

Of the few isolated buildings of any consequence dotted about at this time between the Crown and the Brewery was the cottage, currently known as Vine Cottage, standing opposite College Street and a hundred yards further on The Ring o' Bells, a beer and cider house; adjoining this was the local pound and a substantial building owned by the parish officers and

Early shot of Ring o' Bells showing cob front wall – note no licensee's accommodation.

Later shot of Ring o' Bells. The white building on the L is the Licensee's accommodation – all that remains in 2010.

overseers and used by them as their headquarters and possibly the parish poor house. This property stood on land which seventeen years later was to become part of the Burnham Gas Works complex; opposite, stood Seaton House. Beyond this small group of assorted buildings lay Rose Farm, the farmhouse of which stands at the corner of Jaycroft Road and later

Section of cob wall exposed during demolition of Ring o' Bells.

Reed and plaster ceiling at Ring o' Bells – probably original, and contemporary with cob walls.

General view of brewery which extended back as far as the railway line. The old windmill shown on the tithe map was probably pulled down to make way for the track – note the sign for Holimarine, indicating that this shot was taken before Marine Drive was laid out.

which became part of the Convent of the Sacred Heart[38]. Southward and adjoining Rose Farm was another owned and occupied at that time by George Tucker. The farmhouse, a substantial building surrounded by orchards, gardens and shrubberies was known for many years as the Rookery; even after it became the convent the Mother Superior used it as her postal address.

Between the Rookery and Sandyway Farm there were two properties of good size which have since been redeveloped. Pillsmouth Farm became Holimarine, now Burnham Holiday Village; and the brewery, Broadhurst Gardens. There was a third, much smaller, property consisting of a house and garden which together with a small parcel of land backing onto the railway line was acquired around **1960** and demolished to make way for the Catholic church of Our Lady and the English Martyrs which was consecrated on 19 of April **1967**.

Sandy Way Farm on what is now known as Old Burnham Road has also been redeveloped although the farmhouse remains. Unlike many of the old farm houses which are simply described as 'House and Garden', there is no ambiguity in the description of this property as it is listed as 'House Garden and Barton', a barton being a farmyard (usually surrounded by a wall).

Although it was little more than a hamlet, with nearly all of the buildings following the line of the turnpike and being mostly cottages and agricultural structures (now long gone), Highbridge itself was

Pillsmouth Farm, where Richard Locke was born.

Part of Tithe map showing central Highbridge.

38 See Chapter 8.

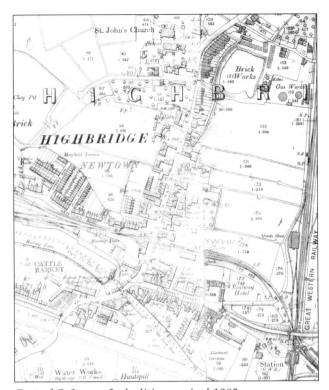

Part of O S map, 2nd edition, revised 1902.

The old (high) bridge over the lock gates which kept the river/canal navigable up to Glastonbury.

View from similar viewpoint in 2010.

Other side of bridge, looking east in 2009.

growing in importance as the most accessible point on the turnpike to Glastonbury and was the terminus of the Glastonbury Canal. Much of the land along the north bank of the River Brue was wharfage, with Market Street, known at that time as East Wharf Way and being almost entirely devoid of houses; there were certainly no shops or hostelries of any kind, although it was almost fully developed by the time of the **1883** survey.

Being on the turnpike (now the A 38) means that Highbridge has been well blessed, over the years, with coaching houses and inns. Travelling south from the building that became the Bristol Bridge Inn (**1875**)[39] there were those of the White Hart (demolished **2003**) both of which were beer houses the latter not being mentioned by name until **1939** when it was listed as a public house with Fred. Morgan as the licensee. The Lamb (now a Chinese takeaway **2010**), as a building appears in the **1838** survey although it is not listed as an inn until **1866**. Mrs Ann Davis, the licensee, is later given as a beer retailer. The George Hotel and the Highbridge Hotel were both long established coaching inns at the time of the survey, although the Highbridge Hotel which closed its doors in **2008** in preparation for re-development was at that time in the parish of Huntspill.

Early shot from similar viewpoint showing ships laid up on the mud. Note the lock abutments.

---

39 The dates in parenthesis against the name of licensed premises is only a rough guide as to when it first opened as it is the first date that it appears in any local directory and does not preclude the possibility that the business was trading much earlier . Many of the public houses that were well known during the twentieth century were originally only beer houses or retailers with the old directories listing the names of the licensee and the street or road rather than the establishment. We may be reasonably confident, however, that the date against the Bristol Bridge Inn applies to those premises as there was none other as suitable in the area at the time.

The only other buildings of any consequence, still standing from that time are the stone and brick building on the north side of King Street which for many years was a feed mill, although not shown as such on the map; and the Baptist chapel which was the first custom-built place of religious worship in the town.

The Railway Hotel followed close on the establishment of the Bristol to Exeter Railway and was in operation by **1848**. The advent of the Somerset and Dorset Railway with its shipping interests and railway works, heralded the further expansion of Highbridge.

The Somerset coastal strip with its abundance of high quality clay had ensured that most of the local houses constructed during the preceding centuries, were built of brick and roofed with tiles, rather than of stone walls under slate roofs. Known for many years as Hunt's Pond, the expanse of water that is bordered by Rectory Drive and the roads off it, with the caravan park to the south is shown on the **1884** O.S. map as 'brickworks (disused)'. Many older properties were built of bricks that had been fired on, or near, the site of construction. A short distance along Red Road is a field that is named on some early maps as Brick Field or Brick Pits Field.

The number of brick and tile works in the locality grew with the opening up of potential markets along the Bristol Channel coast and further afield. Newtown really was a new town with Newtown Road, initially, being aptly named Prospect Place which together with Ritson's Row and the terraces off, provided homes for the workers of the docks, railway, and timber mill as well as the brickyards, as did Market and Walrow Terraces. This led to the establishment of several more inns and beer houses. The Anchor, the Globe and Somerset Vaults (known as the Top House),

A tile maker in Colthurst and Symonds's yard making hand-made roof tiles.

in Newtown Road, together with the Rose and Crown and the Cooper's Arms in Market Street all date from around that time. The Globe, the George, and the Cooper's, being the only ones still plying their trade in **2010**.

The spiritual needs of the workers were not neglected as in addition to the building of Saint John's church in **1859**, several more, non-conformist, places of worship were also established[40].

Returning to Burnham, it was during the period immediately following the survey of **1838** with the

Colthurst, Symonds and Co's Burnham yard with its own railway siding, from a company catalogue.

40 See Chapter 5.

Lott's Commercial Inn, shortly after being built on what is now the corner of Cross Street and High Street.

development of Regent and College Streets that the built up area of the town began to spread slowly across the fields towards Highbridge. Slowly was the operative word for oddly enough the extension of the Somerset Central Railway line from Highbridge to Burnham in **1858** did not immediately attract building to that part of town, in fact some twenty-five years or so passed before the Abingdon Street area became built up. The row of houses which make up Abingdon Terrace being the first to be put up followed shortly afterward by Osborne Terrace **1883**, Windsor Terrace **1884** and Jubilee Terrace[41] in **1887**.

By the mid **1850s** the built-up area, with gaps here and there had reached the north side of Cross Street, John Lott's new Commercial Inn being completed circa **1853**. By **1879** Alfred Street (High Street) had been extended southward on each side as far as 'Tuppeny Tube'[42] (South Terrace) on the east side and South Street on the west side; the old Methodist chapel Sunday School[43] which since being built in **1860** had stood apart from the built up part of the town to the north, was now close to the centre of it as development spread southward.

Before the shop fronts were installed, the row of private houses between lower Cross Street and Adam Street were known as Arundel Buildings (**1839**) and those between Adam Street and Tuppeny Tube, as Oriel Terrace. At this time most of the land between South Terrace and the railway station and extending eastward from Alfred Street (High Street) to Oxford Street was laid out as pleasure gardens which included a maze were very popular with both residents and visitors alike. Over the years, they became progressively smaller as Jubilee Street, Hudson Street and Technical Street were built on them until finally they were so reduced in size that they were restyled as tea gardens and used largely for the entertainment of children and parents from many of the surrounding villages who, up to the outbreak of the Second World War came on their Sunday School outings, year after year, to enjoy a day at the seaside.

The building of the terrace known as Alexandra Villas between South Terrace and the railway station between **1880** and **1885** more or less completed the building up of High Street, with some minor in-filling being carried out at later dates.

* * *

The fact that the level of many of the old Somerset river beds, in places, approximate to that of the low-

---

41 Now the east side of Jubilee Street.

42 Tube or Tuppeny Tube is one of the local colloquialisms for a footpath between buildings as 'Gullet' or 'Jowler' is in other parts of the country. Another local name is 'Drain'.

43 See Chapter 5.

lying land beyond the retaining banks, creates a situation whereby the co-incidence of tide lock with heavy rainfall results in the overflowing of the banks and the consequent flooding of large areas of the Levels gives some idea of what it would have been like in those early days. Certainly without the work of the old monks, the eighteenth century Dutch engineers combined with the development of the first coastal defences, the land for miles inland from the coast would have been regularly inundated, and Burnham could not have developed as it has. A map published in **2007** by the Environment Agency shows the area which we might expect to be submerged in the event of global warming and which closely resembles that won back from the sea since the monks of Glastonbury commenced their activities.

Contemporary depiction of the 1606/07 floods. There were not two separate floods, but because this was the time that we changed from the Julian to the Gregorian calendar, both dates occur on documents of the time and refer to the same incident.

In respect of draining the levels, one benefit to the locality, derived from the Second World War, was the cutting of the Huntspill River and enlargement of the Kings Sedgemoor Drain and other drains in the area. The decision to build the Royal Ordnance Factory at

Puriton meant that large quantities of water would be required and so the Somerset Rivers Catchments Board received the funding it needed for a major drainage project that it had wanted to implement for many years. In cutting the Cripps River which allowed water to be pumped from the Huntspill to the Brue the engineers were following in the footsteps of the monks of Glastonbury who were probably the first people to attempt any drainage improvements in the area by digging the Pilrow which ran between the Brue and the Axe from a point east of Cripps Farm, to somewhere west of Rooks bridge. This has been replaced and/or upgraded into the Yarrow Yeo Rhine, Pilrow Wall Rhine, and the Mark Yeo.

We have a constant reminder of the Dutch engineers responsible for much of the drainage work carried out during the eighteenth and nineteenth centuries, both in the system of rhines[44] that they were responsible for digging, as well as such names as Dutch Road, and Swale[45] House (originally Swell House) that they built for their own use, and is remembered in the name of Swell Close.

Because the land is so flat, all natural watercourses tend to meander and precipitate large quantities of silt thereby reducing their depth and water carrying capacity and increasing their tendency to overflow. This was overcome to a large degree by the construction of dykes, or dikes, as the Dutchmen would have called them. The banks of the Mississippi in America have the same sort of thing but on a much larger scale[46].

Until **2007** the expansion of Burnham was largely on greenfield sites that in-filled between Stoddens Road, Love Lane, Worston Lane/Road and Burnham/Highbridge Road with many lesser developments on smaller enclosures or fields around the area. Similarly in Berrow with the Ash Tree Road and Church House Road developments and the land between Golf Links Road and Links Gardens. There was no large scale demolition and redevelopment in either Burnham or Berrow, other than for industrial purposes. Even in the case of the Broadhurst Gardens development, that required the demolition of the brewery, by far the greater proportion of the land used was open fields which once provided grazing for the brewery horses. The only residential development of any size in Burnham that might be looked on as a brownfield site is Marine Drive and Willis Court which largely follow the line of the old railway track.

In Highbridge, with its industrial nature, both

---

44 A network of deep drainage channels fed by numerous smaller ditches. The name probably coming from the German via Dutch.

45 Swale in this context can be interpreted as rushing stream.

46 The flood scenes for a film called Floods of Fear, about the Mississippi levees bursting were shot at Pills Mouth and Huntspill.

William Welland's blacksmith's shop in Oxford Street. Joe Lynham, one of his men is filing the horse's hoof.

past and present, the development was mixed, brick and tile works, railways, shipping and timber together with housing for the influx of related workers. The twentieth century saw the demise of the Somerset & Dorset Railway, the Locomotive Works, docks and all the brick works, some of which had exported their products around the world. Most of the largest developments were, at least partially, on brown sites, most of which were either old brickyard or railway land which has been used both for industrial redevelopment and residential purposes. The two main exceptions being Poplar, and Moreland estates with land to the east of the town as far as Isleport Road being re-developed for light industrial and commercial usage and the old railway land between the station and the locomotive works being used for housing.

Notwithstanding the march of progress there continued to be a need for blacksmiths. There was sufficient work to keep a couple of them employed around the end of the nineteenth century and into the twentieth. Several members of the Welland family plied their trade as such in Burnham and Highbridge as well as a Tucker, who worked in premises at the back of Church Street, Highbridge – Richard Henry made the wrought iron gates for Highbridge cemetery, and was sufficiently proud of his handiwork to stamp his name on them.

The Welland family forge was in Oxford Street, opposite Dunstan Road and was in operation up to the beginning of the Second World War. A modern detached house now stands on the site.

Chapter 4

Social Development (And Changing Values)

Of the long list of medieval Somerset wills that have been recorded many include bequests to the church of St Andrew at Burnham and of these, the following in abbreviated form are interesting examples, showing as some of them do the use of words still in common use but in an entirely different context.

The will dated 26 December **1486** of Richard Swan of Wells testifies as to his regard for the church of St Andrew's at Burnham to which he bequests the sum of £10[47].

Dame Isabell Linton of Wyke (Wick) in her will dated 18 March **1498** bequeathed to "Thomas Kenne sonne of John Kenne all lands and tenements at Brentmershe if called Berrough Grene and at Burnham to his exhibicioun to schole during teams and yeres that John Broke gentilman late hath made of the gift and feoffment of John Kenne gentilman by his charture indented prose date is the 10th of June".

In his will proved at Axbridge on 14th July **1544** Richard Jennett of Burnham states, "… desire that I be buried in the church yard at Burnham. To St Andrew's of Wells IIIJd (4d, otherwise 4 pre-decimal pence). To St Andrew of Burnham half bushel of beans. To my daughter Katerine a cow and to my daughter Agnes a cow. All my wool to be parted among all my children. The residue to my wife Isabell …" Similarly, expressing in her will the wish to be buried in the churchyard of St Andrew at Burnham Isabell Wall bequeathed thereto half bushel of malt, to the high altar half bushel of malt and to our Lady's service IJS VIIJd (Two shillings and eight pence) the residue to Richard my son whom I make executor, witnesses Sir Peter Manfylde my ghostly father[48], John Hart clerk and others" dated 15 September **1544.**

The wills made by members of the Dod family who owned farms in the Burnham area for more than three hundred years appear from time to time in the records at Taunton from one of which the following extract is made:- "John Dod of Burnham … To Robert my son, my best wain with wheels iron bound" dated 8 March **1555**, proved in the church at Axbrydge 10 May **1555**. From the short space of time that often elapsed between making and proving it would seem that many of these old wills were made on the death beds of the testators, an indication, maybe of the natural aversion some people had, and still do, to anticipate their own demise of which event the making of a will seems some how to them to be brought closer.

Although the feudal system as such had ceased to exist by the seventeenth century, much of the land was still in the possession of a relatively small number of people with the bulk of the populace subservient to their demands. By the end of the eighteenth century local land values had increased substantially, due in no small part to the activities of Richard Locke, a celebrated agriculturalist of the time and relative of the philosopher John Locke. The value of the parish increased enormously. In Domesday book Burnham's 4000 acres were values at £4, in **1688** at £1,248 and in **1796** the figure has risen to £10,000, which even after making allowance for a decline in the value of money represented quite a substantial increase.

"The farmers too became wealthier. In the early eighteenth century they were content with the title of yeoman, only one was worth £1,000, with only five qualifying as jurors. By **1796,** 50 were worth £10,000, and of these, 10 were each worth £100,000. and 35 now acted as jurors; 15 of these were styled Gentlemen and served on the Grand Inquest of the County at quarter sessions[49]". In **1792** a survey showed that at that time there were only three other land owners in Burnham with property of greater value than Locke's.

---

47 It is only necessary for us to consider how much the buying power of the pound has diminished in our own lifetimes to have an idea of the relative wealth of Richard Swan in 1486.

48 Not as one might expect, a deceased parent, but an adviser or confessor.

49 Appendix to *Life of Richard Locke* by F. Madeline Ward 1939.

Describing what Burnham and its inhabitants were like in the early **1700s** Locke wrote, "an inconsiderable parish of poor renters and cottagers who existed without hot dinners, silk clothing, carriages of pleasure, mahogany furniture, clocks, watches or even tea kettles[50]. – The farmers carried their dinners to market in their pockets as the labourers did at the end of the century, and their clothes as well as their blankets were made of homespun material, the produce of their flocks combined with the industry of their wives and daughters[51]".

Of all the many diverse and invaluable contributions that Richard Locke had made toward improving the quality of life for his fellow man his efforts to form and get established a mutual benefit society in Burnham must surely rank among his most successful achievements. Although, primarily it was the intention to provide those attending the monthly meetings with the opportunity to exchange opinions and to address those present on a variety of subjects for the mutual instruction of all, the need to make provision for financial help to members in times of sickness was also not the least of the society's' aims. Its formation was mainly the result of an illness of some severity suffered by Locke in **1769** during which he vowed that if he recovered he would take such practical steps as lay within his power to alleviate the lot of others less fortunate than he in time of sickness and misfortune. Called the Burnham Society, it was officially formed in **1772** although it does not appear to have become active until the following year. The exact location of the society's headquarters is not known and it may at times have been moved. An extension of Homebush in Manor Road and marked 'Locke's Room' (now demolished) is shown on an old map of Burnham.[52]

Initially the meetings of the society proved to be popular and the subjects discussed at the monthly meetings frequently became matters of general conversation between members and non-members throughout the district, thereby creating a widespread interest which resulted in a rapid increase of membership. As a consequence of a regularly large attendance of members at the monthly meetings it was necessary to limit to five minutes the time allowed each member to address those present if another wished also to do so.

Some two years or so after its formation as a forum for debate the early enthusiasm shown by the members waned somewhat, and the original ethical and academic aspirations of the founder members gave way to the discussion of matters of more practical consideration, such as the planting and maintenance of orchards, the subjects of agriculture and horticulture and also the cultivation of willows which were in great demand at that time for the making of the butts used in the important local salmon fishing industry and the no less important consideration of providing financial and other help to sick and distressed members who mainly consisted of artisans, labourers and tradesmen and who at that time numbered about one hundred. Great care was taken to see that the funds of the society were not in any way depleted by any 'lead swinging' behaviour and each and every member had in his turn to undertake the duties of sick visitor two new ones being appointed to this office every three months. Each member in the club was visited at both the beginning and end of each week until he either recovered or died. Richard Locke was appointed first President of the Burnham Society to which office he was re-elected for twenty years in succession. One of the duties of this position was the selection of other trustees from the membership to assist him in the running of the society.

The income of the society was derived from various sources with each member's weekly contribution being two pence, usually paid at the monthly meeting. A somewhat complicated system of fines was also drawn up which covered so many different ways by which a member could be in breach of the society's rules that the funds of the society were considerably increased thereby. The following are typical: failure to pay his monthly contribution on time cost the offending member two pence, while neglect to pay his contribution to the widow of a fellow member cost the offender two shillings. If after being elected to serve as an officer of the society a member declined to do so, his refusal was assessed at a half guinea. The rules of the Burnham Society were instituted for the assistance of poor persons when sick or old were printed by William Pine at Wine Street, Bristol and stated in the preamble that at the meeting room, securely fixed to the floor by bolts is a strong box made secure by iron bands to which are fitted five different locks, each having a different key. 'In this box there is deposited £20 for the purpose of lending to any member, such amount to be maintained or increased if found necessary and each key shall be held by a different member. After one complete year's

---

50 Bath and West of England Society papers.

51 *The life of Richard Locke* by F. Madeline Ward as an appendix to Collinson's *History of Somerset*.

52 This is now among the MSS etc collected by the late Mr Arthur Ruscombe Emery, in addition to which there is other evidence that lends support to the possibility that these premises were at one time the Burnham Society's headquarters.

membership each person shall, subject to the society's articles, be entitles to a payment of 6/- per week until better, or if incurable and unable to work to 3/- per week for life. There were many other benefits for members which were now limited to one hundred in number.

In certain approved cases a member was also able to borrow from the society to purchase livestock, if a farmer, or if a labourer a sum sufficient to meet extra expenditure incurred on the birth of a child or to pay rent charges. Such loans could be re-paid by easy stages and were made interest free, a facility which undoubtedly made life for members a great deal easier in those times when an insufficient income often resulted in slow starvation, a state of affairs which was by no means unknown to the very poor in the Burnham area during Richard Locke's lifetime.

It is not known for exactly how long the Burnham Society remained in existence; but certainly, in the closing years of the eighteenth century when legislation affecting all friendly societies came into force, it is recorded that at the quarter sessions held at Wells on 30 April **1794** all the rules, articles and regulations of the Burnham Society were allowed and confirmed as being in order. J.R. Churchill writing in **1903** stated that the Burnham Friendly Society registered under that name and having its headquarters at the Crown Inn was founded during the nineteenth century with aims and principles so like those of the original Burnham Society that he was in no doubt that it was the direct lineal descendant of the society that had been founded by Richard Locke.

Although Burnham was fortunate in having the Burnham Society, the people in many towns and cities had no such help. With the advent of the industrial revolution and the resultant decline in cottage industries, the working class were, more than ever at the mercy of their employers who, unlike Joseph Fry, Titus Salt, and some other Quaker families, had little or no regard for the wellbeing of their workers, and generally viewed them as expendable. The growing need for mutual aid and benefit societies was met by the formation of what might be described as consortia, combining several smaller societies under one large umbrella. One of the largest and oldest of these was the Manchester Unity of Oddfellows, founded in **1810**, a branch of which was established in Burnham in **1878**. Among the eleven founder members was John Bodger, one time gardener to George Reed at the Manor House, but by then in business on his own account as a florist and already preparing the foundations of an enterprise which after he emigrated to America some thirteen years later grew to become a business with world wide connections.

Although many people benefited from membership of these mutual aid societies, there were many more who were excluded because they were unable to afford the subscription. Such people had, for centuries, been taken care of by the Parish with money from the local Poor Rate; this care took the form of 'indoor relief' or 'outdoor relief'. As the term implies, the former involved the persons concerned being taken indoors, that is, into the Parish Poor House. This occurred when the claimant (usually a man) was unable through no fault of his own, to earn sufficient to pay the rent on the family home, and support his family. Outside relief was given to those families who could manage the rent payments but little else. So the overseers paid them what was deemed necessary to feed and clothe themselves; this was paid in cash or kind, as best suited that particular occasion. In many parishes benefactions were created whereby money or property was left to the parish to help support the poor. Few older parish do not have such benefactions, details of which are often to be found displayed on boards or stone tablets somewhere about the church. Saint Andrew's is no exception, with Henry Rogers's gift being recorded with that of the Rev. John Golden among others on boards in the vestry, some details of which may be seen in Appendix One (Time Line).

The New Poor Law of **1834** compelled parishes to sell their poor houses and hand over the money and any other relevant assets to their local poor law union to finance the building and operating of union workhouses run by Boards of Guardians with different criteria for establishing the qualification of the needy (Burnham was part of the Axbridge Union). Generally with regard to these establishments, one was either in, or out, there being little opportunity of outside relief. This resulted in those families that could have been kept going with a loaf of bread and a couple of pounds of meat a week in the old days were outside the scope of most unions. They became known as the 'Second Poor', and special funds had to be created to

Axbridge Union Workhouse, where the poor of Burnham were sent – now luxury apartments.

help them as anything left for the poor of the parish, after the **1834** Act, went straight to the local union. By specifying that a bequest was for the benefit of the second poor it was possible to retain it for use in that parish.

Alms houses were another, long established, way of helping the less fortunate members of the community. Ellen's Cottages, on the Berrow Road to the South of the High Lighthouse come into this category, having been built and endowed by John Saunders for ten single women, in memory of his wife Ellen[53].

Ellen's Cottages – an early engraving.

Ellen's Cottages.

RULES.

1. That no person shall be admitted as an inmate unless she shall have proved to the satisfaction of the Trustees that she is not less than sixty years of age.
2. That no person shall be eligible as an inmate who has ever been a lunatic or had epileptic fits, or who is at the time of seeking admission, labouring under any chronic, contagious or incurable disease.
3. That each inmate upon admission shall have a livingroom and a bedroom; and such apartments shall be occupied by her as inmate only so long as the Trustees shall think fit.
4. That every inmate, unless hindered by sickness, shall attend once every Sunday some place of worship.
5. That persons of all creeds shall be eligible as inmates.
6. That any dispute or difference of opinion arising between any of the inmates shall be referred to the Trustees, whose decision shall be binding upon all parties.
7. That if any inmate shall marry after admission, she shall cease to be an inmate.
8. That if any inmate shall become entitled to receive in possession for her own benefit a sum of money that will produce a clear weekly income of seven shillings per week, she shall cease to be an inmate.
9. That no inmate shall solicit pecuniary assistance elsewhere.
10. That, as the apartments will be suitably furnished and kept furnished at the cost of the Founder, no inmate shall bring or introduce any article of furniture or other article, except a box or boxes containing her clothes, without special permission being granted by the Trustees.
11. That no inmate shall exchange her apartments, or remove any fixture or article of furniture therefrom.
12. That each inmate shall every day sweep and clean her rooms and dust her furniture, and also keep clean every article in daily use.
13. That once in every week each inmate shall, unless prevented by sickness, scrub out and well clean the floors of her living room and bedroom.
14. That the porch entrance, steps and passage, common to each double cottage shall be thoroughly scrubbed and well cleaned once a week, the two inmates of such cottage alternately doing it.
15. That, as cleanliness is a great promoter of comfort and preserver of health, each inmate must be careful to observe that no slops, filth, ashes, or refuse of any kind, be allowed to remain in her rooms.
16. An inventory of the furniture and other articles will be handed to each inmate, or hung up in some part of the rooms or passage.
17. That each inmate shall replace any article that is broken in her rooms; but all articles that from fair means or use require to be replaced, will be provided by the Trustees without expense to the inmates.
18. That any inmate absent, except under special circumstances, from her rooms for more than one month in the year will cease to be a recipient of the Charity.
19. That no inmate shall allow any person to lodge or sleep in her room, or to remain there later than nine o'clock in the evening, and all inmates shall be in their rooms not later than nine o'clock at night.
20. That each inmate shall avoid giving any provocation to the rest or any of them remembering that mutual forbearance and kind offices performed towards each other are the best means for promoting peace, happiness and comfort, and also of fulfilling the wishes of the Founder of the Cottages.
21. That any inmate guilty of misconduct or who infringes any of these Rules is liable to instant dismissal.

Dated this 15th day of August, 1930.

Ellen's Cottages, rules, 1930 copy.

The feudal system having, theoretically, gone it was the turn of the last remaining anachronism, the payment of Tithes[54], if not to be swept away then at least be replaced with a more equitable system with the Tithe Commutation Act whereby all tithes were converted into pounds shillings and pence[55]. There had been much dissatisfaction with this arrangement for many years, both on the part of the people and the clergy (some of whom were prepared to come to an arrangement with the people of their parishes for an agreed monetary equivalent). Witness of this is to be seen in the church of Saint Decuman at Watchet where a board commemorates the fact that in **1777** the Earl of Egremont was instrumental in negotiating and implementation of such an arrangement for the locality.

Tithe apportionment board – Saint Decuman's church, Watchet.

Times gone by have often been referred to as 'The Good Old Days' – which they were – especially for those members of the landowning classes who had taken advantage of the Enclosure Acts to enlarge their estates by incorporating much of the common land on which the peasants had been wont to graze their animals as well as forage for food and wood to feed their families and their fires. Matters were made even worse by the, often harsh, administration of the Game Laws under which all game belonged to the owner of the land; even tenant farmers without the necessary licences and permission could be, and often were, prosecuted for killing animals on the land that they rented.

Evidence as to the misery endured at this time by the poorer inhabitants of Burnham is provided by correspondence which appeared in the *Bridgwater Times* during **1846**. Writing from 3 Brunswick Place[56]

53 See Chapter 7.

54 Where land owners and tenants paid a tenth of their produce/income to the church towards the maintenance of the fabric and any incumbent.

55 Before 1971 when British coinage officially became decimal, the pound consisted of 20 shillings. A shilling being worth 12 pence. For smaller denominations there was the half-penny and the farthing (fourth thing).

56 Now Brunswick Terrace, 2 - 8 Berrow Road.

in November of that year a Mr John Adams refers to a local family known to him who with a total income of 6/- per week to provide food, clothing and shelter for father, mother and six children found it an impossible task with bread at 8d per loaf and with no potatoes available, and to make matters worse with the eldest child dying of a rapid consumption. A letter from another correspondent appearing in the same issue makes reference to the wages of an able-bodied man being so miserably low here in Burnham and the adjoining parishes and made worse by the fact that they were obliged to pay high rents for the most wretched dwellings that had neither drainage nor water. The following example showing the income and expenditure of a labourer in this part of Somerset around **1846** is by no means atypical.

Married with five children aged 28, 25, 15, 12, 10.

Employment constant except on wet days, wages 7/- per week with three pints of cider a day. Wife gets six weeks work in a year at 1/6d per week. One son earns 4/6d per week the four other have no employ. Estimated value of garden allotment 3/- per year.

Weekly Expenditure

Rent	1- 9 1/2d
Coal and turf	7d
Bread	7- 0d
Potatoes	1- 4d
Soap etc	3d
Candles	1 1/2d
	11- 1

Clothing Bought

For the man		For his wife	
A coat 4 years ago		A cloak 2 years ago	
2nd hand waistcoat	1 – 0d	2nd hand gown	1 – 3d
Trousers	2 – 0d	Shift	8d
2 shirts @ 1/-	2 – 0d	1 pair stockings	6d
1 pair stockings	1 – 0d	1 pair shoes	1 – 6 d
2 pairs shoes @ 5/-	10 – 0d	3 yards calico	9d
Hat	2 – 6d	Needles & thread	2d
	18 – 6d		**4 -**

10d

For the boys	
1 shirt	10d
1 pair stockings	8d
1 pair shoes	4 – 6d

For the girls	
Pair stockings	6d
	6 – 16d

The family used burnt crust instead of tea or coffee and say they have eaten no butter for three years nor can they ever look upon meat or bacon.

Some indication as to the length of time that the number of those existing at poverty level in the Burnham area had been living on short rations was provided ten years earlier by a notice widely distributed throughout the parish in September **1836** and signed by all the leading landowners warning that anyone found in pursuit of any game on the lands of the forty-one signatories would be vigorously dealt with[57]; not the prime cause, but certainly a contributing factor. According to Bragg[58] in **1840**, the popula-

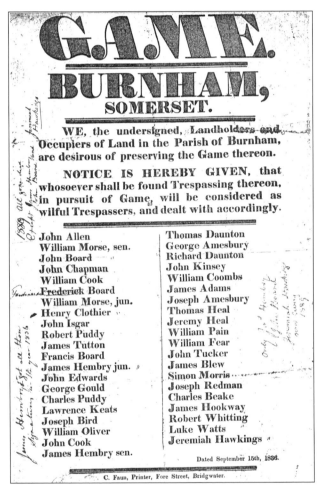

Game poster – descendants of many mentioned still live in the area.

tion of Burnham was a little in excess of 1100 souls which was made up of six gentry and private families, about thirty craftsmen and shopkeepers together with seven yeomen and their respective families. The remaining nine hundred or so, presumably being of the labouring class, were not considered worthy of individual mention – quite a large pool of potentially desperate people who might be forced to turn to

57 The new Game Bill which repealed 27 earlier laws became law on 1 November 1831. Under it, it became illegal to sell game without a licence which cost £2 and there were severe penalties for anyone possessing game that they could not account for. Anyone found in possession could not only have the goods confiscated but also any dogs or equipment used for its acquisition. A tenant farmer was not even allowed to take a rabbit he found eating his crops without authority from his landlord.

58 One of the earliest, but by no means comprehensive, directories for Somerset.

poaching to keep their families fed. William Cobbett in his *Rural Rides* recounts a meeting with a man breaking stones for a roadway who when asked how he managed to live on such a small wage said that he could not and that he supplemented his family's needs by poaching on the basis that he would prefer to hang for a rabbit than starve for the lack of one. Even tenant farmers without the necessary licences and permission could be, and often were, prosecuted for killing animals on the land that they rented.

Again, according to Bragg, there were three inns or hotels in Burnham, the Clarence, the Bell (long gone, but believed to have been in Regent Street) and the Crown (demolished **2009**), with one in Highbridge, the George. At that time the Highbridge Hotel was in Huntspill. There were however, numerous unlisted beer and cider, houses such as the Ring o' Bells in Oxford Street, that catered for the common herd, and which, as their name implies, were not permitted to sell spirituous liquor. At one time during nineteenth century there were eighteen hotels and public houses operating in Burnham alone with another dozen or so in Highbridge. The poor had to have somewhere to drown their sorrows and the traders and artisans somewhere to get their entertainment.

Places the size of Burnham did not have theatres and the only entertainment the masses had that they did not make for themselves was the occasional itinerant troupe or individual, most of whom only visited the larger towns such as Taunton and Bridgwater or anywhere that was on their direct route. Burnham would have been too far off the beaten track and too small to justify many such visits.

The Puzzle Gardens Inn, still standing, but no longer a pub, was built in **1842** and known originally as Lucerne Cottage. Owned by George Reed it was he who had the adjoining land attractively laid out as pleasure gardens[59], complete with maze for the entertainment of both visitors and residents alike. It was situated in the Berrow Road nearly opposite the present junction with Poplar Road, quite isolated from all other licensed premises which were within a close radius of the town centre. The Crown Inn and Ring-o'-Bells in Oxford Street and Mason's Arms in Victoria Street. Regent Street in those days had two inns, one at the side of the Clarence Hotel, a spit and sawdust affair known familiarly to its habitués as the

Bloodstain, and the Bell which had but a brief existence. A short distance away, College Street was able to boast three public houses, the Albion and the Rifleman's Arms in upper College Street, followed some years later by the Railway Hotel, still going strong in **2010**. Lott's Commercial Inn, the upper floor and roof-line of which is still easily recognizable stood at the junction of upper Cross Street with High Street. John Lott, its first landlord, and for whom it was built in **1853**, successfully combined such diverse activities as publican and fisherman for most of his life[60]. At the corner of upper Adam Street, the South side of which

Cheque from the local burial board to Frederick Hookins for work carried out enlarging the cemetery (see footnote 60).

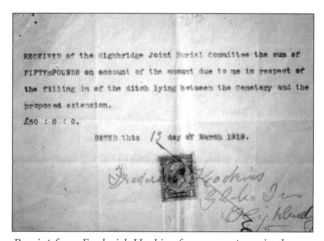

Receipt from Frederick Hookins for payment received

was then known as Frederick Place[61], stood the Royal Marine public house which, with the innumerable small panes of glass in its windows and entrance doors, but for the unmistakable character portrayed on both sides of its sign could have been mistaken for something from Dickens or a Christmas card. Not far

---

59 At a time when folk had simpler pleasures a garden was a place of recreation where one might walk and indulge in social intercourse. Contemporary with the Puzzle Gardens was a pleasure ground in Berrow belonging to Mrs Mary Johnson. By 1884 another had been established at the other end of the town on land now largely occupied by Jubilee Street and Hudson Street.

60 Many licensees, especially those who were beer retailers, had more than one occupation or undertook other jobs as they became available; Frederick Hookins, the landlord of the Globe Inn in Newton Road, Highbridge, is another example, who was paid £50 by the local burial board for filling in the rhine in 1919 when they extended the cemetery.

61 Prior to that it was known as Alfred Place.

The Steam Packet – now York House.

away, on the corner of South Street and the Esplanade, stood the Steam Packet.

Situated prominently in the centre of the esplanade is the Royal Clarence Hotel which without doubt is the oldest of the licensed premises left in Burnham[62]. Built as a coaching inn, it is not difficult to imagine the relief that must have been felt by the passengers as the coach and its team of horses passed under the archway into the hotel yard after experiencing the bumps and jolts occasioned by the shocking state of the roads then leading to Burnham from the Bridgwater turnpike. Over the many years of its existence there have been many landlords, but the one best remembered by the older inhabitants of Burnham was the late George Pruen whose memorial gates are at the west entrance to the churchyard. His 1896 chain-driven solid-tyred two cylinder 6 hp Daimler wagonette known affectionately over a wide area as Fiery Liz[63] was for many years driven by him as the hotel bus to meet guests arriving at Highbridge Station.

The Reed's Arms Hotel[64], together with its one time tap the Pier Hotel, were built for George Reed , to provide accommodation and refreshment for the anticipated flood of visitors from South Wales who were confidently expected to make good use of the paddle steamers to be used on the Burnham-Cardiff ferry service shortly to be established and in which venture he had a considerable financial interest. The Somerset and Dorset and Railway Hotels followed within a few years. The progression of Richard Avent from Grocer to Grocer, Linen Draper, Wine and Spirit Merchant and agent for 'Henry Brett & Co's Eau de Vie' took twenty five years, from **1850** to **1875**. Quite when the premises were first known as the Victoria Hotel is uncertain as the first mention of that name

Richard Avent's, grocer and off licence premises 1875, shortly after Princess Street was opened up – later to become the Victoria Hotel.

---

62 Its earliest known deeds date from 1792.

63 This vehicle is now part of the Bristol City Museum collection.

64 Later known as the Queens before reverting to its original name.

Victoria Hotel pre 1913 – the building opposite, next to the bank, where various chemists have traded since the early 1920s, was at that time, an estate agent's.

does not appear in any directories before **1902**, when Thomas Huish held the licence.

The Ocean Wave was another short lived public house, trading for a few years at the end of the nineteenth century. It was situated in some old cottages at the junction of Oxford Street with Abingdon Street. It

closed when the old couple who ran it both died of natural causes on the same day. It was, shortly afterwards, pulled down and the present property Clifford House built on the site.

The Lighthouse Inn, opened in **1970**, is the only new one that was built during the twentieth century

Royal Clarence Hotel – the oldest surviving hostelry in Burnham.

although several existing premises such as the Rosewood, Chaplains, Dunstan House and the Chapel, acquired licences for existing properties.

Great efforts were made during the nineteenth century to promote Burnham as a place for holidays and recreational trips with pleasure gardens and golden beaches, not forgetting the Rev. Davies's spa, the waters of which compared more than favourably, when analysed, with those of many of the great spa towns such as Bath and Buxton.

The introduction of the motor char-a-bancs, fore-runners of the modern long distance luxury coaches, with their solid tyres and collapsible canvas hoods, bearing such names as Lorna Doone, Greyhound, Dorothy, Maid of the Mountains, and others provided the means whereby even the poorest of people could afford the fares charged to convey them from city squalor to the seaside for a day's outing. The drivers of these uncomfortable vehicles, supposedly limited to a speed not exceeding 12 mph overran that figure at their peril, all too frequently falling victim of the ubiquitous police trap which in those days was considered to be an occupational hazard by any motorist on the main road.

During the summer months of those years which followed the end of the First World War hundreds of people from the one time slum areas of Bristol were daily brought by char-a-banc to Burnham to enjoy an inexpensive visit to the seaside. It was not unusual on such occasions for whole families, mother father and children together with grandparents uncles and aunts to come on these trips. After one or two glasses of the local brew had rid the women folk of any inhibitions, they often took to dancing their own particular version of the can-can on the pavement or in the street, outside of whichever public house they happened to be visiting, to the accompaniment of the inevitable concertina with occasionally that of a barrel organ for good measure. Most of these women were dressed alike, long black alpaca dresses and coats, black shoes and stockings, the whole outfit being completed in most cases with a large nondescript black straw hat. How they managed to execute the high kicks of the can-can dressed as they were must remain a mystery, and although, as seen through the eyes of a very small boy[65] they appeared to be very old women, such could not have been the case as many of them were nursing mothers and would afterwards sit on the pavement's edge suckling their babies in the full view of the passing public. While all this was going on the older children would sit at trestle tables set up for their benefit in the hotel yard regaling themselves with ginger beer and cockles, with sometimes a locust[66] bar or medlars for desert.

Charabanc, 'Dorothy' outside the Crossways Inn, Withy Road, West Huntspill.

65   Editor's note: I remember my father describing such scenes which he would have been ideally situated to observe as the family home was on the corner of Cross Street and High Street opposite Lott's Commercial Inn.

66   The fruit of the carob tree. A reddish brown pod somewhat larger than a garden pea with seeds, used for flavouring or eaten on its own.

The arrival of closing time at 2.0 o'clock[67] meant for most of them removal to the beach, where if the weather was fine and the tide suitable paddling was indulged in, mostly by the children but often by those adults who were not under the necessity of 'sleeping it off'. This afternoon interlude came to an end for everyone with the return of opening time and for a brief period drinking was resumed with musical entertainment again provided by concertina or coin-operated barrel organs. The raucous noise which all

Women enjoying a donkey ride.

Paddling near the jetty.

too frequently occurred during these musical inter-ludes was sometimes euphemistically described by the police as singing when action was taken by them against offending landlords on whose premises 'singing' was not permitted.

As with the bigger breweries, the Burnham brewery had tied houses as well as independent customers, spread over a large area, which were serv-iced by horse drawn drays until well into the **1920s** when these were superseded by motorised transport. Their round canvas hoods drawn together at each end with rope, caused them to look something like the covered wagons used by the pioneers when crossing the American prairies. These brewery horses were kept in a large field extending from St Peter's church to Worston Road and also in the smaller field oppo-site, upon which the present Lighthouse Inn now stands. With the advent of mechanical transport, a single horse-drawn wagon was retained and used for local deliveries[68].

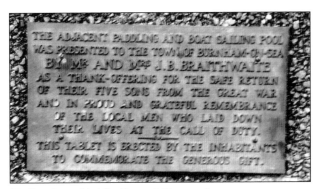
Dedication tablet for the paddling pool.

Paddling and boating pool viewed from the Esplanade near the church. Given to the town by J.B.Braithwaite in grati-tude for the safe return of his sons from World War One.

---

67 In those days there was no 24 hour opening. A few hours around noon and during the evening was all that was allowed.

68 Editor's note: I can remember when as a small boy during the school holidays Mr Sweet the old dray man who lived down the road from my home would take me on a trip to Berrow. I have often wondered since, whether he and his horse were retained on the grounds of cost effectiveness or he was a long serving worker who could not drive a motor vehicle, so was allowed to finish out his working life for the firm (something that employers would often do in those days).

Antonio's ice cream barrow at the top of Seaview Road.

Ernest Brewer in the doorway of his fish shop at 63 High Street between the wars. Note the cigarette in his mouth – no food hygiene regulations then!

With the development of the Esplanade and other streets for residential purposes, the need for suppliers to service the needs of these new homes grew steadily. This need was partly satisfied by an influx of traders and partly by many of the locals wearing more than one hat; farmers opening butcher's shops or dairies were a natural extension of their existing businesses. But often there was no obvious link between some people and their second business, John Lott, for example, who opened Lott's Commercial Inn, was a fisherman and also operated a 'Toy Warehouse'. Many cottagers turned their front rooms into small shops, from which they sold a variety of goods and services for a few pence in order to boost the family income. Others built shops over their front gardens – two, easily recognised, examples of this are still to be seen in Victoria Street (**2010**).

During the early part of the twentieth century, not forgetting the First World War, it was possible to source almost any product or service without going out of town. Potential customers could choose from several grocers, and boot makers (who actually made boots), as well as butchers, fishmongers and greengrocers, many of whom had shop windows that slid up, allowing the goods to be best displayed to any potential customers without the need for them to enter the premises. There was even locally made real ice cream.

The latter half of the century brought great changes to Burnham, with its expansion and the invasion of supermarkets. At the end of the first decade of the twenty-first century, Burnham and Highbridge have no independent butchers where once there were over half a dozen and the numbers of greengrocers and fishmongers have been reduced to one of each.

For many years prior to **1939** the north end of the town that is to say Berrow Road and others adjacent to it closely resembled Cheltenham in so far as the lifestyle the majority of those then living there was concerned. Why it was de rigueur to live north of the church is not clear although in all probability it was the fact that to the south was the nearby industrial town of Highbridge with its docks and railway works. Love Lane being the town's other link with the main road would also have been busy with commercial traffic. The Berrow Road, however, led nowhere in particular except Berrow and Brean or Brent Knoll, and would therefore be much less frequented by the hoi polloi.

As in that, much larger, one time haven of impoverished gentility, many of those residing in the Berrow Road end of the town were army and navy officers retired on half pay, who could not afford Cheltenham and could barely manage Burnham; while among the others were to be found ex government officials and one time members of the Indian Civil Service, of widely varying degrees of importance, as well as tea and coffee planters who were all similarly situated. They were 'returning home' from large houses standing in their own grounds well away from the homes of the working classes. Land along the Berrow Road fitted the bill admirably and was much cheaper than in Cheltenham.

Although some were financially well able to maintain, in their retirement, the same standard of living to which they had for so long been accustomed, many others, being quite impecunious for a variety of reasons and unprepared to adjust their lifestyle to accord with their means took advantage of the local tradesman, to many of whom they were permanently in debt paying off so much on account in order to ensure the continued supply of goods or services. Doubtless the local tradesmen did the same as their counterparts in Cheltenham, and loaded the prices charged to such customers in order to make it worth their while to give the extended credit that such people expected[69].

Throughout this period of time many local girls, on leaving school at the age of 14 or 15 years, went immediately into domestic service, being employed in varying capacities by these people. The size of the staff employed by the local 'gentry' was usually determined by either the number of persons in the household and size of premises, or the ability of the employer to pay the appropriate wages, the last mentioned item in many instances being the one to receive the least consideration.

Thursday by common consent was the day when most of these girls had their afternoon off, and from 2 p.m. onward they could be seen streaming into the

Indoor staff at the Towans.

---

69 Editor's note: My late father told the story of an occasion during the 1930s when he was in Cheltenham. Intending to purchase a scarf priced at 17/6 he tendered a £1 note, whereupon the shopkeeper said that as Father was paying cash the correct price was 12/6.

town to do their shopping or to meet their boyfriends, many of whom were members of that now extinct species, the tradesman's errand boy. Such was the economic situation generally prevailing between the wars that many local boys on leaving school were obliged from sheer financial necessity to become errand boys at about £1-00 to £1-10s (£1.50) a week (a job with no real prospects) instead of becoming indentured apprentices to some worth while trade with good prospects, but with little or no wages for the first four to five years. More or less hand in hand with the demise of the errand boy was that of the customer's account book, in which was entered the next order, which was then priced up back at the shop ready for delivery.

Errand boy with bicycle, this one was the butcher's boy, but similar lads were employed by most other retailers.

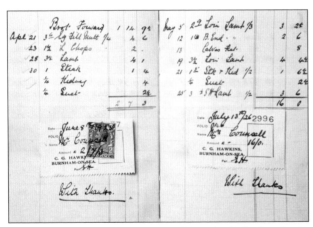

Customers a/c book for C.G. Hawkins who had a butcher's shop at 14 High Street. Note the L/H page where the receipt is signed over a postage stamp, which was obligatory at that time for any amount in excess of £2.

In spite of a considerable difference in the size and extent of their financial resources many of these retired people had one thing in common, a predilection for the playing of bridge, in some cases obsessively so. Bridge parties were regularly and frequently held in each others houses at which they gossiped about each other and criticised or praised the goods or

services of the local tradesmen, justly or otherwise according to personal whim. 'My husband is a perfect Gentleman he has never soiled his hands with work', was the comment made by the lady of one Burnham household to workmen carrying out repairs at her home, a remark indicative of the thought processes of not a few people of that time. They have now all gone, together with the lifestyle and attitudes of which they were so representative; swept away at the end of the Second World War by a political awareness and an undeniable demand for radical social changes on the part of returning service men and women. The war and its aftermath brought many changes, both physical and social. The people of Burnham continued the British tradition and celebrated the end of hostilities with street parties in spite of the restrictions of food rationing. The posts that had been set in the beach as a defence against enemy aircraft were removed; the only plane to fall foul of them being an American Flying Fortress that was forced to ditch in the sea.

All men were now equal, at least that was the theory, but as time passed it had become quite evident, with the creation of a new elite, that in fact that was all it was, a theory. To be in trade or to work

Street party at the end of World War Two. This one was in South Street.

Posts projecting from the beach. These were set at intervals above low water-mark to make it impossible to land an aircraft without wrecking it.

manually for one's living had now become respectable and more widely acceptable socially. Many of the larger houses in the Berrow Road area were converted into flats after the war, while others, by a strange quirk of fate were in later years bought and occupied by the very tradesmen who had at one time supplied goods and services to the pre-war owners and occupiers.

In the twenty or so years immediately preceding and following the Second World War large numbers of council houses were built in towns and villages across the country, which provided well-built homes at a reasonable rent with a degree of security in respect of tenure for the many people unable to afford to purchase a home of their own or pay private rental charges. This went a long way toward alleviating overcrowding in the towns and reducing the thraldom of farm labourers living in tied cottages, to their employers. Burnham was no different – Killarney and Sutherland Avenues were built, together with Moreland and Poplar estates in Highbridge; the immediate result of which was to provide homes for those families who had been temporarily housed in the Nissen huts of the then

The old manual telephone exchange at 13 Cross Street, shortly before its closure around 1951/52

defunct POW camp and elsewhere in the area. This increase in the number of homes meant that the telephone exchanges in Cross Street, and Newtown Road Highbridge, were no longer able to cope with the demands on them; so they were replaced with a brand new STD exchange built in one corner of the old camp site.

At the time of the Tithe Commutation Act in **1838** most of Highbridge was a part of Burnham which was bounded on the north by Brent Broad, with the old River Brue marking its southernmost limit. It stretched inland as far as the beginning of Mark Causeway at Watchfield. With the consecration of the church of Saint John the Evangelist, Highbridge became a parish in its own right in **1859**. In **1896** it acquired Urban District status which lasted until **1933** when new local government legislation brought the two towns together again. This change in local government set up was understandably greatly resented by many Highbridge people. After a few years the feeling of injustice has died down although persisting among some of the older residents.

Throughout Victoria's reign and that of Edward VII drunkenness in public places was a fairly common sight locally, as elsewhere, but became increasingly less so during the reign of George V. Burnham beer was cheap, but the local farmhouse cider, a most potent drink, being made much cheaper still was consumed in enormous quantities. During the last half of the twentieth and the beginning of the twenty-first centuries, drunkenness became more common again aggravated by the use of recreational drugs which often made many people not just uninhibited but often violently aggressive[70].

Cricket has been played in Burnham since Victorian times. In **1884** the large field adjoining the gas works and part of Love Lane Farm, was designated as a cricket ground[71]. Burnham Cricket Club held its inaugural meeting at the Royal Clarence on Monday 8 February **1887**[72]. Some years later the location changed to a field north of Pillsmouth Farm where it remained until it removed to the Gardenhurst sports field in Rectory Road. When Gardenhurst

Burnham Cricket Team 1895.

closed and the land was sold for redevelopment the Cricket Club, in company with several other sports clubs moved to the Burnham Association of Sports Clubs ground at the bottom of Stoddens Road.

Highbridge C. C. came into being later, playing initially on a field belonging to Hatcher's Farm before moving to the 'Cricket Field' shown on the **1928** revision of the O. S. map as being where Poplar estate now stands.

Over the years Burnham and Highbridge have supported a considerable number of football teams,

often several at the same time (not counting junior teams). Many of these also used the Coronation Field and the Pillsmouth ground[73] when they were not being used for cricket[74]. In **2010** football is still being played at the Recreation Field) in Highbridge which was acquired by the local council in **1933**.

Football match on the Pillsmouth ground – Burnham Albion v Burnham Adult School. Note the Queen's and Pier Hotels in the background.

1898 saw the foundation of a local cycling club with Edwin Horril as the captain. A hockey club was also formed in that year. Other, relatively energetic and popular outdoor pastimes in the area, which have since been legislated against were Hare Coursing and Fox Hunting.

Hockey team 1920.

---

70 Interviewed for a local paper, a resident of South Street (which runs along the South Side of York House between the Esplanade and High Street) stated that he was fed up with washing the blood off of the pavement and road outside his house.

71 The Home Ground belonging to Love Lane Farm part of which, during the early years of the twentieth century became the site of Kingsway and Dunstan Roads, with the remainder being known as the Coronation Field.

72 In January of 1911 the club held a '*Smoking Concert*' at the Town Hall in order to raise funds.

73 In those days, the sporting seasons followed each other without the degree of overlap found during the twenty-first century.

74 Editor's note: It is interesting to note that on the various revisions of the O.S. maps of Burnham and Highbridge various fields are marked as Cricket Fields, even when they served a dual purpose, suggesting that cricketers took preference, and were somehow superior to footballers.

Hare Coursing Club at Brean.

Fox hounds meet at Berrow.

Avenue L.T.C.

Tennis was both popular and fashionable during the early part of the twentieth century. The Avenue Croquet[75] and Lawn Tennis Club was formed in **1909** and established on land, initially leased, from Hart House School which was selling off the land on the west side of the property that, when redeveloped eventually became the Grove and the east side of Berrow Road. The first pavilion was a disused railway carriage from the Somerset and Dorset Joint Railway. It seems odd and strangely refreshing, in these days of Political Correctness and anti-discrimination laws, to read that male and female players were segregated and that the club was unashamedly elitist with new members having to receive a minimum of seven votes in their favour after being proposed and seconded, with one black ball being sufficient to override all the white ones. The needs of those who could not or would not join the Avenue club were catered for by

Opening of Baptist tennis courts in 1922.

various other tennis courts around the town, provided by other organisations such as the local Adult School, who also had their own football team.

75　Croquet was dropped from the name in 1911.

45

The Burnham and Berrow Golf Club links extend from the westward end of Saint Christopher's Way northward to a point some distance beyond Berrow church. From quite modest beginnings the links were extended to eighteen holes in **1897**. Initially, ladies

Burnham and Berrow Golf Club – the original clubhouse, opening ceremony.

Golf demonstration match between Taylor and Braid – Taylor being the club professional and Braid a player of national repute.

Ladies Golf Championship 1906. Miss Bertha Thompson driving off. She went on to win the championship.

were not allowed to play other than on their own links which were established between Saint Ann's and the Mount where they also had their own clubhouse. When a large part of the links were lost to the sea they ceased to be viable and after remaining unused for years the Trinity Rise development was laid out on the land after an earlier application for planning permission to use the land for a holiday park was refused.

Ladies golf links club-house – the houses in the background are in Gore Road.

Being a sea-side town, there was a higher proportion of water related recreations. Around **1912** there were changing rooms standing near the head of the jetty, that were used by the local swimming club when

Swimming Club changing rooms.

Marine Lake with diving platform, mid/late 1930s.

the tide came in[76]. Alternatively if one lacked the patience to wait for a stupid fish to swallow one's hook, there was skimming, where the skimmer pushed a net through the water and scooped out shrimps, flat fish, and even the occasional eel. For those who enjoyed messing about with water, but

---

76 This consisted of only a few hours per day when the tide was coming in.

Skimming for shrimp or flat fish. The best place was N of Allandale Road inshore from where the old sewer outfalls discharged.

preferred to keep their feet dry, there was the Burnham Model Yacht Club, founded in **1921** with Leonard Lott as its first chairman. The one for owners of full sized models came later.

Members of the model yacht club – 2nd from L front row is Leonard Lott the founder chairman.

The Burnham Bowling Club green and clubhouse was established between Saint Andrew's Road and the Manor Gardens (from which there was at one time an access). The club was founded in **1906**.

Bowling Club pavilion.

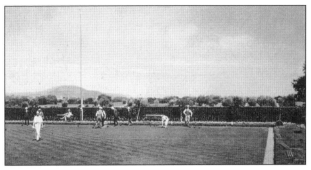

Bowling green with view of Brent Knoll, before Saint Andrew's Road was developed.

Burnham was not alone when it came to sporting clubs and facilities, Highbridge Swimming Club predated the one in Burnham. The Cricket Ground and pavilion were on land behind Church Street, later developed as Poplar estate. The local tennis courts were on land between Brue Farm and the river. There was also a large angling club that had its headquarters at the Highbridge Hotel.

Highbridge Angling Club, outside the Highbridge Inn. John Charles White was the licensee from around 1910, but had gone by 1919. Note the bottles of beer in front of the club officers, and the poultry hanging from the front of the table – competition prizes, perhaps?

One thing that Highbridge had that Burnham did not was a Motor Cycle Club although little seems to be known about it, other than its emblem was a pair of spoked wheels, on a circular white ground with a black border, inscribed **HIGHBRIDGE M.C.C.**

Highbridge Motor Cycle Club badge.

From time to time the people of Burnham have participated in many less strenuous activities with clubs and societies dedicated to model yacht building, stamp collecting, debating, archaeology and local history, as well as a wide range of the performing arts.

Pageant Society performance.

Early carnival float.

Carnival walking entry (1927 photo taken in what is now GH Tyres depot in Adam Street).

The Pageant Society put on a variety of shows during the early **1900s**, usually if not exclusively out of doors, in the grounds of Hart House or on the lawns of the Manor Gardens. The only other form of outdoor theatricals, apart from small-time professional entertainers during the summer months, during the first half of the century was the Summer Carnival that was run on August Bank Holiday in conjunction with the 'Hospital Fête' which provided funds for the local hospital which had been built to commemorate the dead of the First World War. The floats for this event bore little resemblance to the hundred foot long illuminated monsters that we know today, sometimes being nothing more than a decorated hand cart. Enthusiasm for this waned in the **1950s** as did that for the Highbridge Guy Fawkes Carnival. As the Highbridge Carnival necessitated the closing of the A38 through the town, when it revival was mooted several years later a different route had to be found so Burnham and Highbridge Carnivals were combined into one and run over a much less contentious route.

Albert Chevalier's Recitals, 1905.

Operatic Society, 1925 production of Rebel Maid. *The group photo was always taken in front of the Infant School opposite the Town Hall.*

Madam Watson's Poppy Orchestra, circa 1911.

In addition to numerous choirs and choral societies Burnham had, in the closing years of the century, six amateur theatrical companies covering most things from light opera to pantomime. One of these was the Burnham Amateur Dramatic Society which had been going strong since the beginning of the century, although like other organisations they took time off for the wars. Of these groups the only one to survive into the twenty-first century is the Pantomime Society although a number of small groups with varying degrees of talent have come and gone during those hundred years.

During the summer seasons a variety of professional performers, ranging from circuses to orchestras, brass bands and pierrot shows entertained locals and visitors alike.

Freddy Fay's Dinky Dots on the stage in the Manor Gardens Enclosure, 1933.

In the run-up to the Second World War, Burnham boasted two cinemas and a 'chippy'. The cinemas were the Majestic (originally the Burnham Electric Theatre) at the southern end of High Street, adjoining Sunny Lawns; and the Ritz in Victoria Street, on the corner of Vicarage Street, both, at that time being part of the Trueman Dicken circuit.

Smedley's Military Band, 1908.

John Baker outside his Fish and Chip shop at 4 Cross Street accompanied by 'Titch' King (a local salt) with his parrot.

The Fish and Chip Shop was in upper Cross Street. Until a few years before it ceased trading in the late **1930s** it had been given as a restaurant, unlike the 'Star Fish and Chip Bar' which operated at 79 Oxford Street circa **1911** and had ceased trading by the outbreak of war.

There was a third cinema, of a similar vintage to the Majestic, that was in Highbridge. It rejoiced in the highly unoriginal name of the Picture House, later to be known as the Regent. After its closure it became the Regal Club before being demolished to make way for a small housing development. Most of the above activities would have been advertised or reported on in the local newspapers, of which the *Burnham Gazette* is the longest running title having been founded in **1864** and remained in the possession of the Patey family until it was bought by the *Bridgwater Mercury* in the latter years of the twentieth century; by which time it had become the *Burnham Gazette and Highbridge Express*. For a few years prior to the Second World War there was a second paper, the *Herald*, which for most of its life was published in conjunction with the *Highbridge Echo* which first hit the news stands in **1894**[77]. Later, during the late **1900s**, came *The Burnham and Highbridge Weekly News*, the last of the non-free papers.

77 Both of these papers were published under a variety of names throughout their lives.

Churches and Religion

As it is difficult, at times, to make a clear divide between Churches as a body of worshippers and churches as the buildings where they worship, this chapter makes no attempt to treat them separately; therefore, in the interest of expediency and minimal confusion, church, and parish halls, as well as Church organisations are dealt with herein, excepting only the old Vicarage which is a building of some interest in its own right.

Because England has been (at least notionally) a Christian country for well over a thousand years it follows that many of its churches are of great age, often with the documentation to prove it. In the absence of a castle they were the hub around which the life and activities of the community were centred, and being so much more substantially built than any ordinary dwelling they have lasted many hundreds of years longer. It therefore follows that, as the priesthood was the only consistently literate class, there is much more recorded information available about them than almost any other category of buildings.

CHURCH OF ENGLAND CHURCHES
SAINT ANDREW'S

The Rev. T. C. Dupuis who was vicar of St Andrew's church at Burnham **1867-1914** who carried out extensive research on the subject, stated that the earliest notice relating to Burnham in the Cathedral archives at Wells was undated, but indicated by the subject matter of its content that it had been written prior to **1292** and showed the parish of Burnham to be a satellite of the Greater St Andrew's under Mendip.

These records show that at that time the church at Burnham was valued at 25 marks[78] out of which a pension of 10 marks was to be paid to the Bishop at Wells. This was later appropriated to the Dean and Chapter of Wells in **1336** in which year a vicarage was ordained. From the absence in their records of any information relating to the physical characteristics of

the village of Burnham at that time or on matters secular concerning the inhabitants it must be assumed that the old monkish chronicles were more concerned with the re-establishment and development of the church at Burnham than with such mundane matters as did not directly affect their spiritual responsibilities and/or those of the local community.

In a charter dated 12 April **1305** Walter de Hazelshaw Bishop of Bath and Wells granted to John Dean of Wells 2 acres of land at Burnham together with the advowson[79] of the church of St Andrew's in the same village In the following year he issued another in which he called for an annual payment of £10. by the church at Burnham as a contribution toward the great expenses incurred by the Dean and Chapter of Wells who had all but impoverished themselves in building their Cathedral Chapter House.

In other documents reference was made to the fact that Bishop Burnell in **1292** and Bishop Hazelshaw in **1308** took over the revenue of the church at Burnham to found their orbits or endow chantries, where masses might be celebrated for their souls, at an income of some ten pounds per annum. One such chantry might well have been set up on Steart Island where many years ago ancient graves were exposed in which lay skeletons which from the manner in which they were buried indicated that they were the remains of former priests. The late Canon Robert Sellers of Wells had since his retirement to Burnham commenced researching the subject of local chantries and was investigating the possibility of this being so. There is evidence of a chantry being long established about this time near Burnham but which was closed by Thomas Stede rector of Burnham at the time.

It was six years later in **1314** the year of Bannockburn that Bishop Brockensford rebuilt the parish church at Burnham 'in a clearing of the sand dunes among the cottages of the farm workers and fisher folk'. The implication being that he was responsible

---

78   At that time the mark was a monetary unit used primarily for accounting purposes.

79   OED 'The right of presentation to a benefice.'

for the construction of the current building as a replacement for an earlier structure. In the summer of the following year it was dedicated to the honour of St Andrew by Bishop Brokensford who at that time declared that "Those who frequent it with due contrition, confession and votive oblations shall thereby be accorded forty days indulgence".

The construction of the tower, which was added around a hundred years later must have caused much anxiety and worry to the builders and church authorities alike because, almost from the outset substantial settlement took place which resulted in the whole structure taking a considerable list to the north. To minimise the damage that might occur to the fabric of the remainder of the building in the event of the tower falling over, a false joint was inserted between the tower and the nave instead of the usual tie-in of timber and masonry; this allowed for independent movement of both structures.

The most likely cause of this settlement was running sand the presence of which over the years has caused subsidence to occur in other parts of the local-ity[80]. The mineral springs discovered in later years close by might well have been a contributory factor in creating the instability of the subsoil beneath the tower. The inclination of the tower to the north of some three feet is most apparent when viewed from a boat out in the bay. Although the angle of inclination from the vertical in no way compares with that of the leaning tower at Pisa the overhang of the tower of St Andrew's was considered to be sufficiently far from perpendicular as to make it necessary to take down the masonry and rebuild the upper part of the tower in **1887** in what would appear to have been a completely successful attempt to arrest any further movement beyond the limit reached at that time. This work, which called for a very high degree of practical expertise, was carried out by the brothers Harding, members of a family with roots in the locality since the time of the conquest and whose ancestors had followed the craft of stonemasons for generations.

Within the basic shell of the building, little remains of the original interior work, due in part to the considerable amount of modernisation and restoration work carried out in England on so many ecclesiastical buildings during the reigns of Henry VIII and Victoria, as a result of which nearly all vestiges of earlier work in the church at Burnham have disappeared. One of the few remaining examples of the earliest work is the late twelfth century Lady Chapel dedicated to St Nicholas. This according to expert opinion given at the time of the **1875/9** restoration was built originally to contain two tombs each one being overhung with a canopy the chapel window being similarly adorned. At the time of this restoration work, remains of a similar canopy were found built into the wall of the chancel; these were removed and placed by the well in the garden of the Old Vicarage where they remained for over twenty years. In addition, there also remains the arch of the south doorway and the Holy Water stoop. The scratch sundial on the left side of the south door is believed to have been originally built into the wall of the church which preceded the present structure. The consecration cross on the east side of this entrance arch is the only one surviving. The most recent restora-

Saint Andrew's church, leaning tower – from the W.

Scratch sundial to L of church door, suggesting that the S porch was not part of the original construction.

---

80 See also Ritz Cinema, Chapter 7.

Holy water stoop to right of church door.

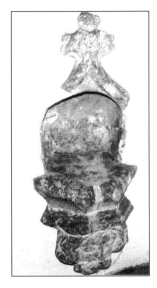

tion work to be carried out to the Lady Chapel was the insertion of the completely new stone window in **1975**.

It was during the incumbency of Dr Walker King **1799-1827**, that it was found necessary to replace the bells in the tower. These were five in number and so broken as to be quite unusable. All five had been in use for many years and having served the community well were taken down and replaced in **1823** with a peal of six new bells which were set up in the tower after being transported in two vessels by sea from London to Bridgwater for transhipment by road to Burnham a team of oxen was employed to haul them into the bell chamber. The names inscribed on these bells make interesting reading, being those of the forebears of some well known local families long resident on the Burnham area :-

John Buncombe, a local landowner, surveyor and parish councillor, James Blair and Samuel Daunton, Richard Hardwidge and Edmund Board, Thomas Hembry, John Allen, William Morse and William Adams.

Most of the above being farmers and landowners, the name of the last one being perpetuated in Adam Street after Adams' Orchards on which land this thoroughfare was laid down in the opening years of the twentieth century. The sixth bell was inscribed with the names of James Clothier and John Dod, the latter whose ancestor Henry Dod had acquired Pillsmouth Farm in **1668** from the Brodripp family.

For eighty years these bells rang out their Easter and Christmas message to the townsfolk of Burnham and at other times of public rejoicing as well as on more sad and sombre occasions – the Golden and Diamond Jubilees of Queen Victoria, her death in **1901** and on the news breaking of the relief of Mafeking. Whether the exuberance of the ringers on this occasion was in any way responsible is open to question, but, certainly, it was about this time that the bell cage and bells were found to be in need of extensive repair. So successful was the appeal for money to cover the cost of this work that sufficient funds were raised enabling the church authorities in **1902** to have the existing bells re-hung in a new bell cage with the addition of two new bells at a total cost of £350.

This work was carried out by Thos. Nears, bell founders of London the same firm who had made and installed the earlier six bells in **1823**. On 25 March **1902** the new bells were dedicated by the Bishop of Bath and Wells Dr George William Kennion. One of the new bells was inscribed to commemorate the long reign of Queen Victoria and the other the coronation of her son Edward VII. The names of the vicar the Rev. T. C. Dupuis appear on these bells as also do those of Richard Brice and Alfred Whitaker (churchwardens) and G. B. Sully and Henry Marchent chairman and vice chairman of the Burnham Urban District Council. Except for the period covered by the **1939-45** war, when the ringing of church bells was banned, they have been in regular use ever since.

Victoria and Edward bells arriving at the church on a farm wagon.

In **1824** St Andrew's church became the recipient of a truly magnificent gift. This was the presentation by the blind Bishop of Rochester Dr Walker King, of the beautiful marbles designed by Inigo Jones and sculptured by the master craftsman Grinling Gibbons and his pupil Arnold Quellin. These marbles had originally been commissioned by King James II whose intention it was that they should become part of the altar piece being constructed for the chapel of the Palace of Whitehall. After his death in **1701**, on the instructions of Queen Anne, the altar piece was dismantled and removed to Westminster Abbey where all the component parts were placed behind the high altar and where they remained for many years being considered as unsuitable for re-erection there on the grounds of not being in accordance with the surrounding architecture; in consequence of which they were offered to Bishop Walker King by the Dean and Chapter of Westminster and out of kind regard for the parishioners of Burnham whose vicar he had been for 25 years dedicated the gift he had received 'To the greater glory of God within these walls'.

When first placed in the chancel at St Andrew's they were erected in such a manner that the whole of the east window was obscured. The installation of this masterpiece aroused a great deal of interest among parishioners who were encouraged to visit the church and inspect them, and in so doing contribute to church finances. According to a contemporary account this invitation to the people of Burnham to inspect the celebrated marbles however regretfully introduced a somewhat sour note to the whole proceedings when an announcement was made to the effect that especially produced for the persons of "condition" an illustrated book printed on superior paper and enclosed between hard covers giving a complete history of the marbles was available at a cost of 5/- per copy, which covered the cost of admission to view the chancel which at that time was shut off from the rest of the church by a gate under lock and key. Persons not of condition to pay less for admission and to have a guide book of inferior quality

In **1838**, the local population having greatly increased in numbers, it was thought desirable that additional accommodation should be provided and this object was achieved by demolishing the north wall and extending the structure in that direction by some fourteen feet, thereby creating a north aisle with a gallery above. The six columns supporting both this and the roof above stood on the foundations of the original wall. The whole scheme was considered by many to be an architectural and aesthetic disaster, the previously long and comely nave being debased by a sham colonnade and a skied gallery;

Sketch from the Dupuis Diaries showing a possible rearrangement of the panels around the E window.

the architect a Mr Carver being described as more of a builder than a professional expert.

The year **1867** marked the commencement of what was to prove to be the third longest period of ministry served by any vicar at St Andrew's Burnham when Rev. Theodore Crane Dupuis was appointed to the living at a stipend of £100 per annum. It was during his incumbency that further repairs and renovations were put in hand. These works were carried out by the Ecclesiastical Commissioners as lay rectors and although not of the order of those carried out in **1838** were never the less of considerable importance and the merit of the handiwork of those who contributed to this work is still in evidence.

Until **1875** the Grinling Gibbons carvings as erected by Bishop Walker King occupied almost the whole of the east wall of the sanctuary. These were removed in their entirety and the most suitable of them re-arranged and re-erected to form the present surround and reredos. Those not used for this purpose were then placed at the west end of the church beneath the tower and a smaller group of figures in one of the north wall windows. The re-disposition of these carvings made it possible for a new east window to be constructed this portrays the Transfiguration of Christ and was provided by public subscription at a cost of £79. 6. 0d.

The 'Grinling Gibbons' altarpiece as originally arranged – obscuring the E window.

One of the two angels on new plinths, flanking the tower arch, after restoration in 2010.

For many years, in common with most country churches, no seating accommodation was provided at St Andrew's. The floor of the nave consisted of well trodden earth which was covered and re-covered with reeds from time to time as was considered necessary. There is, however, evidence that at some time during the eighteenth century efforts had been made to provide limited seating accommodation for the parishioners which was later extended to the whole of the nave area. This accommodation consisted of totally enclosed high backed pews for which those appropriating them paid pew rents. These were removed in **1875/6** and the present free and unappropriated pews installed.

When the flooring beneath the old pews was removed a number of stone coffins without lids were found, each containing a female skeleton. It was suggested at the time of their discovery that they were those of the foundresses of the original building, although there is no evidence to support the claim. It was also while the old pews were being removed that the opportunity was taken to lift the ancient slabs with which the chancel floor was paved and re-level the surface and lay down the decorated tiles that now cover it. The first of the enclosed pews to be constructed were most likely to have been the ones installed by those wealthy farmers of Burnham

referred to by Richard Locke in somewhat scathing terms as by their selfish monopoly of so much floor space depriving many of the poorer inhabitants of the facility to worship in comparative comfort. A first hand account of the conditions under which parishioners worshipped at St Andrew's church in the mid nineteenth century is given by Mrs Dupuis in her journal.

Some attempt to alleviate the acute discomfort experienced by those attending divine worship during the winter was made in **1870** when a gill stove was installed near the south entrance. This, while better than nothing at all, provided only limited relief, for when operating at maximum capacity almost roasted anyone sitting near it, while leaving those beyond its area of radiation little or no warmer than before. This stove, however, remained the sole source of heating within the building for many years and even this innovation was strongly opposed by some, actuated possibly by the commonly held belief that there was merit in mortifying the flesh and that to suffer personal discomfort was essential to ultimate salvation and should be accepted without question by all good Christians. In **1906** church members were at last able to worship in comfort when the old gill stove was removed and, prejudice having long since been overcome, replaced by the installation of central heating.

The circumstances which gave rise to the removal of the ancient font from the Baptistry in **1881** are not at all clear but it is known that it was given in that year by the Rev. Dupuis to a one time curate of his the Rev. Peppin for use in his church at Horrington. The old font which had been presented to the church by the family of Austin Board whose memorial tablet is close by was replaced by one made of various marbles erected in **1883** and given to St Andrew's by Dr Board of Clifton in memory of his family and is the one at present in use (**2010**).

For many years, forming part of an ornamental window at the old vicarage there were three glass panels bearing the date **1618** and incorporating in their design the arms of what had long been thought to be those of the Roche family of which the Earl of Rochester was a member and who for a period during the sixteenth century had resided here. The accuracy however of some of these statements was disputed by Mr W. B. Brassington who had carried out extensive research on the matter during the early part of the twentieth century which resulted in the arms being declared as those of the Allen family – a gold shield whereon was a black chevron between three black bloodhounds passant. The inclusion of the date **1618** was accepted as a confirmative factor. These items were removed from the old vicarage by the Rev.

Arms of the Allen family in the S window.

tower were taken down and rebuilt by William and Gabriel Harding; the date for this work being commemorated by the casting of the date **1887** in the cistern heads of the rain water pipes draining the lead roof of the tower.

Date on cistern head beside the clock face.

Dupuis and placed for safe keeping in the church where they were set up in a glazed frame for protection and kept in the vestry until, eventually, being fitted into the centre of the nave window between the south porch and the tower where they may still be seen.

The year **1885** saw the fulfilment of a long felt need when it was decided to dispense with the antiquated organ which had been built by Beals of Bridgwater and which had been in use for so many years at the west end of the church, and replace it with one of more up to date design. Made by Vowles of Bristol the cost of the new organ was £315. To enable it to be installed in the most suitable position permission was obtained from the Ecclesiastical Commissioners to open a great hole in the chancel wall from floor to wall plate to provide an aperture of sufficient height to accommodate the 16 foot stop. Because of its size the new organ, when installed, reduced considerably the already limited space in the old vestry; an inconvenience that was endured for over forty years until **1926** when the present vestry was built during the incumbency of the Rev. Hereward E. Wake. This vestry and offices, together with the much criticised north gallery of **1838** comprise the only additions to the church structure since the building of the tower.

Coinciding with the installation of the new organ was the establishment of the choir in the newly constructed stalls in the chancel, and which are those at present in use. It must have been highly diverting for the choirboys sitting opposite when shortly after the new organ was installed strange noises were heard coming from its interior during the singing of the psalms and upon the music stopping a cat appeared through a gap in the panelling and interviewed the organist, according to witnesses of the incident.

The final phase of this particular period of restoration work was in **1887** when the upper sections of the

After the completion of these major works almost a century was to pass before further restoration work of any magnitude was carried out to the actual fabric of the church when in **1975**, during the incumbency of the Rev. Raymond Dean, extensive works costing in excess of £20,000 were carried out. This work included the total redecoration of the inside in pastel shades of green, ceiling bosses and relief work being highlighted with gold. These decorations, completely different from any previous work did not meet with general approval, particularly among the more conservative minded.

In addition to restoring and maintaining the fabric it has also been necessary over the years to renew and add to the various fittings and installations within the building. Few additions to the church can have had a greater impact on the inhabitants of Burnham as a whole than the installation of the clock and subsequent provision of the Westminster chimes. The clock mechanism was originally commissioned by the Dean and Chapter of Wells in about **1830** for the purpose of driving the automata of the famous cathedral clock, but although well constructed was found to be of insufficient power to do so.

Desiring to dispose of these clock works they were offered by the Dean and Chapter at a low rate to the Rev. Dupuis who, after having them examined by Mr Fisher, an expert, bought them on his recommendation. Additional parts, face hands and figures were obtained from the London makers and the complete clock was installed in the tower in **1890**. A photograph taken at the time by one of the mechanics carrying out the work shows the suspended scaffold and a mechanic working on the clock face while another showed Juliet Dupuis as a small child peeping through the clock face which was then resting against the foot of the tower. It was not until fourteen years later that the now familiar Westminster chimes were installed and linked to the clock mechanism. They were first heard by the townsfolk of Burnham at Easter **1904**.

Saint Andrew's Church Hall, not long after it was built in 1912.

Until the early years of the twentieth century most church activities were still limited to those that it was considered could properly be carried on within the church itself or in the vicarage, or, as a less satisfactory alternative, in the National School buildings which at best were not ideally suitable for the purpose of holding religious social events. With a rising population and the formation of such affiliated bodies as the Mothers Union, the Church of England Missionary Society, the Church Lads Brigade and others. The need to acquire a building where these and other more secular activities could be carried on but still mainly under the auspices of the church became ever more pressing, a fact which had been recognised for a long time.

For many years the Burnham Pageant Society had directed its efforts almost entirely to the raising of money for church purposes, and towards that end had organised various events and devoted the proceeds to defraying the cost of specific items of

expenditure incurred from time to time by the Parochial Church Council such as the bell cage restoration and many others. Their most ambitious project ever was to raise sufficient money to cover the cost of building a hall which would enable all such church activities to be carried on in comfort and for the enjoyment of the parish as a whole. Pageants with mainly medieval themes were held in the spacious grounds of Hart House School and in the Manor Gardens. The beautiful trees and ornamental lake of the former providing a most attractive backdrop to many of the scenes. One particularly spectacular different enterprise called for the construction in the Town Hall of a Swiss village, with miniature snow-covered chalets, in which a fair was held on two successive days; this particular event producing a profit of £268. 'Converiatziones' and other events of a less spectacular nature were also arranged and altogether raised enough money to cover about three quarters of the total cost, which amounted to £1,200.

The hall was dedicated and opened on 1 March **1912** by Dr Kennion, Bishop of Bath and Wells after a service in St Andrew's church. By a sad quirk of fate the man who had worked the hardest to bring the project to fruition E. P. Davis, a local businessman, died suddenly shortly before the hall was opened.

Apart from the Mother's Union, Men's Society, and the usual children's organisations, Saint Andrew's also supported a thriving and highly competent drama group during the early post-war years until a disagreement with the church authorities over 'artistic policy' forced its closure. It re-formed under the name of the Phoenix Players and continued for many years to win awards at local and national drama festivals.

MISSION CHURCH
Edithmead
(The Tin Church)

Consecrated in **1910** as a chapel of ease. Its name and nickname tell us a lot. It is a small building with corrugated iron walls and roof over a timber frame. It was built to fill the needs of the small, largely agricultural,

The mission church at Edithmead (the Tin Church).

community most of whose members would, otherwise, have had to walk about two miles to worship at the mother church.

SAINT PETER'S

Built on land owned by the local brewery and donated by Thomas Holt the head of the family. It was proposed in **1920** that some of the money donated towards a memorial to Preb. Hayes Robinson who had been vicar during the war years be put towards this project. Pollards of Bridgwater tendered £2,225 for the work. When no longer required as a church, it was sold to the local Roman Catholic Church for use as a hall in **1976/77**. Planning permission was granted in **2008** for it to be replaced with a block of flats. It was demolished in March **2009**, together with the bungalow next door.

Saint Peter's church, Highbridge Road.

Interior of Saint Peter's church.

SAINT JOHN'S
Highbridge

The story goes that when passing through the town, possibly on her way to, or from her home at Badgworth Court, Mary Ann Luttrell noticed the conditions of the place and the people and noting the lack of a church, decided to build and endow one. After the consecration of the church of Saint John the Evangelist in **1860**, Highbridge became a parish in its own right. Hitherto it had always been part of the ecclesiastical, and later civil, parish of Burnham.

Saint John's is the only building in Highbridge that Pevsner bothered with, and then, only to the extent of four lines. Being so relatively young, as churches go, it has not been around long enough to have acquired any benefactions or memorials of note. Perhaps the most interesting piece of its history is that when it was first built it possessed a quite elegant spire which unfortunately was constructed in such a way that its weight caused the top of the tower walls to spread and become dangerous, thus necessitating its removal in **1911**.

Saint John's church, scaffolded for the removal of its spire, 1911.

ROMAN CATHOLIC CHURCHES

Following the reformation, there was no established place of worship for Catholics in the locality for something in the region of three hundred years. Initially there was only a small mission chapel in Bridgwater serving the area until **1871** when a branch mission was established in Highbridge with visiting priests from Bridgwater, the Bishop arranging for them to celebrate mass once a month. During the intervening periods the church members assembled for united prayer under the leadership of laymen who were most assiduous in instructing the children in their catechism. Until the nuns came to Burnham and established their convent of the Retreat of the Sacred Heart of Jesus this was the only way that the religious needs of the local Roman Catholic community could be met without travelling to Bridgwater or Weston.

The first thing that the nuns did after getting their convent 'up and running' was set about building a proper chapel in which to carry out their devotions and from the start, made it available to the Catholic community as a whole for use as their parish church. The centre for Catholic worship in the district then moved from Highbridge and the mission there was closed. There was no formal opening when the church was used for the first time on Sunday 27 April **1890**. The Bishop of Clifton the Hon. William Hugh Clifford being away at the time on a visit to the Holy Land, the service of consecration was not held until 1 July after his return. In his absence the new buildings were blessed by an ordinary priest who celebrated mass on a temporary altar.

In **1902** the convent chapel was re-decorated in a highly ornamental style by Davenport, most of the wall surfaces being covered with a stylized, stencilled fleur de lis design which although most artistically executed imparted for the next seventy years a some-what sombre appearance to the interior. However, during the winter of **1975/6** the chapel interior under-went considerable renovation in a manner more in keeping with current tastes and requirements. The sanctuary was separated from the nave by an open-work wrought iron screen and the altar and tabernacle therein replaced at a lower level. A secondary altar was placed across one corner of the nave and the seating was re-aligned to suit this new position. The whole interior was made much brighter and the requirements of personal comfort were contributed to by the installation of a modern heating system.

The church of the Sacred Heart continued to be used by the Catholic community as a whole until the church of Our Lady and the English Martyrs (built on the site of an old cottage (*BUR 360*) was dedicated in

Convent chapel, post 1976.

April **1967**. The new church was built at the time of the Rhodesia Crisis when Prime Minister Ian Smith made the Unilateral Declaration of Independence. Unfortunately, Rhodesia was at that time a major copper producing country and the church had been designed with a copper roof. Fortunately this did not affect the cost of the building as all the metal had already been delivered but it did cause a headache for the contractors as, with rapidly escalating copper prices, their site became a potential target for metal thieves. The problem was solved by distributing the precious rolls of metal at a number of locations around the area with only two people knowing where it all was – the managing director of the company and the man whose job it was to collect and deliver enough for the day's work to the site[81]. The church was built on the site of a ramshackle two-storied house with a long roof that sloped down to ground floor ceiling level at the back and had been standing at the time of the **1838** survey.

Interior of convent chapel, circa 1911.

Our Lady and the English Martyrs nearing completion in 1966.

81 Norris Mercer was the M.D. of W.J. Pople, the contractor and "Gill" Young the other.

Our Lady and the English Martyrs, interior – a service of ordination.

When the C of E church of Saint Peter was deconsecrated the parishioners bought it for use as a parish hall and youth club in place of the prefabricated building which had stood behind the church.

NONCONFORMIST PLACES OF WORSHIP

With the clergy of the established church being made up largely of lesser sons of the aristocracy or, at least, men of 'good family', an 'us and them' culture was inevitably prevalent, with the humble workers being made to feel of little account, especially as the major-

ity of churches were established in the more well-to-do parts of the towns. There can be little doubt that such circumstances contributed substantially to the development of nonconformist worship which usually started in the poorer and rougher areas that were mainly populated by the labouring class where elaborate ceremonies and rich vestments were inappropriate and of little meaning as well as being largely incomprehensible to any potential worshippers.

BAPTIST CHURCH
(Burnham)

1843 saw the erection of the Baptist chapel in Burnham. For some time it stood alone surrounded by warren until the school buildings nearby were put up by George Reed twelve years later. In those times it was not necessary to obtain planning permission and building control approval. Soon after the land had been purchased from William Clements who owned the Royal Clarence Hotel and a lot of the surrounding land the construction work was commenced. It is interesting to note the degree of trust between the parties as the conveyancing documents were not signed until 10 August **1843**, two days before the chapel was opened for its first service. Prior to that date, in common with most other groups of dissenters, meetings for worship had been held in the private houses of its members. The church was regis-

Early engraving of Burnham Baptist church standing alone on the sand dunes.

Baptism in the sea.

tered with the Bishop of Bath and Wells as 'a place set aside for the public worship of Almighty God by a congregation of Protestant Dissenters' on 11 July **1844**. In early days baptisms by total immersion were conducted regularly in the sea, a practice which has continued at infrequent intervals, even after the construction of the chapel with its indoor baptistery for which (according to the records) a new well was dug in **1874**.

Unlike so many, chapels and small churches of similar age which have been sold to be re-used as homes, engineering workshops or auction rooms, this one entered the twenty-first century on a very positive note. In **1980** Elnathan[82], the most easterly of a terrace, originally of five houses, adjoining the chapel was demolished to make way for a new extension providing the up-to-date customised facilities that even the most devout and forbearing worshippers seem to expect in this day and age.

BAPTIST CHURCH
(Highbridge)
Hope, Baptist church, Church Street.

Hope Baptist church was the first custom built place of worship in Highbridge and the first non-conformist church in the parish of Burnham. It opened its doors on 19 April **1819** although the church, as a body of worshippers, began only two years earlier in **1817**. A plaque in the front gable records the date when the building was enlarged and extended in **1868**.

Hope Baptist church, Highbridge – Rev. Smith's jubilee celebrations.

BAPTIST CONGREGATIONAL CHURCH
Huntspill Road

When this was constructed it was in the parish of Huntspill. The inscription on the tablet in the gable end of the building gives the date as **1895**. One year before the Civil Parish of South Highbridge was created, incorporating that land which was between the old River Brue and what is now known as Alstone Lane. For many years since, it has ceased to fulfil its original function and has been used as a garage or an engineering works.

METHODIST CHURCH
(Burnham)

The earliest written record of a Wesleyan Methodist church building in Burnham states '… the Chapel was

---

82 It had been purchased in 1883 to provide accommodation for the pastor, the Sunday School, and other facilities for the church.

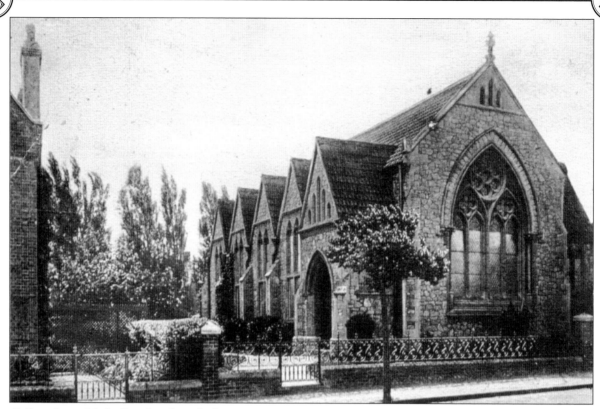

College Street Methodist church, early days.

New entrance to College Street Methodist church, 2010.

opened by the Rev. J. Rattenbury. January 17th **1860'**. When built, this building stood in isolation to the south of what was the main part of the town but now marks the corner of Adam Street and High Street. It continued in use as such until a replacement was built in College Street after which it served as a venue for the Sunday School and other church activities.

The new church was built in **1879** at a cost of around £1,300, all the costs and expenses being recorded in a new ledger which cost two shillings and three pence (a little less than 12.5 p). When in **1906** the church was enlarged and new Sunday School room and other facilities built on the back at a total cost of £1,250 the trustees agreed to offer the old building for sale in the evening of 25 October **1906** and it was bought within a few hours by Mr D. S. Watson on behalf of the local Unionist Club. The money thus raised being nearly half the sum required to pay for the new work. While the building work was going on provision was made for the Sunday School, sewing meetings and the like by hiring the Lifeboat Pavilion and the Adult School as required.

The original Methodist church as the Unionist Club on the corner of Adam Street, decorated for the coronation of George V, in 1911.

After the Unionist Club, the old building has been used as a wholesale tobacconists warehouse and been home to a number of amusement arcades, and night-clubs.

2010 saw the latest extension and modernisation of the College Street building with the addition of a new main entrance and an upgrading of the facilities.

METHODIST CHURCH
(Highbridge)

As nonconformist churches were a relatively recent concept in respect of Divine Worship and very much, the churches of the people unlike the established church which was of the 'Gentry', they had had neither the time nor the opportunity to amass gifts of land or benefactions. It therefore followed that as any place of worship had to be paid for and funded by the members of that church it could take many years before sufficient funds were available. During that time many good people had no option but to travel some considerable distance to worship with others of their faith. So it was that two Highbridge men took steps to remedy the situation: Thomas Hicks, a local land-owner, in his seventies who was obliged to worship in Burnham, and John Buskin, a saddler, who worshipped at West Huntspill. The foundation stone was laid by Thomas Hicks on 11 July **1864** and the chapel opened on 25 May **1865**. The building still stands but, like so many others in this increasingly secular world, lacking the necessary money to survive, it was sold in **1988** and converted into flats.

(Plymouth) BRETHREN
(Burnham)
Shaftsbury Hall, Technical Street

Up until **1902** the Brethren Meeting Room was in Princess Street, probably in a member's house as this was common practice with many groups that were not part of the established church. Meetings were held on Sunday and Tuesday evenings at 6.30 and 7 pm respectively. By **1902** meetings had been transferred to the, recently opened, Lifeboat Pavilion which is given in Kelly as the address of their meetings as late as **1910** although the Shaftsbury Hall was advertised by name in Mate's Guide of **1905** where it was described as providing tea gardens, refreshment rooms and a stage equipped with scenery and electric lighting. It was probably around **1914**,when Marchent's Bakery was established in the adjoining buildings that the hall was split off from the rest of the site by the simple act of sealing up the door which linked it to the tea-shop next door; this door remained in evidence until after a period of use as an antique shop it became an office for a conveyancer. Since when it has been a private house. The hall remains in regular use.

(Plymouth) BRETHREN
(Highbridge)
Gospel Hall, Newtown Road

The Gospel Mission Hall is shown on the 25 inch O.S. map which was surveyed in **1883**. It appears in most of the local directories up to **1939** and was still in use after the war. Oral history suggests that it was originally a seamen's mission church, which would make the date of its origin no earlier than **1873** when the first ship is recorded as docking at the wharf. It seems that it only came under the wing of the Brethren at a later date. Certainly it is identified on the O.S. map of **1887** as a chapel of no particular denomination. It is first referred to as a Brethren meeting place by Kelly

Old Mission Hall, Newtown Road, Highbridge, 2010.

in the **1889** edition which was the first one in which places of worship were listed. Because of the restrictions imposed by the size of the site, enlargement of the building and improvement of facilities were both impossible, and the building fell into disuse; the congregation removing to the old Salvation Army Citadel off Old Burnham Road.

JEHOVAH'S WITNESSES

The first Kingdom Hall was in Cross Street at the rear of the Commercial Hotel. When the site was sold the hotel became offices and the hall building, lock-up shops (8/10 Cross Street). When the Witnesses left the Cross Street premises, they moved into the old bakery behind what had been Marchent's bakers' shop at 2 High Street. From High Street they moved to custom built premises in Oxford Street on part of old gas works site that they purchased from Sedgemoor District Council in **1986**.

RELIGIOUS SOCIETY OF FRIENDS (Quakers) (Burnham)

The Religious Society of Friends was active in Burnham long before **1890** when the Adult School was built in Adam Street, where they met for many years. The Tithe apportionment register of **1838** shows Henry Clothier (a leading Somerset Quaker) and other members of his family with significant land holdings in Burnham. Sometime around **1795**, Magnolia House at Watchfield[83] is believed to have been built by one Henry Clothier (whether the same or an earlier namesake is not certain); Pillmore Lane that runs beside it and links Mark Causeway (B 3139) to the Bristol Road (A 38) being then known as Quakers' Way with the orchard on the opposite side (also belonging to the Clothier family) being known as Quaker's Plot Orchard.

Adult School, Burnham.

---

83   At that time the parish of Burnham extended Eastwards as far as the B 3139 at the beginning of Mark Causeway, with Magnolia House being number 1059 on the tithe Apportionment Register, with Watchfield windmill number 1125.

With an improvement in general education, the need for basic education of adults diminished and the Adult School buildings were put to different uses. When no longer required as an A. R. P. Report Centre after the Second World War, the back room was used to house the local library when it moved from the Town Hall. Later, the library moved to the front part of the building and the Friends met for some years in the back part before the library took over the whole building until **1985** when it moved to its present location in Princess Street. The building then became a carpet shop.

Quakers' Plot Orchard, last remaining grave marker, 2010.

Having disposed of the building the Friends now (**2010**) meet in the Community Centre.

(Highbridge)

The Highbridge Adult School (**1891**) like its Burnham counterpart provided a centre for religious meetings and adult learning and similarly became the local branch of the County Library. It has since been converted into apartments.

SALVATION ARMY

Towards the end of the nineteenth century and during the first half of the twentieth, the Sally Army, as it was popularly known, had a strong following in Highbridge as it did in Bridgwater and many other similar places where a large proportion of the populace were engaged in rough manual work such as brick and tile making, shipping, both on the docks and as seamen, as well as heavy engineering in the railway works and the like. Such men, having received, at best nothing more than a very basic education and living in a world of the survival of the strongest where arguments were settled by fighting. When the Army taught them to 'fight the good fight' without the need for bloodshed they began to believe that He was on their side as well as that of the richer folk, it was speaking in a way that they could understand, and made more sense to them than the elaborate rituals of the established faiths.

Like so many religious groups they progressed from meeting in members' houses to having their own premises in a corrugated building on or near the site later occupied by the local cinema. On 9 of January **1932** a custom built citadel was opened by General Higgins the Army's Commander in Chief who was 'a local lad made good'.

Chapter 6

◇

Education

EARLY SCHOOLS

Since **1850** or thereabouts many 'progressive' scholastic establishments of one sort or another have been opened in Burnham, but from examination of such records as remain available it appears that throughout the preceding fifty years or so the only facilities for the academic education of the local children were those provided, mainly by either the National Society or by small concerns sometimes referred to as Dames' Schools, the latter often being euphemistically described as Academies of Learning. These establishments were usually run by women of widely varying ages, who, being either unmarried or widowed, were compelled by circumstances to augment their often meagre means by instructing their charges in the rudiments of an elementary education; an exception being James Lovibond in **1848**.[84] Such was the number of these establishments that making a fully detailed record of them all would go some way to filling a separate volume, as many of them appear to have operated for only a few years. If we accept the premise that they could not all have been incompetently run, we can but surmise that the marital status of their principals had some bearing on the matter and that matrimony was largely responsible for their closure on the basis that, at that time, it was considered to be the duty of the husband to provide the home and the wife to look after it.

In addition to these small schools, conducted more often than not in the parlours of private houses the educational requirements of the children of the more affluent members of the local community were met by such establishments as that of Mrs Swan's Academy for Young Ladies whose principal in a somewhat pretentious advertisement in the *Bridgwater Times* of **1846** "... begs to announce that she has removed from Brunswick Terrace to larger and more commodious premises at Prew's Terrace (now Kinver

Terrace) and begs to add that she has secured the services and aid of a lady in every way qualified to assist in the education of the pupils entrusted to her care. Music and singing taught by a master from the Royal Conservatory of Music Paris". No entries for this, much vaunted, establishment appear in any of the directories of the time suggesting that like many other such establishments this academy made no lasting mark on the town.

The existence of such educational establishments as Mrs Swan's tended to be fleeting, as was the preparatory school run by the Misses Weaver which according to Kelly was at Steart House, Vicarage Terrace in **1897** but had gone by **1906**. Similar, equally short lived, small scale schools were run in Highbridge during the '80s and '90s by the likes of Charlotte Cox, Ellen George, and Martha Ford, unlike the boarding school for girls run by the Misses Hobbs.

The Misses Hobbs' school was at Alfred House situated at the junction of Alfred Street with Lower College Street. This property was pulled down in **1910/11** and the new premises for the Wilts and Dorset

The Misses Hobbs with pupils outside their school at Alfred House.

---

84 It is not certain whether this is the same James Lovibond recorded later as being the postmaster, and then as Assistant Overseer and Rate Collector, but in those days it was common for individuals to wear more than one hat and all these occupations require more than a basic education.

Bank erected on the site. Ann and Hannah Hobbs first appear as two ladies running a school (address unspecified) in Hunt's Directory for **1848**, with Slater giving us Ann and Fanny in **1852**; neither Hannah nor Fanny appearing after that date. The **1861** Kelly makes the first mention of College Street and gives Ann (Miss) as the principal. The entry for **1875** is the first to specify that the service is for young ladies at that address[85]. Whether the Miss Hobbs shown in the **1910** edition is one and the same, or a younger sister is not clear, certainly, although not impossible, Ann would have been a very old lady by then.

Although such educational establishments as Mrs Swan's and the Misses Weaver had been superseded by the expanding state schools and the numbers of larger private schools for both boys and girls that had come to the town, there was still room for a few. As late as the early **1950s** a Miss V. P. Stewart-Graham ran such an establishment in part of South Myrtles[86].

NATIONAL / FREE / STATE SCHOOLS
Burnham

National Society Schools were within the control of the Church of England and although instructing their scholars in 'the three R's' and other secular subjects their main and declared purpose was the promotion of Religious instruction and from their inception Scripture exams were a regular feature of the school curriculum. Set out in some detail the early records, though incomplete, show that the first National School to be opened in Burnham was circa **1814**. The location of the premises is not known for certain, but was most likely to have been in that part of Homebush (since demolished and now St Andrew's church car park). Certainly the **1851** census indicates the presence of a schoolroom at that address.

In **1814** there were fifty children on the school roll, while four years later the parochial returns for **1818** record that there was now accommodation for a further twenty five. Eight children were then being instructed at the expense of the vicar Dr Walker King and six other by a vote of the vestry. At the time of the **1833** Education Enquiry there was a school with 35 boys and 25 girls, which was supported partly by subscriptions for which 20 children were taught and partly by payments from the remainder of the children. There was also a Sunday School attended by 44 boys and 46 girls which was supported solely by subscriptions.

The Sunday School appears to have been started some time between **1772** and **1780** and to have first assembled in the reading room of the Burnham Society (possibly the same Locke's Room at Homebush as shown on A. Ruscombe Emery's plan) where it remained until being transferred to St Andrew's church. Julia Dupuis, in her journal states that in **1800** the Sunday School was continuing to meet regularly in the chancel.

For many years religious nonconformity has received considerable support in Burnham. The Baptists who built their own chapel in College Street in **1843** and the Wesleyan Methodists worshipping at that time temporary accommodation close by, were no less mindful than were their counterparts in the parish church of the need for active and well attended Sunday Schools. In later years the absence of so many nonconformist children attending their annual Sunday School treats made it necessary to close the National School for that particular day. There were also occasions when these children, in deference to the wishes of their parents, were excused attendance during religious instruction because of their objection to reciting the Creed.

The return to the National Society's Church School Enquiry of **1846/7** records that there were at that time 45 boys and 48 girls attending on weekdays and on Sundays with an additional 10 boys and 12 girls who attended on Sundays only. They were taught in one large schoolroom by a mistress whose salary was £30 per annum. The total annual expenditure of the school, including the teachers salary was estimated to be £45 and this amount was raised by subscriptions and the children's pence. As this schoolroom was not legally conveyed for the purpose for which it was used and there was no residence provided for the mistress, the premises presumably were either rented or provided by a benefactor. Although from the outset the school was affiliated to the Diocesan National Society the only record of any request for financial assistance being made to the Society on behalf of this school, resulted in a grant of £2. 10. 0 (£2.50) being made for books in **1814** which appears to be the extent of the assistance given. The income from a bequest made by a previous vicar, the Rev. John Golden[87] in **1797,** made possible the occa-

---

85   The appearance of Samuel Hobbs, Solicitor, at Alfred House at this time and earlier suggests that the property may have been a family home and that the Hannah may have been the mother or sister-in-law, rather than a sister.

86   Editor's note. I have fond memories of Miss Graham. She was a large, lady in all respects, especially to small boy. She was strict but fair, and I learned a lot from her, not the least of which, was my love of the English language.

87   The gift of the Rev. John Golden, together with those of Henry Rogers and others are recorded on three benefaction tables, currently in the vestry.

The National (old Saint Andrew's) School from the air, showing Paxton House, Royal Parade, and the Clarence to the L, with College Street and Beach Terrace to the R, with the Pavilion opposite.

sional supply of books to the school. In October **1844** an application to the Society to recommend a suitable mistress was made, but no-one was available on their books at the time. Henceforth the school seems to have gone into decline, there appear to have been no Government inspections and there is no record of it in any official reports, although the school was 'National' by the terms of the deed.

Such was the situation prevailing in Burnham as far as provision for child education (or lack of it) was concerned up to the mid nineteenth century, although for some years previously a number of the less well off members of the community had made strenuous efforts to raise sufficient money to build and equip a school for their children but without success. Being well aware of the pressing need of a school for the many underprivileged children in the locality (illiteracy being then quite common place) George Reed, a prominent local resident accepted personal responsibility for meeting that need. On the death of Sara King, widow of Dr Walker King, George Reed purchased from the trustees of her estate various lands and properties which included Sand Warren held by them under the Dean and Chapter of Wells. Wishing to free these lands of existing restrictions he stated that if the Dean and Chapter would enfranchise this land he would give the parish a National School Room, and thereby advantage both the parish and living. When making this generous offer he had been given to understand that the charge for enfranchisement would be a purely nominal one, but in the event the commissioners exacted their pound of flesh by charging him the maximum amount possible for relieving the lands of these encumbrances. Notwithstanding these charges George Reed went ahead with his plans and had erected entirely at his own expense the original buildings in **1855** at a total cost of £907. 10. The land cost £100, the builders account £765 and sundry items which included the provision of coke stoves for heating £42.10. 0.

On their completion, the school buildings and land were conveyed by George Reed to the vicar and trustees, for ever, for the benefit of the parish, thereafter becoming known as the National School. Writing on 12 August **1856** to the Council of Education (subsequently the Ministry of Education) at their offices in Downing Street, George Reed requested their Lordships 'To now assist this poor Parish in their efforts to fit up the school rooms and the Master's residence by granting a sum to help them in that object in order that the advantages of a Church/National School be no longer be wanting in this place where for some time past the dissenters have had a flourishing Sunday School attended on average by 160 children." This request resulted in a grant by the Government of £200 towards the cost of the new building so that George Reed was able to recoup some of his initial outlay. In **1876** a further Government grant of £124. 16. 10 was made towards the cost of improving facilities at the school. The school as originally built by

National School playground.

George Reed consisted of the elevation facing south to College Street, one large class room divided some years later by a moveable screen. The west elevation consisted of the end of this room plus one two storey gable ended section in which the memorial tablet was set. This latter section was the Headmaster's residence which on the ground floor also contained a small infants classroom.

At one time the parents of scholars contributed two pence per week towards the cost of the children's education, but in cases where this was not possible owing to the poverty endured by some families the amounts were paid out of public funds. Entries in the early school log books recalled that the relieving officer called to pay the fees of the pauper children. In other instances the weekly twopences of some other poor children were paid on their behalf by some well disposed persons who had some regard for these favoured few. Other charitably inclined persons from time to time provided such things as exercise books and suitable literature for the scholars and on other occasions gave materials for the girls to make

Pupils in class at the National School with Mr May standing in the doorway. Note segregation of sexes.

pinafores for themselves, a practical gift enabling them not only to attain some degree of proficiency in sewing and dressmaking, but at the same time providing for themselves a tidy-looking garment to wear in the manner of a school uniform.

In spite of these occasional gifts some children regrettably were kept from attending school because of their parents' inability to provide them with decent clothes. Even more regrettable was the fact that in the early years of the school others were kept at home, the parents objecting to their children having to associate with those from the poorer families in the town. This persisted for many years, at all levels of social strata; until comparative recent times the children of tradesmen were considered as being unacceptable for admission to many of the private school in the neighbourhood.

Regardless of all that George Reed had done to provide the means whereby their children could now be given an elementary education many parents failed to understand or appreciate how much their children could benefit from his endeavours, and on the slightest pretext children were kept from attending school: open defiance of the education authority being quite commonplace, even after attendance at school became compulsory following the Act of **1870**. Truancy was prevalent, condoned in many cases by the parents.

"This fearful disease is deep rooted in many children abetted by parents who have no desire to see their children educated", was the Headmaster's entry in the log book on 30 August **1870**.

On the matter of homework one father wrote "I object to my child having to do such litter". This lack of co-operation on the part of some parents concerning the education of their children was a matter of great concern to the school management and in September **1864** in an attempt to overcome this attitude of mind, evening classes for adult education were organised and run in connection with the school. In addition a lending library of over a thousand books was set up. Suitable books being made available free to all children punctual in their attendance at both day and Sunday School. For exactly how long these evening classes continues is not clear, but the need for their continuance was very great, the incidence of illiteracy among the adult population being considerable. Awareness of this by the Society of Friends resulted in an Adult School being built and equipped by them in lower Adam Street in **1882** where the good work started at the National School was continued. A few years later a second school was built in Highbridge.

At times so large was the number of children absenting themselves from school that certain annual events were made the occasion of an official holiday and it is interesting to note that among such to receive approval was the anniversary of the founding of the Burnham Society which event, was commemorated in the town for many years. The anniversary of Guy Fawkes gunpowder plot was also such a great occasion for enthusiastic celebration by both young and old that this event too received official recognition by closure of the school. There were also a number of non recurring events of local importance that were made the occasion of an official holiday and among these was that of 17 November **1869** when the scholars were excused attendance at school so that they could witness the laying of the foundation stone of the Market House and Town Hall in Princess Street by Mr J.B. Thwaites. Another such occasion was the arrival of the *Cheltenham* lifeboat in the town. There were also unofficial 'holidays' when pupils were conspicuous by their absence, as on 3 April **1882** when the re-opening on of the steamship ferry service between Burnham and Cardiff was celebrated in great delight by a public demonstration. Very few children were present at school that day, being en fete for the occasion.

From the very beginning, Religious instruction was considered to be of paramount importance, and the effectiveness of the teachers' efforts in this direction is evident from the satisfactory reports from the inspectors entered in the log books after the Scripture exams had been held. Comments elsewhere in the school records also provide an interesting side light on the life style and living standards of the local working class section of the community during the latter half of the nineteenth century. Wages were low and families generally large in numbers. Entries frequently record the fact that boys were regularly kept from attending school at seed time for the purpose of planting potatoes and other vegetables in the family garden, while their fathers were at work. Girls, too, were kept from school on many occasions to assist with domestic duties either in their own homes, or those of other people. The importance of agriculture to the local economy is shown in the school records by such entries as "closed for the harvest holidays", during which time many of the children were employed on local farms at haymaking, lifting potatoes and general farm work as well as picking blackberries on their own account to augment the family income and to provide themselves with a little pocket money. Blackberrying was also a frequent explanation for non-attendance at Saint John's School in Highbridge, although this was not an activity that was engaged in 'en masse'. Where possible most of the local schools endeavoured to organise their holidays with regard to the seasons, on the basis of 'if you

can't beat them then join them', there were, however, special holidays that were officially sanctioned in term time for some occasions of local significance; one such event being in **1904**, when the Somerset County Show was held on land off the Berrow Road opposite where it is now joined by Golf Links Road.

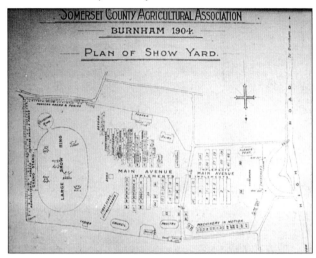

Somerset County Show, plan of showground.

Somerset County Show, programme of events.

Somerset County Show, equipment on display.

Somerset County Show, celebration arch across Oxford Street, outside the Crown Hotel, looking N – note the absence of houses at the bottom of Manor Road.

The winter of **1895** was so cold that the ink used in the school froze solid so that no written work was possible the children being sent home as a consequence, while in complete contrast on 19 July **1901** it is recorded in the entries for that day that the temperature in the playground rose to 118 degrees F and in the classrooms to 100 degrees.

In **1872** and again in **1885** cases of smallpox among the children and adults made it necessary to close the school for the period of the emergency, also, as was frequently mentioned in the early school records, so many children were affected by the recurring outbreaks of whooping cough, measles and scarlet fever in those 'pre-jab' days that the school was obliged to close anyhow on account of the parents keeping their children at home whether they were infected or not.

Among important events in the school's history were the establishment of a cookery centre for the first time in September **1906** by the County Education Committee, the changing of the name in the following December from the National School to St Andrew's School, the opening in Princess Street of a temporary

infants school (the Tin School) on 6 September **1910** under the Headmistress Mrs Randell. On 7 December **1910** a centre for the manual instruction for the older boys was opened at Highbridge.

Other matters of less concern to the school but considered to be worth recording appear from time to time in the log books;-

22 January **1872** each child was given two buns and an orange in thanksgiving for the recovery of the Prince of Wales (Edward VII) from his grave illness.

14 November **1879** private venture schools on the increase in Burnham.

27 March **1882** Many children absent owing to the White Ribbon Army[88] coming to Burnham.

9 October **1891** Under the tuition of Mlle Bland, French language lessons were given after normal school hours.

6 December **1894** An exhibition and demonstration of Thomas A. Edison's invention, the phonograph, given at the school was greatly appreciated by the children.

1 March **1900** The relief of Ladysmith by General Redvers Buller was celebrated by a half holiday.

4 May **1904** So many of the bigger boys got employment at the County Agricultural Show or assisting local tradesmen, that it was decided to close the school for the week.

3 May **1906** it was decided to close the school for 5 days from the 10th in order that the pupils might caddy for the international golf tournament.

3 November **1913** General Sir John Fryer K.C.B. son in law of George Reed, founder of the school, visited the school and spoke to the scholars.

Of the several headmasters appointed over the years the most outstanding was undoubtedly William Henry May. At the time of his retirement he had been Headmaster for almost 43 years from 21 September **1880** to 29 March **1923**. His four predecessors had shared the first twenty five years of the school's existence between them, neither having remained long enough to leave a lasting impression of individual personality on the school.

When William May took over as Headmaster there was an almost complete lack of discipline and obedience among the scholars. Patiently he slowly but surely asserted his authority and in due course, apart from very isolated instances put an end to insubordination. Held in great respect throughout the commu-

88   Part of the British Women's Total Abstinence Union.

nity he is still remembered with some regard by the older generation of Burnham folk[89]. He was succeeded on 10 April **1925** by Mr A.V. Holley who, freshly returned from the war, had been his assistant since May **1919**.

Although discipline was maintained in a more robust manner than would be tolerated today, there is little evidence to suggest that the children grew up any the worse for it. Apart from 'ear clipping' and a knuckle rapping, corporal punishment had always been, and still was, administered by the Headmaster when considered to be appropriate. When given to boys it generally took the form of being across the palm of the hand or in cases of serious misbehaviour the offender was commanded to "touch your toes"[90]. In only exceptional cases were senior girls ever punished by the Headmaster, and then only by hand caning.

It was during A. V. Holley's time as Headmaster that sport became a regular item in the school curriculum, some of the boys achieving a sufficiently high standard of skill in football as to merit their being selected to play for the County.

During the **1914-18** war a small number of children had left London to avoid the Zeppelin raids. These together with a few Belgian refugee children who were living in the old vicarage became temporary scholars at St Andrew's School. Their numbers however were completely eclipsed by those from some London schools that were evacuated in their hundreds to Burnham on Sea at the outbreak of war in September **1939**.

The old school buildings together with the exposed position they occupied on the sea front had for a long time concerned both the Church and secular authorities. The necessity for the school to be re housed in a new purpose built premises with surrounding playing fields being now accepted, the old town football ground known for so many years as the Coronation Field and which, in Victorian times had been the Cricket Field, was acquired and provided the site for the new school. On 26 March **1973**, the Headmaster (Mr Heywood), the staff and scholars assembled as usual, for a final farewell service in the old buildings which had served the community for 118 years. The following day being the first full one in the new school commenced with a special service which was taken by the vicar assisted by Rev. Philipson (Methodist) and Rev. Andrew

New Saint Andrew's School in Dunstan Road.

New Saint Andrew's School, interior.

(Baptist) and Rev. Tookey (Curate). The marble bust of George Reed was removed from the original classroom and now stands in a small courtyard surrounded by the new school buildings

In March **1980** the old school buildings on the sea front were demolished. The exterior memorial to George Reed was taken down and together with the smaller one in the original classroom removed to St Andrew's Junior VC School where with the bust of George Reed they are now grouped together in the courtyard; a visible reminder of that school's antecedents.

BURNHAM ON SEA COUNTY INFANTS SCHOOL
(Princess Street)

The temporary accommodation provided by the buildings in Princess Street to which the infants section of St Andrew's School had been transferred in

The 'Tin' School in Princess Street, long after it ceased being a school. The adjoining building (now the Community Education Centre) was its successor, and continued in that role until a new infants school was built in Winchester Road. The old building was demolished to make way for the new library in 1985.

September **1910**[91], continued however to be used as such until **1914**, when the new infants school built by Pollards of Bridgwater was completed on adjoining land. The following excerpts from the school log give a flavour of those early days:-

1 March **1911**. Dr Gibson Parker gave the first medical examination at this school to 38 of the children. Three were temporarily excluded by reason of Scarlet Fever and one for Ringworm.

20 March **1911**. Total number of children entered on the school register at this date is 127.

3 April **1911** 30 of the children in the top class were transferred to the C of E School on the Esplanade.

27 November **1914**. The children contributed £1 for sending Xmas puddings to Somerset soldiers at the front.

11 June **1915**. We are moving today into our permanent building. We shall start work there on Monday next.

14 June **1915**. Our first day in our new premises .... we are waiting for furniture .....

16 June **1915**. New furniture arrived today.

For over sixty years this infants school under the direction of various Headmistresses provided for the educational requirements of local non-Catholic children attending school for the first time, but, even with additional temporary class rooms it became necessary to move, once again, to larger premises in Winchester Road.

Mrs Randall, the Head Mistress, and pupils outside the Tin School.

91 Being a corrugated iron structure it was dubbed the Tin School. For a number of years after it ceased to be a school it was used to accommodate the local branch of the county library before seeing service as a central kitchen for the provision of school meals. This use ceased when all schools were provided with their own kitchens. The building was demolished and a new custom built library was erected on the site in **1985**.

BURNHAM-ON-SEA COUNTY INFANTS
(Winchester Road)

Like Saint Andrew's, the County Infants moved from its restrictive town centre premises to a greenfield site in the centre of a new housing development in Winchester Road.

SAINT JOSEPH'S PRIMARY & NURSERY SCHOOL

In **1889** the nuns of La Retraite started work to build a day school on land adjoining their convent to provide elementary education and religious instruction for children of the local Roman Catholic community some of whose children had, until then, attended at George Reed's National School or been obliged to travel to Bridgwater. It welcomed its first pupils in the **1890/91** school year. An entry in the National School (later to become Saint Andrew's) log reads, 12 September **1890** A number of scholars left to attend at the new Roman Catholic school.

Saint Joseph's School. The part with the tiled roof is the original building.

Although much extended and altered during the twentieth century, the original building can easily be distinguished. Access was from Oxford Street via two gates, one of which led into the boys' playground and the other into the girls'. There was a third, smaller, play area at the back, for the nursery class.

TECHNICAL INSTITUTE
(Technical Street)

Although not a 'free school' in the same way that the old National Schools had been conceived, it was run for the benefit of the community with all charges kept to a minimum. Built in **1910** at a cost of around £1,000, it catered for the needs of adult learning at a time when the levels of adult literacy and numeracy were low. It also provided tuition in basic practical skills needed for people (both young and old) to improve themselves. It was there that girls from St Andrew's attended cookery and domestic science classes. There were also courses in shorthand and typing, accounting and business management, as well as science and general technical subjects. When the infant's school moved from Princess Street the institute moved in and became the Community Education and Adult Learning Centre and the old building was renamed Belmont House and became a drop in and counselling centre.

NATIONAL / FREE / STATE SCHOOLS
Highbridge

SAINT JOHN'S JUNIOR SCHOOL & BEECHFIELD INFANTS
(Now Churchfield School)

Less than ten years after the building of Burnham's National School, the foundation stone of the original Saint John's School was laid in May of **1863** by Eva Luttrell, whose mother had also endowed the adjoining church. As with Saint Andrew's, it became necessary to move the infants to other premises. The new Highbridge Infants School that came to be known later as Beechfield School, was built in **1913**

Again, like Saint Andrew's, Saint John's removed to a new building in **1973** on a site adjoining Beechfield School on Burnham Road. In **2009** it was proposed to recombine both schools under one administration to be known as Churchfield School.

KING ALFRED'S SCHOOL

The provision of educational facilities for local children was advanced considerably when the new King Alfred County Secondary Modern School (since re-classified as comprehensive school) was officially opened by Admiral Sir Mark Pizey G.B.E. C.B. D.S.O. on Friday 6 June **1958** under the headmastership of W.N. Edge B.A. Since then, the buildings have been extended and facilities expanded to include an indoor sports centre, opened in **1977**, which is also available for use by the general public.

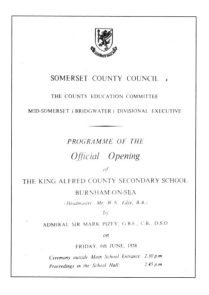

King Alfred's School, programme for opening ceremony.

Saint John's School, a classroom, circa 1920 – Mr Jordan, standing top L was the headmaster.

King Alfred's School, front of original building.

PRIVATE SCHOOLS

Like many of the Dames' Schools, some more substantial private schools came and went, having an almost equally ephemeral existence. Those that survived for any noteworthy length of time were Ravensworth House, Hart House, Naish House and St Dunstan's schools. Each one being conducted exclusively for the education of boys, although St Dunstan's became co-educational during its later years.

The education of girls was catered for by La Retraite, Gardenhurst, Brean Down House, St Margaret's and Oakover Schools. Although they were primarily for girls the latter two had a kindergarten at which small boys attended up to the age of about eight years.

BREAN DOWN HOUSE SCHOOL

Of the four girls schools previously mentioned, the earliest was Brean Down House which, from the scanty information available, seems to have been opened as such with a nucleus of pupils brought with her from Newbury, by Miss Fanny Dows, its first principal (possibly in partnership with Miss or

Fanny Dows, first principal of Brean Down House School during the decades either side of 1900

Mrs Saunders) roundabout **1877**. The school when first established occupied two or three premises in Julia Terrace but in later years it contracted somewhat and latterly occupied only one building at the Maddocks Slade end. The original two ladies were later joined by Miss Owens. Although mainly for boarders, like most of the other private schools in Burnham at that time, a limited number of day pupils was accepted.

Hockey matches were mainly played on the beach in front of the school although there was a recreation ground (now entirely built over) situated at the back of the school in Maddocks Slade. The school, which in **1903** had a write up in the *Girls Realm,* had many accomplished musicians among its pupils, and for several years a full orchestral concert was given annually in Burnham Town Hall. Of all the local girls school, Brean Down House appears to have been the only one where cricket was for several years played by the girls on a regular basis. Although still functioning for some years after the Great War the school continued to contract and as far as is now known closed down in the late **1920s**.

Brean Down House School, playground at the rear of the premises.

BURNHAM COLLEGE

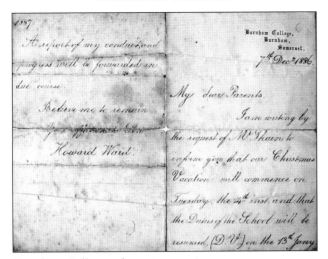

Burnham College, a letter to parents.

One other private boys school about whose comparatively brief existence little is known, but of which some mention should be made was Burnham College[92]. Situated at the corner of Pier Street and Alfred Street (High Street). It first appears in Kelly for **1883** under the Headmastership of Ernest Albert Russell. By **1889** Its principal was a Dickensian char-

acter, one Osborne Thain by name. An early photograph showing a group of pupils and staff, assembled outside the building, all wearing the traditional academic headgear of mortar boards is believed to date from his period.

GARDENHURST SCHOOL

Founded around **1899** by the Misses Hains in the building which later became Oakover School and subsequently Oakover Flats, at the junction of Westfield Road and Berrow Road. The school moved to custom-built premises in Rectory Road sometime around **1902/03**[93] notwithstanding that its address continued to be shown as Berrow Road, until **1906**. Over the years it became an internationally renowned school, including the daughters of many foreign royal families among its alumni. In its heyday it had expanded into several other large properties in Rectory Road and the Grove. With the exception of Rectory House (now Beaufort House) most of these buildings have been demolished for redevelopment.

Over the years a number of initials came to be incised into the brickwork to the right of the front entrance. Whether these were put there clandestinely

Burnham College, corner of Pier street and High Street, pupils and staff.

92 Although there was no obvious connection, the name Burnham College was used for a brief period during the mid-1930s by J.V. Browne when he took over Oakover School.

93 When the school closed, Knoll House as it was known was bought by Allendale Nursing Home and continued as such until its demolition in 2003 to make way for Allendale Court.

Burnham, "Gardenhurst".

Gardenhurst School.

by individual girls, or whether, as at some other well known educational establishments, such as Eton, a small fee was paid to the school is unclear. Certainly the confining of the work to a specific panel suggests official involvement or, at least, acquiescence.

Initials carved into the brickwork of the front entrance.

It is possible that, in its embryonic state, Gardenhurst occupied only one of the two buildings comprising Oakover, as Clifford Wade, a Professor of

music, gave his address as Oakover at about the same time.

HART HOUSE SCHOOL

Hart House school was founded in the early **1800s** by a Mr Hart and established by him in Tregony in Cornwall, some ten or eleven miles from Truro. It was acquired in **1861** by Rev J. Thompson who in **1880** was joined by his son H.J. Ker Thompson as junior partner. A disastrous fire in **1893** completely destroyed the buildings and the school removed to Burnham and took over a large building known, at that time, as the Grove. This house described at the time as a 'Noble Georgian Mansion' had for many years been the residence of Mr J. B. Thwaites, a man very prominent in local affairs.

After seeing the school re-established at Burnham and the property re-named Hart House, Thompson senior retired from active participation in the affairs of the school, handing over control to his son who then became Headmaster.

Although many of the boys were boarders from homes far distant from Burnham some coming from Scotland, East Anglia, London, Wales and Cornwall, quite a number, as with Ravensworth House, from the surrounding district were accepted as day boys;- many of whose families bearing the names:- Palmer, Frost, Hutchin, Glanville, Rich and Wills are still resident and well known in the Burnham area. At one

Hart House VAD hospital, with group of staff, patients, and matron's dog.

Hart House VAD hospital, recovering amputees and other patients.

time 158 boys were on the school register and in regular attendance.

Over the years the school achieved a very high standard of academic distinction but also established a reputation over a wide area in the realm of sport, excelling particularly both at cricket and football (association). Its crowning achievement being that of **1902** when the 1st XI beat the best team that the Somerset FA could field against them. J. Ker Thompson retired as Headmaster in **1906**, when the school was taken over by Mr W.E.D. Potter, who remained as principal until the school closed down in **1911**.

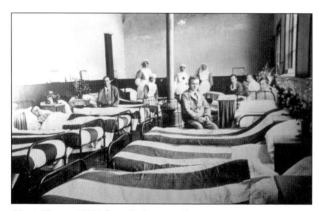

Hart House VAD hospital, a ward.

Hart House VAD hospital, recovering patients on a trip out.

Although at this time, far distant, storm clouds were already gathering over Europe when war did eventually break out in August **1914**, Hart House (the name remained although the school was gone) was, converted into a V.A.D. (Voluntary Aid Detachment) military hospital in less than six months. It became fully operational on 7 January **1915** under its commandant Mrs Duncan Tucker and its chief M.O. Dr Nesbitt Burns MD. A total of 1,782 casualties passed through its wards before it closed on 25 June **1919**.

Following its closure as a military hospital the old house underwent considerable renovation and refur-

Are we Downhearted?
NO! Not at Hart House
V. A. D. Hospital.

Hart House VAD hospital, comic post card. Whether it was intended to cheer-up the patients or their relatives is not clear.

bishment when it took on a new lease of life as the Manor Hotel opening as such in July the following year. Surrounded by well-wooded grounds, and fronted by an ornamental lake, the whole combined to make a most attractive setting. This was apparent when during the summer of **1923** a well known company of Shakespearean actors and actresses known as the Ben Greet Players performed a series of plays in the grounds directed by Sir Ben Greet himself. By special invitation many children from local schools were able to see performances of *Twelfth Night* and *Midsummer Nights Dream*.

As an echo from its past, in November **1937** a reunion of old boys of Hart House School was held at the Manor Hotel at which 56 old Harthusians were

Old Harthusians reunion dinner menu.

present. At the reception and dinner which followed, the guest of honour was their one time Headmaster the Rev H.J. Ker Thompson.

It continued in use as a hotel for many years until for a time it became part of the complex of buildings that made up Gardenhurst School. After the closing down of Gardenhurst, the building was demolished and the site redeveloped in **1977**.

LA RETRAITE
(Convent School)

Established by the nuns of the convent of the Retreat of the Sacred Heart of Jesus. The school catered for fee paying girls, most of whom were boarders. It grew in size and reputation until well into the twentieth century (see also under Convent and R C Church).

La Retraite, showing the original convent building centre, before the top floor was added. The E end of the church is on the L with the first school building on the R.

NAISH HOUSE, AND SAINT CHRISTOPHER'S SCHOOLS

Originally established at Clevedon, the school removed to Burnham in **1904** after, as in the case of Hart House, a fire had completely destroyed the school buildings there. Situated on the Berrow Road half a mile northwest of Hart House with its extensive playing fields adjoining the Burnham and Berrow Golf Links, it was built expressly for use as a boarding

Naish House School.

school for sons of gentlemen. The original buildings were put up in **1904**, and opened in June **1905**, by the Very Rev. Dr. J. Blake, Dean of Wells and one time Headmaster of Rugby School.

Naish House School was well known for its success in preparing boys for entry to the Royal Naval College Osborne, and to public schools generally. Boys of a younger age group were accommodated and taught at the annexe Lowerfield a large house in Golf Links Road, which was also the Headmaster's residence, until they were old enough to be transferred to the main school.

Following the outbreak of war in September **1939** Naish House School was closed down, and for a brief period, another school under an entirely different management occupied the premises, but after a stick of bombs dropped from a lone enemy aircraft fell quite close to the school buildings, this short-lived venture came to an end, and then for the duration for the war the school buildings were occupied by American troops.

After the war was over the premises were, once again, used for the purpose for which they had originally been built when after extensive renovations they were taken over by St Christopher's School which had previously been in Rectory Road.

OAKOVER SCHOOL

In **1902**, the same year that Gardenhurst moved to Rectory Road, Oakover School is shown as being under the proprietorship of Mr and Mrs. F. C. Webb. Just before the First World War the Misses Archer took over and remained in charge until around **1930** when they presumably retired. Their last entry in the local directory shows them in the section for private residents rather than the commercial section, as previously, but at the same address; although the school continued for some years after.

RAVENSWORTH HOUSE SCHOOL

Around **1880** Ravensworth House was converted for use as a school, and by **1888**, when it had become well established, was accommodating 30 borders in addition to which a number of local boys were attending as day pupils. The Headmaster was Mr William Clarke and the school prospectus stated that apart from teaching such basic subjects as the three R's "the object of the School is to provide a practical training which shall prepare pupils for the active duties of agriculture, manufacturing and commercial life". There were holidays at Christmas and mid summer, but not at Easter or Michaelmas. The fees, which in **1880** compared with those of the present day, seem absurdly low were £6 per quarter, or £6. 10. 0 if over

Ravensworth House School, picture post card with details of services and fees.

11 years of age, and were inclusive of board, tuition and laundry. The standard of education provided seems to have been quite high, a number of examples of work by some of the boys still exists as evidence of this. Some of the pupils after leaving, grew up in the

Ravensworth House School, example of student's work.

neighbourhood, later becoming successful tradesmen and farmers. Between **1883** and **1889** he removed his school to 1 Catharine Terrace. Kelly for **1889** gives Bertha Clarke, a Professor of Music as resident at that address. William Clarke's school continued there until around **1902**, sharing it with Hamilton William

Ravensworth House School, Certificate of Merit.

Clarke, another teacher of music, whose final entry in Kelly is for **1906**.

SAINT DUNSTAN'S SCHOOL

Founded **1897** by Charles Strong and Kenrick Bird as a boarding school for boys, it was located in Grove Road. It later took a number of local boys on a daily basis. By **1906** Kenrick Bird had a new partner, Edgar Sellman. The school was taken over by Ewan Stokes

Saint Dunstan's School, before the land W of Herbert Road was developed.

in **1919**. It relocated to Rectory Road when Gardenhurst closed and became co-educational in **1977**, before closing in **1983**.

SAINT MARGARET'S SCHOOL

St. Margaret's first appeared in **1910** at 7 & 8 Julia Terrace, later to become 64 & 65 the Esplanade. By **1919** the school had expanded to include no. 66.

When the Lysaght family disposed of The Gables in Poplar Road after the war, during which, like Hart House, it had been used as a V.A.D. hospital, St Margaret's moved in, and remained there until the school closed in the mid **1950s** after which, the building was converted into flats and the single storey gymnasium/classroom turned into a small arts centre

for use by the local amateur theatrical groups. After these buildings were later demolished to make way for a more modern apartment block the only remaining part of the original Gables site was the stable block which ran parallel with Herbert Road.

Saint Margaret's, from the air. Note 'Bellfield', now the site of Bellfield Court, bottom R.

Saint Margaret's, shortly after moving to the Gables, taken from the dunes on the opposite side of Poplar Road, before the house known as 'Bellfield' was built. The stable block and glass-house are that remain in 2010.

This single storey timber-framed building was an addition that has since been replaced by a brick built bungalow.

Saint Margaret's School, original premises in Julia Terrace.

Chapter 7

Buildings

Although churches and chapels are significant local buildings they are dealt with in Chapter Five, Churches and Places of Worship, as their stories are also those of the people who worship in them. Apart from a small number of large houses or mansions, the buildings of Old Burnham consisted mainly of brick-built farm houses of varying sizes, and labourers' or fishermen's cottages, mostly of cob.

Burnham first came to the notice of the outside world with the development of the spa by the Rev. David Davies during the first half of the nineteenth century. With the coming of the railway and the building of the jetty in the **1860s** it became known, and popular with more than the relatively few people who could afford to come and 'take the waters' and began to grow. It is easy to spot the few buildings on the original sea front that are not Victorian or earlier. Much the same can be said for the rest of the old town although that expansion went on into the twentieth century and is continuing today. The post war housing expansion started with Killarney and Sutherland Avenues in Burnham and the Morland and Poplar estates in Highbridge[94].

Letters in italics beneath a property name identifies the ecclesiastical parish that the property was in at the time of the Tithe Apportionment Survey. The following number and names are the property number on the Tithe Register and map with the name of the owner and occupier at the time, thus:-

> *BUR 921 Sully, Joseph / Coombes, Thos.* indicates that the Bristol Bridge Inn is No. *921* on the Burnham register and belongs to Joseph Sully, and that it is occupied by Thomas Coombes. Similarly, *BER* = Berrow; *H/S* = Huntspill; *S/B* = South Brent (Brent Knoll).
>
> # after a name indicates an owner/ occupier or an untenanted property.

LIST OF PRE 1838 PROPERTIES NOT DETAILED IN THE FOLLOWING PAGES

71-85 Oxford Street *BUR 342-343 Adams, Alice and others*

81/82 Church Street H/bridge *BUR 464 Day, James / Bragg, Samuel*

83/84 Church Street H/bridge *BUR 462-463 Wilkins Robert #*

1-3 Coronation Road H/bridge *BUR 461 Wilkins, Robert #*

Cottage between 15-25 Highbridge Road *BUR 360 Allen, John / Lancaster, John*. (Site of Catholic Church)

Bow Farm: *BUR 531, 532 etc. Adams, James #*

Ivy Farm: *BER 271,272 etc Dawbeny, George / Counsell, George*

Laburnum Cottage: *BUR 74 Crandon, William / Adams, Joseph*

London House *BER 177 Hodges, Richard #*

Middle Burnham Farm *BUR 200 Carde, Joseph / Dibble, Henry*

Middle Burnham House *BUR 204 Morse, William / Morse, Henry*

Overseer's Buildings *BUR 317 Parish officers / Overseers*

Rich's Cider Farm *BUR 1122 Blew, Sarah / Hookway, James*

Worston House *BUR 540 etc. Dean, Kabel Arthur / Daunton, Thomas*

* * *

ALFRED HOUSE

Built not long after the Peachy Williams survey, it appears to have been occupied for the duration by members of the Hobbs family. **1848** sees Samuel listed as a Solicitor & Proctor in Burnham, but not at any specific address. In **1861** and **1866** the address of the Misses Hobbs' school is given as College Street. By **1875**, Alfred House is given as the residence of both Samuel and his sisters. In **1889** the school is being run

---

94   The local council won an award with Poplar estate for the best development of a small site.

Alfred House, L, on the corner of College Street and High Street with the Railway Hotel opposite.

by a Miss Ann Elizabeth Hobbs with a Miss Hobbs (presumably one of her sisters) listed as a private resident. There is no further listing for the school after **1906** although a Miss Hobbs remained in residence until **1910** when the property was sold to Wilts & Dorset Bank – later Lloyds Bank and subsequently

Wilts and Dorset Bank, now Lloyds TSB, built on the site of Alfred House. During the Second World War an air raid shelter stood on the fenced off area.

Lloyds T.S.B. Prior to that date they had traded from premises at 2 & 4 College Street, on the corner of John Street. The Wilts & Dorset were in upper College Street from at least **1883** before moving into the new custom-built premises that were still occupied by their successors in **2010**.

BELMONT (HOUSE /HOTEL)

The building now known as Belmont House started life as the local Technical School and only acquired that name in the **1980s** when the community educa-

tion facility relocated to the recently vacated Princess Street School.

The building that most of the older residents think of as Belmont House, or the Belmont, stands on the corner of High Street and Pier Street. The earliest photograph shows it as Burnham College, since when it has been among other things, an hotel, restaurant, supermarket, and a shoe store. The name first appears in **1897** when it was the private residence of George Sully J.P. The name was retained by J.H. Puddy when he opened his refreshment rooms on the premises circa **1902**. Sometime in the mid thirties, Henry Russell, having previously run refreshment rooms at the other end of Sunnyside, as Pier Street was still known, took over and expanded the business, incorporating the chip shop he already had around the corner in High Street. In those early days this building stood alone surrounded by undeveloped land, the nearest premises then being the Pier Hotel and the houses in Sunny Lawns.

BERROW (HOTEL / INN
(See Wellington Hotel)
BEVERLY COTTAGE
(See Marina House, Daviesville etc.)

THE BREWERY
BUR 375 etc Allen, John #

From details shown on the Tithe map it is clear that the business had been in operation for some time before the survey when John Allen is given as the owner. Apart from a few minor alterations, the layout

The brewery, front entrance.

The brewery, mineral water bottling department.

Way, for obvious reasons. An old round wind mill (Allen's Mill) stood for many years a short distance from the main brewery buildings and was most likely demolished when the railway line was extended to Burnham in **1858**. The brewery's wind-operated water pump which delivered water from their own well stood on land later occupied by Margaret Crescent and was removed in **1951** when house building commenced on the site.

The Brewery, wind pump, located in the region of Margaret Crescent. It pumped water from the brewery's own well.

Richard Shackel was the next owner between **1872** and **1883,** when the Holt Brothers acquired the business. It remained in their possession until it was

The brewery, iron bung hole inscribed, R W SHACKEL BURNHAM SOMERSET, attached to an oak barrel stave.

of the buildings at that time differ little from that appertaining at the time of its closure in **1966**.

Initially the address was Church Street[95]. It is reasonable to assume that the large field on the opposite side of the road (jointly owned by John Allen and Robert Evered) was probably used for grazing the brewery horses as a stable block and yard had been constructed on part of it by **1884** when the OS survey was carried out.

The private house which had always stood within the brewery grounds was known as Sand(a)way House, no doubt taking its name from that of the track leading to Highbridge which was known as Sandy

95   At that time Church Street was what are now, Manor Road, Oxford Street, Highbridge Road, finishing just past the brewery. The road on into Highbridge was known as Sandy Way – adjoining the brewery was Sandaway House, Sandy Way Farm being near the Highbridge end with some parcels of land adjoining the road being recorded as 'at Sandy way'.

bought by Starkey Knight and Ford. The end came when Starkey's were, in their turn, taken over by the Whitbread group which used the premises as a distribution depot for a few years before selling the site in **1966**, retaining only a small parcel of land to build a new pub on – The Lighthouse Inn (the only purpose-built pub to open in Burnham during the twentieth century). The bulk of the land was redeveloped as Broadhurst Gardens.

The brewery, advertising ash tray for Holt Brothers who took over from Richard Shackel around 1880.

BRISTOL BRIDGE INN
Bur 921 Sully, Joseph / Coombes, Thomas

It is possible that the James Coombes who is first listed as a beer retailer at Bristol Bridge in **1875** was a relative of Thomas Coombes who occupied the house and garden with the orchard behind, although this has yet to be established. He was followed by William Vincent in **1883** who held the tenancy until a year or so before the beginning of the Great War.

BRUE FARM
HS 504 Sparrow, Letitia / Jones, Ann

Located on the south bank of the river about 150 metres east of the main road. Since **1883** it has been known also as Highbridge Farm and Huntspill Farm. Letitia Sparrow also had substantial holdings of land in Burnham. At various times, the local water works,

fire station and tennis courts were located between the farmhouse and the main road.

Notwithstanding that Brue Farm was never in the parish of Burnham, it became part of Highbridge when the parish boundaries were re-drawn. It is of some interest in that Letitia Sparrow was an absentee landlord in both parishes

BRUNSWICK COTTAGE
BUR 111 Adams, John / Comer, Ann
and
BRUNSWICK PLACE / TERRACE
BUR 112 &113 Adams, John #

The enclosure with stage show and audience.

All that remains of the buildings on the site of Brunswick Cottage, door and window openings in the enclosure wall.

It was in the grounds of this cottage that John Adams built the four houses that were first called Brunswick Place which later became known as Brunswick Terrace. At the time of the survey, only the first two were completed. Brunswick Cottage remained until the local council purchased the Manor House and gardens, when that was obtained as an optional extra. It was then pulled down and the 'Enclosure' laid out with a concert stage backing onto the Berrow Road. This building was modified to become the local information bureau, since when it has become a veterinary surgery.

BURNHAM NURSING HOME
See under Convent

Burnham Electric Theatre, the first custom-built cinema in the town.

Lifeboat Pavilion, where, among other things, the first regular exhibition of films took place. Note the back of Prew's Terrace.

Burnham Electric Theatre, after converting to a Woolworths store – note the disused projection box on the flat roof.

CINEMAS

The first purpose-built cinema in the area was the Burnham Electric Theatre which opened on Whit Monday 27 May **1912** with a film of the *Titanic*. It was located at the South end of High Street between South Street and Pier Street. The main part of the building that contained the auditorium, remains although the frontage bears little resemblance to the original, other than being a single story structure. By **1931** it was part of the Trueman Dicken circuit and by **1939** had been renamed the Majestic, just in time to be requisitioned by the Ministry of Food for use as a flour store. When the building was de-requisitioned after the war it was sold, as the Ritz which Trueman Dicken had built in **1936** was adequate for the town's needs. Initially converted into a branch of Woolworth's the Majestic later became a supermarket, and then a shopping centre.

The Ritz was designed and built as a cinema/theatre. It had a good sized stage with curtains independent of those used for the screen and up to date lighting. The projection box even incorporated facilities for follow spots when the stage was being used. The design called for dressing rooms beneath the stage, but excavating for this purpose, the builders hit running sand which meant that the hole had to be filled in, resulting in no more than four feet of headroom beneath the stage.

It was officially opened on Monday 13 July **1936** by the well known actress of the day Miss Binnie Hale who was introduced to the waiting crowds by Ben Travers the playwright who at that time was living in Burnham. It was built on the site of the Lifeboat Pavilion which was a very ornate but substantially constructed timber building that had been designed and erected by Boulton and Paul[96] at the turn of the century to better fulfil the function of the temporary structure, erected at the other end of Victoria Street, by the Lifeboat Coffee Tavern company.

It was intended as a place of public entertainment, with Sunday School parties, bun-fights, school and other concerts; dancing classes and political meetings being regularly held there. The first moving pictures (bioscope) to be seen in Burnham were also shown there: 'The Adventures of Lt. Rose and the Chinese Pirates' were received by the youthful audiences of those times with no less enthusiasm than their more modern counterparts responded to 'Star Wars' or 'Pirates of the Caribbean'.

Burnham Electric Theatre, front of flyer.

Burnham Electric Theatre, back of flyer. Note the special notice – 'ASBOs' are clearly nothing new.

Ritz Cinema built on the site of the Lifeboat Pavilion.

---

96 Boulton and Paul were a firm of specialist joinery fabricators who went on to build military and civil aircraft during and between both World Wars. In the '50s and '60s they manufactured wooden window frames for the post-war housing boom.

During the **1970s** the Ritz was purchased by the local branch of the Royal British Legion and adapted for use as a United Services Club and mini cinema. In **2006** a 70th birthday celebration was organised by Mr and Mrs Scott the current lessees at which Robert Trueman-Dicken the grandson of the builder was the guest of honour. While the building was closed for alteration a temporary cinematic facility was established in the Princess Hall by Kontakt Electrical, a local firm who took over the running of the new cinema when it re-opened as well as leasing the Palace in Bridgwater.

The Highbridge Cinema Ltd first appears in the early **1920s** and operated the Picture House (previously, films had been shown at the Town Hall). By **1935** it had become the Regent Picture House which it remained until its closure in the **1960s**. Two memorable things about this cinema were the shiny brass handrail of the stairway leading to the balcony, and the fact that when trains were using the railway, only a few feet away across Newtown Road, the screen would move as well as the pictures. After its closure it

The Picture House in Highbridge, on the corner of Newtown Road. Note the line gates to the L.

Somerset and Dorset Railway where it crosses Church Street with the corner of the Lamb Inn, extreme L. The RH track runs into Burnham and the one on the L goes to the wharf and sidings. The cinema is just out of shot to the R of the signal box. The small building with the porch, CR is the old mission chapel.

became the Regal Club which had the dubious distinction of being, probably the only night club where the tables had legs that were shorter on one side to accommodate the rake of the auditorium floor which had not been levelled when the club opened. On the closure of the club the building was pulled down and the site redeveloped for residential purposes.

(ROYAL) CLARENCE HOTEL
BUR 6 Clements, William #

Situated prominently in the centre of the original Esplanade, the Royal Clarence Hotel is, without doubt the oldest of the licensed premises still standing in **2010**. Built as a coaching inn, its earliest known deeds date from **1792**. It is not difficult to imagine the relief that must have been felt by the passengers as the coach and its team of horses passed under the archway into the hotel yard after experiencing the bumps and jolts occasioned by the shocking state of the roads then leading to Burnham from the turnpike.

CLIFFORD HOUSE

This building with a curved frontage at the corner of Abingdon Street and Oxford Street was built on the cusp of the nineteenth/twentieth centuries on the site of two old cottages which had been run as a public house by an old couple who died within hours of each other.

CLYCE PLACE

Although there is no definitive date on the tablet set in the wall, it is likely that these houses were probably the first to be built in the road. Many roads and streets started life as 'places' with a small number of properties. Newtown Road, for example, started out as Prospect Place.

THE COLONY
Bur 62 etc. Dod, Henry #

Built by Henry Dod, who was the owner/occupier at the time of the Peachey Williams survey and was known at the time as Dod's Cottages. Whether this was its official name is not clear, although certainly on the O.S. map of **1886** it is identified as the Colony. There are two supposed explanations for the strange shape of the building. One is that he had maritime connections and built the property in the shape of a ship; forecastle at one end, and poop at the other. A slightly less fanciful suggestion is that he had it built thus, in an attempt to keep his warring daughters apart (they lived at opposite ends, presumably with him and their mother in the middle). The Colony buildings have changed little in outward appearance since they were built, other than being re-roofed with

The Colony, an early engraving.

The Colony, sketch dated 1845.

clay tiles after the original thatched roof was destroyed by fire during the nineteenth century, and the subdivision of much of it into flats during the latter part of the Twentieth. Owing to the original shape of the structure, these sub-divisions have resulted in the creation of flying freeholds and (according to some residents) the permanent sealing off of lengths of corridor that once linked parts of the original property that are now in separate dwellings.

CONVENT OF LA RETRAITE[97]
Bur 312 etc. Tucker, George. (The Rookery)
Bur 315 etc. Hembry, Philip. (Rose Farm)

To give it its full name, the Convent of the Retreat of the Sacred Heart of Jesus.

In **1883** the farm house and land known as the Rookery was bought by the nuns of a French order who by **1889**, while still retaining the old building and its name[98], had the convent chapel together with the original extensive school buildings constructed around it.

Apart from such land as was used to provide for their material needs an area of about 1/4 acre (0.1 hectares) was later set aside and consecrated as a burial ground. When the school was closed and the

convent downsized, the remaining nuns moved into Rose Farm in **1985**. The buildings and land, were sold, the original convent and school buildings were converted into a residential and nursing home and the land developed for housing. The burial ground remains, in the centre of the development as an open green space about halfway along Priory Gardens, with a centre section enclosed by hedges as a place for quiet contemplation.

Nuns' cemetery.

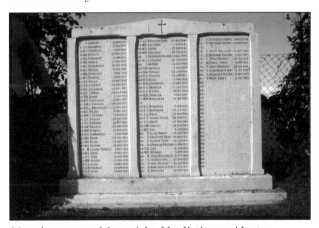

Nuns' cemetery, Memorial tablet listing residents.

COURT FARM
BER 171 etc. Hammond, Mrs Julia.

Other than St Andrews Church in Burnham, or St. Mary's at Berrow, the oldest building of any consequence in this area, until its destruction in **1929**, was probably Court Farm[99], known to the locals as the Old Court House, which stood in extensive grounds on the west side of the Berrow Road, a little to the north of the 'nap[100]'. Its name implies that it was a place where justice was dispensed. Some support for this claim was the discovery of two skeletons, both with

---

97 See also Chapter 5.

98 It was not until just before the beginning of World War One that the Mother Superior ceased using it as her address.

99 The only other structure of comparable age is the pig sty adjoining Barton Close.

100 A local term for a slight rise in the ground. In this case, between Golf Links Rd and Naish Rd.

their necks broken, which were unearthed when the garden was being cleared many years before the building was pulled down; it being suggested, probably as a convenient explanation for the remains, that they were those of rebels, hanged for their part in the Monmouth Rebellion[101]

When advertised for sale this medieval residence was described as a thirteenth century building, constructed of stone, with mullioned windows, flagstones on the ground floor and a Jacobean staircase giving access to the upper rooms. It was said to have at one time been used by the monks from Glastonbury as a fishing lodge which seems more than likely as we know that the abbey had estates in this area.

The property was bought by a local builder who pulled it down and erected a row of semi-detached houses on the site (Nos.183-201). The fact that this represents an odd number of houses is explained by the fact that 183 was built on a double plot with 181 being built on the second plot over thirty years later.

CROWN HOTEL / INN
BUR 32 Hallett, John

Like so many inns and public houses up to the twentieth century the Crown was a Beer House which meant that it was precluded from selling wines or spirits. The number of premises with this restrictive form of licence declined rapidly when no more were issued and applications were being granted for their conversion to 'full on licences', as the tastes and needs of the drinking public changed.

The Crown Inn, originally thatched roofed has been substantially altered over the years until, in **2010**, after the entire site was cleared, it was replaced by the ubiquitous block of flats which appears to be the style of twenty-first century architecture.

CUSTOM HOUSE

The first recorded occupier was William Ward in **1866** whose title was 'Tide Surveyor (Customs)'. How long he had held that post before that date is not clear because in Hunt for **1848** and **1850** the duties were carried out by William Bardo from the Custom House at Banwell. For many years, there was a signal mast with cross arms on the opposite side of the Esplanade giving rise to the building also being known as Flag Staff House.

It would seem that in the nineteenth century government departments job titles and descriptions changed as often as they did in the twentieth – by **1872**

Custom House

William Ward is described as the Examining Officer. Around that time the Inland Revenue was a separate department with its officer in **1883** being given as Alfred Thewles L'Amie who lived in Laurel Villa, Oxford Street. It was not until **1923** that the Examining Officer and the Customs and Excise Officer came under the same roof. Later it was the Customs Officer in Charge and the Customs and Excise Officer. The last officer at the Custom House was called Eggleton who retired when the work came under the jurisdiction of the Bridgwater office.

The building was sold and subsequently used as a restaurant and tea rooms then later a take-away.

DAVIESVILLE
BUR 44-47 Davies, David

Not an individual building but a group of assorted buildings to the west and north of the church developed by Rev. David Davies that cannot be adequately

Daviesville Spa, Early engraving showing entrance and carriage sweep from Berrow Road. Now the beginning of Myrtle Drive.

---

101 Even if they were rebels, they would have been tried at Taunton or Wells; Jefferies would not have come to Berrow, nor would their bodies be intact as hanging, drawing and quartering was the order of the day with bits of the remains being displayed on stakes around their home town or village.

dealt within the confines of Appendix Two as it includes *Steart House, The Myrtles, The Round Tower, Marina (Marine) House, and Marina Cottage.* The first building being his lighthouse (the Round Tower) built in **1815**. In **1827** he completed a deal with the Dean and Chapter of Wells whereby he exchanged (as it says in the deed[102]) a pen of ground adjoining the

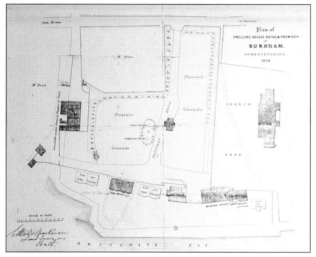

Daviesville Spa, Plan of site when offered for sale in 1856.

Daviesville Spa, Tariff.

Vicarage containing 3 Roods, 34 Perches (slightly less than 1 Acre)[103] for a plot of sand dune contained by an admeasure of 2 Acres, 0 Roods, 18 Perches (the property of the Diocese). This gave him the land he needed to develop the spa with the money he received from the sale of his rights to the lighthouse. The land extended from the north side of the seaward entrance to the churchyard as far as the land where Catherine Terrace was later built by George Reed. Access was from the Berrow Road via a strip of land approximately 50 metres wide between the already existing properties of Tregunter and the Hall. Myrtle Drive follows closely the line of the carriage sweep as shown on the plan when the property was offered for sale in **1856**.

DUNSTAN HOUSE
BUR 118 etc Board, John

At the time of the survey this was a farmhouse with land extending along the north side of Love Lane from George Reed's 'Manor House' almost to the bend where the lane turns north and where Manor Farm was situated. From just before World War One it became the private residence of the Smith-Spark family. After their departure circa **1970**, it became the Dunstan House Hotel.

ELLEN'S COTTAGES

Alms houses on the Berrow Road a little south of the lighthouse. A tablet above the front gate reads, 'IN MEMORY OF HIS LATE WIFE ELLEN THESE COTTAGE RESIDENCES FOR TEN POOR WOMEN WERE ERECTED AND ENDOWED BY JOHN

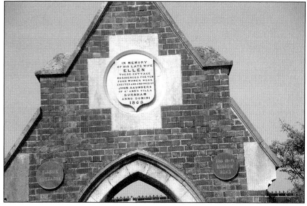

Ellen's Cottages, dedication tablet above front gate.

SAUNDERS OF ST. ANN'S VILLA BURNHAM ANNO DOMINI **1868**'. In **1989** the property was modernised and now caters for only seven occupants.

---

102 Copies of this deed may be seen in the Somerset Record Office and the Hampshire Record Office.

103 To convert Acres to hectares multiply by 0.4047.

THE GABLES
aka St Margaret's

A large house known as the Gables was constructed at the seaward end of Poplar Road and occupied by Gerald Lysaght, a local J.P. whose last entry in Kelly is for **1919**. During the First World War the property (or part of it) like Hart House was used as a satellite of Southmerad Military Hospital although the Lysaght family remained, at least technically, in occupation in spite of their official residence being at Chapel Cleeve. By **1923** Saint Margaret's School had removed from its premises in Julia Terrace and changed the name of the

The Gables, Poplar Road as Lysaght's Hospital, during the First World War.

Lysaght's Hospital staff on the W lawn.

property accordingly. Part of the coach house and stable block, with its staff accommodation over, is all that now remains with its high brick wall abutting the west side of Herbert Road (**2010**).

GEORGE HOTEL
(Highbridge)
BUR 973 Hopkins, William /Hooper, George

Bragg gives George Hooper as the licensee in **1840**. He is shown as the occupier of the premises and the orchard behind on the Tithe Apportionment Register of **1838**. Although the property is described only as a

house and garden at that time, there is no particular significance to be read into this as at the same time, John Hallett is given as the owner/occupier of the Crown Inn which is also described as a house and garden; as are numerous other hostelries. The only establishment within the parish of Burnham described otherwise is the Royal Clarence which is described as Hotel and Garden.

The George Hotel, with portico over pavement. Note the original Jubilee Clock with Tyler's in the background.

Originally, there was a pillared portico over the front entrance, similar to that of the Highbridge Hotel. Unlike that of the Highbridge Hotel, which was on land belonging to the hotel, the one belonging to the George was over the pavement and was removed when the road and footway were altered during the mid-late **1900s**.

THE GLOBE

Of the three public houses built during the late eighteen hundreds to meet the needs of the workers in the docks, the brickworks and the sawmill only the Globe remains. Benita Hicks, the licence in **2010** is the daughter of Jeffrey Philips the last landlord of the Somerset Vaults which was demolished to make way for a local authority development of sheltered housing.

THE GROVE
See Paradise House

THE HALL
BUR 48 King, Sarah

Built circa **1802** for Sarah King, the wife of Rev. Dr Walker King, Bishop of Rochester and Vicar of Burnham. On the **1838** register she is also listed as the owner/occupier of stables **BUR 2** close by the vicarage, and a meadow on the opposite side of the Berrow Road **BUR 108**, known then, as now as Crosses Pen. Until the late **1900s** there was an arched gateway in the wall facing the entrance to the Hall.

The last person to occupy it as a private residence was the widow of the late Thomas Holt a member of the local family of brewers. It then became a residential home for blind persons before it was acquired by the local council who used its greenhouses as the nursery for their parks department, its grounds for car parking, and leased the building to the local community association. The nurseries were later removed to a site in Player's Lane and the site cleared for the construction of the swimming pool.

The Hall. Now the Community Centre.

HIGHBRIDGE (INN / HOTEL)
H/S 4 Butson, Charles / Rogers, Thomas

Known variously as the Highbridge Inn, Highbridge Hotel, and at one time, simply as the Highbridge. Contemporaneous with the George, it was, at the time of the Tithe survey, in Huntspill and remained so until Highbridge became a parish in its own right and the boundaries were redrawn. Together with the cattle market, on adjoining land it was shut down and prepared for re-development in **2008.** The empty building was gutted by fire in April of that year.

HOME (HOLM) BUSH
BUR 35 Buncombe, John #

It was already old when John Buncome[104] lived there, having been known to Richard Locke. Locke's Room, a one-time extension of the property (since demolished) is believed to be the original home of Burnham Society, and later, the first National School, before George Reed built St Andrew's on the Esplanade. The building has been added to and subtracted from over the years and it is probable that the original structure was, at one time, roofed with thatch that was later replaced with locally made 'pan tiles' supported on the original roof timbers which consisted of split tree branches that were still in situ as late as the third quarter of the twentieth century.

----

104 See Chapter 9.

HOSPITAL
See War Memorial Hospital

HUISH
See Sandyway Farm

IVY LODGE
BUR 30 Clements, John / Salisbury, Joseph

A double fronted building certainly in the Queen Anne style, if not of that period with a veranda. Between the end of the First World War and **1930** J. Clement Shuffrey occupied this property as his home, where he also practiced his profession of dentist. Prior to these dates he had lived and worked at the Poplars in Poplar Road. It was demolished to make way for Tucker's Garage, which opened in **1938/39.** The garage and outbuildings were demolished in **2009** and was scheduled for redevelopment as a public open space, with help from a government grant that did not materialise, resulting in the probability of more apartment blocks being erected on the site.

Ivy Lodge in Victoria Street, with Mr Shuffrey, the dentist who lived and worked there.

Tucker's Garage which was built on the site of Ivy lodge, and has itself, now gone.

LAMB INN
BUR 443 Chard, Rev. John / Baker, Thomas

Thomas Baker is listed in Bragg as a Draper and Grocer. It is possible that at that time he was already a beer retailer as this was not an exclusive occupation and was often carried on as an extension of another business, although it was not until Mrs Ann Davis took over, that the premises are listed as the Lamb Inn by Kelly in **1866**. She is specifically described in **1875** as a Beer Retailer. Since its closure as a public house it has been run as a café and a Chinese take-away.

LIFEBOAT COFFEE TAVERN
See Mason's Arms

LIFEBOAT HOUSES

There is no trace remaining of the original lifeboat house which is believed to have stood on land near, and belonging to, the Royal Clarence Hotel. Little is known, either, about the first boat to be kept there, other than it was a gift from Sir Peregrine Acland, a major philanthropist of his day.

The second lifeboat house (still standing in **2010**) is a brick built, gable ended structure standing immediately south of the railway station (demolished in late 1900's)) It was built in **1866** to house the *Cheltenham*, Burnham's first R.N.L.I. lifeboat named

Coxswain wearing his cork life jacket stood in front of lifeboat house.

after the Gloucestershire town the inhabitants of which paid for it. It was also home to the *John Godfrey Morris*, and the *Philip Beach* which was taken out of service in **1930** when the station was closed down.

The building was then purchased by Mr Venn and given as a local scout HQ, as which it remained until **1999**. Subsequently, it was used as adventure play centre for young children and then a coffee shop (**2008**).

The third and fourth lifeboat houses consist of an artificial stone building on the South Esplanade and

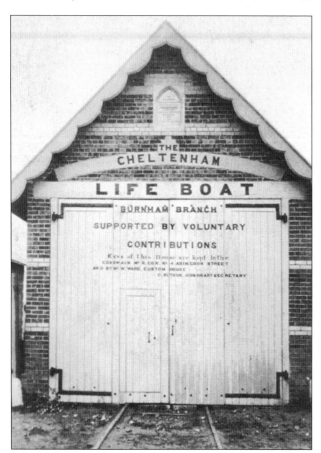

Lifeboat house built for the Cheltenham, *showing the railway lines for the launching trolley.*

Lifeboat house, after 1933, in use as the scout hut.

an industrial building in its own compound behind the *Cheltenham* boat house, respectively. The former, constructed to house the Burnham Area Rescue Boat hovercraft, the latter, housing the R.N.L.I. boats.

New RNLI lifeboat house in its compound behind the Cheltenham's *house, front L.*

LIGHTHOUSES

BUR 72 & 44a Trinity Corporation

The first purpose-built lighthouse in Burnham was that constructed by the Rev. David Davies on land immediately west of the churchyard in **1815**.

In common with many small fishing communities of the period, tradition has it that the wife of one fisherman displayed a light in her cottage window to guide him home on dark and stormy nights. The sexton at that time decided that he could do better and hung a light from the church tower, for which service he was paid a small fee by the local fisher-folk. This was fine for the locals with an intimate knowledge of the waters but of little or no use to the larger trading vessels bound for Bridgwater. The extensive area over which the Gore Sands were spread and their nearness to the deep water channel used by all the shipping entering the river were facts well known to the Rev. David Davies, at the time, stipendiary curate to Dr Walker King, vicar of Burnham. Being a man of some perception and actuated with a desire to take practical steps to alleviate this sad state of affairs he ordered the construction of a tower some forty feet high for use as a lighthouse on land that he owned west of the church and which was later incorporated with other land that he acquired to become known as 'Daviesville'[105].

Although built entirely at his own expense, the Rev. Davies's right to use the light was subject to a statutory lease for which a nominal sum was paid by him annually. He was, however, empowered by an Act of Parliament to receive payment from all ships passing his light and all such dues were levied on a prescribed scale, and under a patent of 20 July **1815** it was decreed that English ships bound for Bridgwater should pay 5/- and coastal craft 3/-. Ships were charged at a rate proportionate to their tonnage, but all foreign vessels were required to pay double the English charges. At the same time Trinity House granted Davies his official licence and another for a period of 99 years at a nominal figure of 20/-.

Several Bridgwater merchants and ship owners complained that the lighthouse was not in a suitable position. A parliamentary committee, subsequently appointed to examine these matters also considered the lease to be most a injudicious one, and in **1822**, recommended that it be bought back, as a result of which in **1829** the remaining 85 years was bought in for the sum of £13,681.

Having taken over the responsibility for lighting the section of coast Trinity House at once commissioned the construction of a new lighthouse, which still stands beside the Berrow Road. Much thought having been given to all relevant factors it was considered that the requirements of shipping approaching this coast would be more effectively served if the siting of the new lighthouse was to be approximately ¾ mile northward of the existing one and that in addition, as a further aid to navigation in avoiding the risk of running on to the Gore Sands, a second one should be erected on the beach. These lights were to be used in conjunction with each other to indicate the line to be taken by vessels entering the river at night, with vertical red stripes on each structure serving the same purpose during daylight.

Both the High Light beside the Berrow Road, and the nine-legged, Low Light standing on the beach, were designed and built by Joseph Nelson an associate of John Smeaton, builder of the third Eddystone Lighthouse. They were completed, and became fully operational in January of **1832**. During its construction one workman fell from the top of the High Lighthouse and was killed. The High Light is a white circular tower approximately one hundred feet high. The structure on the beach supported by its nine legs is in the region of thirty five to forty feet high, depending on the level of the beach which can vary from season to season and year to year. The light from the High Lighthouse could be seen at a range of fifteen miles, and that of the Low Lighthouse for nine miles.

Because of the way in which the sandbanks of the Parrett estuary move and change shape relevant to the lighthouses further navigational aids in the form of additional lights in the vicinity of the church and

Early shot of the High Light from the seaward side. Note the chimney from the lamp room and the weather vane. The pathway, Trinity Path, was used by the keepers to get to the low light on the beach.

The Low Light with the High Light in the background and people walking along Trinity Path. Although the stairs are not the originals, that is not why they now come around the corner of the back leg of the structure, but because the beach is several feet lower than it was when previous picture was taken.

The Low Light with chimney from lamp room. Note that the staircase stops at the corner.

adjoining sea front together with white stripes painted on the sea wall have also been employed. During the last twenty or thirty years or so of the twentieth century these supplementary navigational aids were superseded by an additional, precisely aligned sector light mounted in the High Light and aimed down the river towards the mouth of the deep water channel. This light showed three colours to the ship, red, if she was too far to the left, green for too far right, and white when on the correct alignment, much as the Low Light had done before it. With the advent of G P S navigating systems Burnham's lighthouses were no longer needed by commercial shipping in the same way that world wide maritime radio communication via Portishead Radio was also superseded by satellite communications. The High Light passed into private ownership claiming to be the only lighthouse in the country available for rent as a holiday home. The Low Light was taken over by the local authority and maintained largely for the benefit of local sailors and boat owners.

Projector for the 3 coloured sector light.

LOVE LANE FARM
BUR 338 etc. Board, Ferdinando

A much lower status building and smaller farm than that of John Board on the opposite side of the road (see Dunstan House). The adjoining parcel of land, item *319* on the register, given as Home Ground, is shown on the **1884** map as the cricket ground. Later it became known as Coronation Field after Dunstan and Kingsway Roads were built on part of it at the beginning of the twentieth century. Love Lane Medical Centre and the neighbouring two houses now stand on the site of the old house and part of the paddock

Love Lane farmhouse, site of 15/17 Love Lane.

Love Lane Farm outbuildings, site of the medical centre.

while the Ambulance Station occupies the site of a small barn, with the 'new' Saint Andrew's School taking up most of the remaining land. The last to farm the land were Vivian and Grace Frost.

LUCERNE COTTAGE

Later to become the Puzzle Gardens Inn, now **(2010)** a private dwelling called the Puzzles. It was built in **1842** for George Reed and known originally as Lucerne Cottage. It was he who had the adjoining land laid out as pleasure gardens complete with maze. Located on the Berrow Road near to where it is now joined by Poplar Road, it was quite isolated from all other places of refreshment and relaxation which were within a short radius of the town centre.

In **1866** the Local Board of Health passed the application of Mr Seaman for permission to build a house in the grounds of his puzzle gardens 'below the lighthouse'. Whether this application applied to the Lucerne Cottage site or a different one, further down the Berrow Road, is not clear – certainly, at that time, Kelly gives William Harding as the proprietor in **1866**. At Lucerne Cottage. He was followed by Charles Moore in the **1872** edition, who in his turn was succeeded by his widow. The only way of reconciling these anomalies is on the basis of these 'proprietors' being tenants, in the same way that most licensees were in the twentieth century

The first reference to alcohol is not until the **1883** Ordnance Survey when the premises are shown as a Public House. More recently **(1935)** under Cecil Bett the listing gives 'beer retailer; puzzle tea gardens and camping ground'.

MAGNOLIA HOUSE
BUR 1059 Clothier, Henry

Abutting Pillmore Lane, at that time known as Quakers Way, near its junction with Mark Causeway. Much of the surrounding land belonged to members of the Clothier family who were Quakers. On the opposite side of the lane is what remains of an old orchard which was known as Quakers Plot Orchard, *BUR 854 Clothier, James / Clothier, Henry*. It was used as a burial ground at a time when Dissenters were not allowed to be buried in land under the control of the established church. In **2010** only two grave markers remain, a head stone and a corresponding foot stone.

MANOR FARM
BUR 182 etc. Dod, John and Dod, John / Beak, Edward

Manor Farm was located at the bend where Love Lane turned sharply to the north where the 'Tesco' round-about now stands, at the junction with Queen's Drive and Frank Foley Way. Most of the land between there and the bottom of Stoddens Road, which has now been built on, was part of the farm.

MANOR HOTEL
See Paradise House

MANOR HOUSE AND GARDENS
BUR 109 110 115 Reed, George

No longer occupied as a private residence Manor House with its extension, added in **1968/69** was, since **1905**, in continuous use as offices for administrative purposes by both the old Burnham Urban District Council and its successor Sedgemoor District Council. The land on which it stands together with that surrounding it once formed part of a much larger area formerly known as Gould's Tenements. It is of early nineteenth century construction and was built by George Reed as his principal private residence. It was perhaps with pardonable vanity on his part that he had it styled as Manor House by which name it has been known ever since, although without any inherent right to be so called[106]. It was built on the site of a much humbler dwelling known as Home Field Cottage which because of its name and close proximity, is likely to have been at one time part of the nearby Roper family's farm, the farmhouse of which then stood on the site now occupied by Tregunter. On an indenture of Grant and Demise dated **1787** made between John Carde and Joseph Netherway reference is made to the land on which this cottage stood and which was built on by the latter and lived in subsequently by Elizabeth (Betsy) Cox one time servant to John Dod then owner of Pillsmouth Farm.

After her death the cottage was pulled down by George Reed who then proceeded to draw up plans for a miniature estate and residence for himself. Being a man of ample means, no expense was spared by him in his efforts to lay out and establish the beautiful gardens that were to provide so attractive a setting for his new house. Many varieties of trees and shrubs were planted, most of which for one reason or another have since been cut down. Already of a great age at the time George Reed was laying out his estate, was an ancient mulberry tree, which although for long supported by a number of props became very rotted and unsafe. When it was cut down during the **1970**s it was estimated to be about three hundred years old which, if true would seem to indicate that the land surrounding it had been for a very long time culti-

vated more as a garden than as open farmland. In **1860** the gardens, by then well established, were for the first time thrown open to the public thereby presenting to the visitor a magnificent view of rare exotics. It was said at the time that the Reed's collection of rare orchids and other beautiful plants was unequalled in the kingdom.

After George Reed's death in **1865** Major John Fryer[107] took up residence in Manor House and it remained in his ownership until it was sold at auction in July **1903** at the Queen's Hotel by Palmer Sedgwick.

Manor House, illustration from sale catalogue, 1903.

Typically, the local councillors could not agree on whether to purchase the property, so it was purchased by a local man named Lucas, together with Brunswick Cottage for a total of £3,250. The councillors eventually stopped dithering when he offered to transfer it to them at no extra cost on the condition that he had their acceptance by 4 pm that same day or face it being developed as a private speculation.

---

106 There were three other true Manors in Burnham at the time, belonging to the Dean and Chapter of Wells, Trustees of John Board, and a Mrs Rocke respectively.

107 Later, General Sir John Fryer.

During the next two years the gardener's cottage was pulled down, and the grounds laid out generally in a manner more suited for a public park, as distinct from those of a private residence. A bandstand was erected in the centre of the largest lawn and ornamental wrought iron gates with arches installed at each entrance. The opening ceremony was performed on Monday 12 June **1905** by Rev. T. C. Dupuis, Chairman of the Council, following a public luncheon held in the Town Hall, at which he was presented with a silver key as a memento of the occasion.

In **1912** Brunswick Cottage was demolished, the concert enclosure and borders laid out and the stage and dressing rooms constructed as an annexe to the gardens[108]. Concert parties appearing at the pavilion during the summer season and some of the beach entertainers also gave occasional open air performances there.

During the early post war years such entertainments waned in popularity although the gardens were still frequently used for taking the children and sitting and chatting. The buildings were altered and extended to accommodate the local information bureau together with a kiosk to service the adjoining pitch-and-put and tennis courts in Cross's Pen. In October **1977** after further alterations the bureau was re-opened by Lord George Brown as the first European Information Bureau outside London. Subsequently the bureau was transferred to new premises on the Esplanade and the building sold to

Opening of Manor Gardens, notification of public luncheon.

Manor Gardens, original ornamental gates to Berrow Road entrance.

Relaxing in the park, early days.

---

108 The property was on the N. side of Brunswick Terrace, immediately abutting the footpath running eastward from the Berrow Road. The remains of window and door openings belonging to the old buildings may still be seen in parts of the boundary wall beside the path.

Picnic in the park, 2010.

the Blake Veterinary practice. The Manor House followed a few years later and is now (**2010**) used by a counselling charity although for a few years, the council retained a payment office on the premises.

In recent years, the gardens have been the venue for more ambitious annual events such as Jazz in the Park and similar outdoor entertainments.

MARINA HOUSE
BUR 44 Davies, David / Brice, Ann

Sometimes known as Marine House including the 'Round Tower' and the adjoining Marina Cottage combined with other properties in the block, became Beverley Cottage, a residential nursing and convalescent home, from the latter part of the twentieth century until the first decade of the twenty-first. See also Daviesville.

MASON'S ARMS
BUR 9 Millier, Robert

The Mason's Arms stood at the junction, then, of Regent Street and Victoria Street. When advertised for sale in **1894** by Holt Bros. the local brewers it was described as being a 'most historic building much used as a club by the tradesmen of the town'. Mention

was also made of the fact that at one time the brewing of ale was carried out on the premises. Old inhabitants at that time spoke of seeing the tuns set up for that purpose. It was bought at auction by Mr J.B. Braithwaite, a wealthy local Quaker and philanthropist for £450. After it was pulled down he sold part of the site to the local authority for widening the thoroughfare leading to College Street and thereby extending Alfred Street (High Street).

On the remaining land he built the Lifeboat Coffee Tavern and Restaurant which opened in **1895** filling the gap left by the closure of the Burnham Coffee and Cocoa House Company's premises when the company was wound up in **1886**. Both buildings remain but have been put to different use, the Coffee and Cocoa House entered the twenty-first century with its front half as a dry cleaner's with the other half as an ironmonger's. The Lifeboat is now (**2010**) used mainly for offices and shop premises, unlike the coffee tavern given to the people of Redruth by Lady Jane Vivian in **1880**, which was still selling coffee in **2009**.

Following the construction of the Lifeboat Restaurant a temporary structure was erected on the site at 7 Victoria Street, where a double fronted

Burnham Cocoa and Coffee Tavern and Reading Room, forerunner of the Lifeboat Coffee Tavern. Currently (2010) a drycleaner's and home hardware shop.

Redruth Coffee Tavern. They have been selling coffee there for over 130 years!

Redruth Coffee Tavern. The inscription over the door reads 'OPENED BY LADY JANE VIVIAN MAY 13TH 1880'.

detached property now stands (**2010**) backed by the much older Rock Cottage. The purpose of this structure was to accommodate overflow parties of people from the main restaurant opposite, and continued to be so used until the Lifeboat Pavilion[109] was built and opened in **1901-2** after which time the temporary pavilion was demolished.

THE MOUNT

A mansion built for W. S. Akerman, who lived there from just before World War One until the late **1930s**. Situated on the sand dunes between the Towans and Saint Ann's, it was constructed of concrete, rather than stone or the local brick. Like the 'castle' in Queen Street, Bridgwater it was something of a celebration of the versatility of the material – the Akerman family had connections with the Greenhills of Dunball and were into the production of this new material. 'Greystones' in Rectory Road was a more modest house built of concrete bricks and occupied by another member of the family.

The Mount, on its sand dune.

The Mount, front entrance.

THE MYRTLES
NORTH & SOUTH
BUR 46 Davies, David / John, William
See also Daviesville

Both North and South Myrtles have alternated between single and multiple occupancy, with South Myrtles being the location of Mrs Tucker's school for girls which appears only in Kelly for **1906**. A fleeting existence like so many other similar establishments.

Like Steart House, the Myrtles fronted onto the carriage sweep of the spa complex and had impressive porticos over their front doors, evidence of which could still be seen in **2010**.

NEW FOX INN

The New Fox Inn is shown as Beer House on the O.S. **1902** revision. Charles Baker who was the licensee at the time is listed as a beer retailer at Walrow, continuing to ply his trade up to the beginning of the First World War. Kelly for **1919** shows Ellen Board as his successor, although she had gone by **1923**. There are no other references to beer retailers at Walrow, nor are there any other premises shown as such on other maps of the area.

OCEAN WAVE

A beer house comprising two, possibly more, cottages at the junction of Abingdon Street and Oxford Street. It was operated by an elderly couple up to their deaths at the end of the nineteenth century, when the properties were demolished to make way for Clifford House.

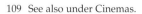

109 See also under Cinemas.

The Mount, interior, main hall.

The Mount, interior, a sitting room.

PARADISE FARM
Bur 75 Fry, Lund Samuel / Hawkings, George

Abutting Brent Broad, which was the boundary between Burnham and the parishes of Berrow and South Brent (Brent Knoll) as well as being, at the time, the route inland from the shore and passing through that part of Burnham known as Paradise which is situated between Brent Broad and Stoddens Road to the west of Stoddens Farm.

PARADISE HOUSE
Bur 85 etc. Blake, Sophia / #

Care should be taken when approaching references to Paradise House as there were two properties so named, although at different times.

The original Paradise House was known as such at the time that Sophia Blake owned and lived in it. It was subsequently owned and occupied by John B. Thwaites, a local dignitary and J.P., during whose occupancy it was known as the Grove. The property extended northward as far as Stoddens Road, bounded on the west by Paradise Road (now Berrow Road) and extending eastwards to a line beyond the bend in Stoddens Road, approximating to that of the north/south section of Rectory Road. It was purchased by H.J. Ker Thompson in **1893** who moved Hart House School there from Tregony near Truro after the buildings there were destroyed by fire.

The other property started out as Paradise Cottage, Middle Burnham and was occupied by one Sealy Stuckey, pastry-cook in Regent Street, circa **1875**, who was presumably responsible for changing the name to Paradise House, which it remained until the early **1900s**.

PAVILION & BANDSTAND

In **1901/02** it was decided to commemorate the coronation of Edward VII by the construction of a bandstand and two public shelters on the Esplanade. One shelter opposite the Custom House and the second opposite the church, with the bandstand approximately midway between them. Each structure being supported on cast iron columns outside the line of the Esplanade. These were removed when the Esplanade carriageway was widened and a new promenade, supported on pillars, and constructed wholly of reinforced concrete was built out over the old sloping sea wall[110]. Two new shelters were built to replace the ones that had gone and a short pier was incorporated in the design. This was to support the Pavilion, a steel framed building intended to provide a covered area for a variety of public entertainments and social activities with a new bandstand on its forecourt. A note in Saint Andrew's School logbook for 26 May **1911**:-

> The noise made by the construction of the new Pavilion and Esplanade extension opposite the school made concentration by the scholars on their lessons almost impossible.

Edwardian bandstand on Esplanade with incoming tide.

110 At the time, a reinforced concrete structure of that size was considered to be a major achievement. Because of the exceptionally high tidal range of the Bristol Channel and the sloping sea wall beneath, steps had to be taken to prevent the surge of water up that slope from breaking up the concrete from underneath. To achieve this, removable gratings were incorporated into the design which allowed the pressure of the water to be released.

Women and children on decking in front of bandstand with National School in background.

Artist's impression of proposed Pavilion.

The Pavilion, Burnham.

Early shot of Pavilion from Beach Terrace, showing seating for some outdoor entertainment. Note the gratings in the Promenade to relieve pressure from below during high tides.

The Sands, Burnham.

Pavilion viewed from beach to the N. Note the gables of the school buildings and Beach Terrace beyond.

The Pavilion on its mini-pier is all that was left of that structure when, as a result of the severe damage done to the Promenade and other parts of the town by the storms of December **1981**, a new sea wall was constructed with a wave-return top. Because of legal complications arising from the fact that the Pavilion had been leased to a third party, it was decided to finish the new sea wall as close as possible to either side of the structure which resulted in this one small example of early twentieth century civil engineering being left to grace an otherwise monotonously functional piece of work.

PIER HOTEL / TAVERN

Built by George Reed at the same time as the Reed's Arms it was aimed at the lower end of the visitors market who came to the town by ship or train. Built before 1/5 Pier Street were constructed, the east facing elevation bore the message 'RAILWAY REFRESH-MENT ROOMS GOOD STABLING BILLIARDS', clearly visible from the station. Many of the words not destroyed by the insertion of a row of windows were still decipherable in **2009**.

PILLSMOUTH FARM
BUR 386 etc. Dod, John

Consisting originally of a messuage and thirty acres of land, Pillsmouth Farm had at the end of the sixteenth century already been in existence for some considerable time. It was situated within the manor of Huish Juxta (Highbridge) which was then part of an estate which had for many years been held in the possession of the Petrie family. During the early years of the reign of Queen Elizabeth the First, Pillsmouth Farm became part of the estate of Thomas Delahoy from whose ownership it eventually passed into that of the Lacey family (John Lacey). From them it was purchased in fee for £25 by Richard Brodria upon whose death it passed to his son Richard Brodria II who although having a son and heir, Christopher, chose to dispose of the farm entirely. This he did when in an indenture dated fifth day of January **1668** the property was conveyed in fee to Henry Dod for the sum of £200 of lawful money.

On his death the farm passed to his son John whose daughter Hannah married Richard Locke the elder who was a second cousin of the well known philosopher John Locke.

Town Hall, c.1900 with council office sign in window.

It was their son Richard Junior who became the celebrated agriculturalist who demonstrated there many of his revolutionary ideas for improving the yield of the land.

Since Locke's death in **1806** there was little change until the last farmer, Edwin Stone retired and sold the property to a holiday and leisure company. Holimarine (now Burnham Holiday Village) opened on the site in May **1968**, taking advantage of the post-war popularity of self catering holidays.

POLICE STATIONS

The police station and magistrates courts were purpose built in **1925** at the bottom of Jaycroft Road and continued in use until court facilities were moved to Bridgwater and a new police station was built on the corner of Broadhurst Gardens at which time the old buildings were put to different uses.

POPLAR FARM / THE POPLARS
BUR 456-460 Hardwidge, Richard

Of these parcels of land and property described variously as:- garden and bartons, home ground, orchard and house, outhouses, and milking pen etc. *458*, the house and orchard gave way to London House Motors, who were followed by Norman's Supermarket / Cash and Carry which, in turn was followed by Foster Court.

457, the home ground was used as the cricket field during the early part of the twentieth century until after the Second World War when together with some adjoining land, it was developed as Poplar estate.

THE PRINCESS (HALL)

Known, for most of its life as the Town Hall – When built in **1868/69** its official title was Market and Town Hall. Notwithstanding that the local Board of Health

Firemen at side of fire station, first half of the twentieth century.

Town Hall with Fire Station doors at E end of building.

and their successors the Urban District Council met and had offices there, it was a product of private enterprise – The Burnham Market House and Town Hall Co. Ltd. The U. D. C. continued using it for offices, even after their acquisition of the Manor House. On several occasions it provided a temporary, and not so temporary, home for the local branch of the County Library until the custom-built premises were constructed opposite, on the site of the 'Tin School'. Two sets of large folding doors were inserted to the left of the main entrance making that end of the ground floor available for use as the local fire station as which it remained until a new station was built near the junction of Marine Drive and Burnham Road.

PROSPECT HOUSE

The town end of Prospect Place, the embryonic Newtown Road. Now 11/11a Newtown Road. From about **1920** it was the offices of E. A. Major's haulage company.

Newtown Road, R foreground is Major's transport depot; the building immediately behind the lorry, is their offices, originally called Prospect House. The houses between there and the tree are Prospect Place. On the other side of the tree is the Globe Inn, the last pub left in Newtown Road, still open in 2010. The fence on the L is made of railway sleepers and bounds the track that runs into Burnham.

QUEEN'S HOTEL

See Reed's Arms

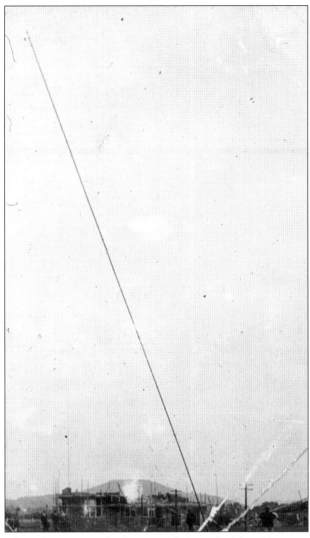

The radio station, the first mast being raised in 1925.

The microwave dishes linking the radio station to the Somerton aerials.

RADIO STATION

Built to provide a ship to shore communication service, officially known as Portishead Radio (one set of aerial masts having been at Portishead), the first mast was raised on the site in **1925**. The Portishead aerials were the first to go, their place being taken by the existing 'Cable and Wireless' installation at Somerton, via a microwave link with Highbridge. Later, the work of the Highbridge aerials was also transferred to Somerton. With the increased use of satellite communication in the **1990s** there was a rapidly diminishing need for its services, so that by **2008** everything had gone and the site was being redeveloped with housing. The development being named Mulholland Park after the last officer in charge.

Although the station was essentially a 'ship to shore' station papers that have become available under the 60 year rule shows that the it also played a vital role in providing communications for SOE agents during the Second World War.

RAILWAY HOTEL
(Burnham)

First appears in Kelly for **1861** as The Railway Inn with James Hallett as the proprietor. It is not clear when it became known as Hallett's Railway Hotel. Certainly, by **1875** when he had been succeeded by John Hallett it was known as an hotel. For many years

Hallet's Railway Hotel, Burnham.

Railway Hotel and Town Hall, Highbridge with captured World War One field gun.
Note, Rose and Crown opposite.

Burnham Station with locomotive, post Second World War, note the Black and White motor coach.
This Cheltenham-based company was one of the first long-distance coach companies.

it had a separate off-licence outlet in High Street which was closed and incorporated into the pub when additional bar space was needed in the late **1900s**.

RAILWAY HOTEL
(Highbridge)

Under the proprietorship of John Anning from around **1848**. John Davidge had it in **1866** – not to be confused with William Davidge at the George in **1875**.

Somewhat confusingly, also in **1866**, John Cooper is given as the licensee of 'The Somerset Central Railway Family and Commercial Hotel'; confusing in that John Davidge was at the Railway Hotel and the Somerset Central Railway had already become the Somerset and Dorset – so where was it? Is it possible that it was an early name for the Cooper's Arms? The location and size are about right and the nearby Railway Vaults would hardly be big enough.

RAILWAY STATIONS
(Burnham)

The small station in Burnham came when the Somerset and Dorset line was extended from Highbridge to meet the paddle steamers coming into the jetty. With the growing popularity of the town as a destination for day-trips as well as longer-stay visitors a second, longer, 'excursion' platform was constructed. This started in line with the front of the

Burnham Station, the excursion platform with passengers waiting. Note the old lifeboat house and the building on the L that became the most recent lifeboat house.

Burnham Station with staff lined up beside waiting train. The small signal box at the end of the platform is preserved at Washford Station as part of the Somerset and Dorset Museum.

The remains of the excursion platform before Marine Drive was laid down. Some idea of the platform's length can be judged from the position of the bungalows on the L.

original station building and extended to a point opposite the bend in Lynton Road. The grass verge on the south side of Marine Drive follows its line at this point. The coal yard and foundations of the station buildings are under Marine Drive and the Lynton Road car park.

RAILWAY STATIONS
(Highbridge)
BUR 1156 etc. Bristol and Exeter Railway Company#
The Great Western, or more precisely the Bristol and

Exeter Railway, came first in **1844**. The Somerset Central Railway, later to become part of the Somerset and Dorset Joint Railway reached Highbridge ten years later although the line was not extended to Burnham until **1858**. In **1962** the passenger service between Burnham and Highbridge was discontinued and the line was finally closed in **1963** with the cessation of goods traffic.

The Somerset Central Railway Company built its locomotive works at Highbridge where rolling stock was constructed and repaired and engines serviced and overhauled – only one locomotive was ever constructed in the works.

It is an ironic twist of fate that after the line to Evercreech was closed and the track pulled up in preparation for the building of the motorway it was necessary to re-lay part of it, as rail transport was the most cost-effective way of bringing in the fly ash from South Wales essential for its foundation.

RAVENSWORTH HOUSE
Bur 15 Clements, William / #
A central block of three stories with lower wings, of Georgian design with an approach from Oxford Street. During the late **1870s** it was the residence of

S & D platform and locomotive works at Highbridge. This was where passengers changed from the GWR main line trains for Burnham.

Interior of the locomotive works, the machine shop. N note the man in the suit – probably the works superintendent. Certainly not a man who expected to get his hands dirty.

The temporary track that had to be laid to bring in the fly ash from Aberthaw power station that was needed to form the foundation of the M5.

Cuthbert Ritson who owned timber yards at Highbridge and Bridgwater. Sometime after College Street was extended to incorporate the West-East section of Victoria Street, the main entrance was moved to that thoroughfare. It is possible that the naming of the street and the creation of the new access coincided with William Clarke acquiring the property and opening his boy's school[111] there, before removing to Catharine Terrace. The building was demolished in the late **1890s** with Ravensworth Terrace and The north side of lower College Street being built on the land the last house to be competed, in **1903**, being number 38 on the corner of Oxford Street.

REED'S ARMS

The hotel, built by George Reed, opened its doors in April of **1860** under the proprietorship of John Gofton. By **1866** he had gone and Martha Wookey is given as the licensee. Between **1872** when Kelly gives James Hatherly as landlord and **1884** (the date of the Ordnance Survey) the name was changed to the Queen's Hotel.

Queen's Hotel between the wars.

With the Reed's Arms and its one time tap, the Pier Hotel, which George Reed also had built he was clearly aiming to cater for the requirements of the customers of all classes from South Wales who were confidently expected to make good use of the paddle steamers to be used on the Burnham-Cardiff ferry service, in which venture he also had a considerable financial interest.

For a short while during the late **1990s** the signs displayed both names but since being bought by the Wetherspoon's chain in **2005** it has reverted to its original name.

RING O' BELLS
BUR 318 Cox, Richard

Unlike many of the beer and cider houses that were to be found in the area at the time, and which have

disappeared almost without trace, the Ring o' Bells survived into the latter half of the twentieth century. A low ceilinged two storey building, the ground floor of which was between 18 inches and 2 feet (0.5 metres) below the level of the pavement. Some idea of the overall height of the building can be gained from the fact that it was possible for anyone of average height to look straight into the upper rooms from the footpath. Originally of cob construction with a thatched roof, the outer walls were replaced with brick and the roof was tiled.

Some time during the **1920s/'30s** a modern extension was built on the North side to provide accommodation for the licensee. A clear indication of its popularity as a public house and its profitability – breweries are not well known for spending more than

All that remained of the Ring o' Bells Nov. 1983 before the site was fully cleared and became a car park.

they need on their tied houses. At one time, when the charges levied on such businesses by the local council was based on 'gallonage' sold, the 'Ring' as it was popularly known, supposedly paid more than any other licensed premises in the town. When the old building was pulled down the extension remained as a private dwelling whilst retaining the old name into the twenty-first century.

ROCK COTTAGE (VILLA)
BUR 15 Clements, William

Occupied during the **1880s** by George Chadwick Wade, Solicitor. Among his clients was the Burnham Coffee and Cocoa House Company Limited of 53 Alfred Street, with his address being given as their registered offices. More recently, the current owner operated a tea room and garden on the premises.

THE ROOKERY
Bur 312 etc.
See Convent of La Retraite.

ROSE FARM
Bur 315 etc.
See Convent of La Retraite.

---

111 See also Ravensworth House School, Chapter 6.

ROSE AND CROWN

An old beer house in Market Street, on the corner with Market Terrace. Built around the time of the railway development to fulfil the needs of the workers. Since the late **1900s** it has been a chip shop and Chinese take-away.

ROSEWOOD FARM
BUR 291 etc. Pauli, Edward / Clothier, James

Like Manor Farm, on the opposite side of the road, this land has been developed for residential purposes as the Rosewood estate and adjoining development. The most recent house on the site replaced a much older building and is now the Rosewood public house.

THE ROUND TOWER
BUR 44a / Trinity Corporation #

The base of the original lighthouse built by Rev. Davies; already taken over by Trinity House by **1838**. See Lighthouses Marina House.

SAINT ANNE'S VILLA
BUR 69 Harwood, Edward #

This Queen Anne style property stood for many years in splendid isolation on the sand dunes to the north of the town until Henry Dod built the Colony. The next neighbours came in **1832** when the lighthouse was constructed for Trinity House.

W (seaward) elevation of Saint Anne's Villa at the top of Gore Road.

John Saunders who built Ellen's Cottages lived there during the **1860s**.

During most of the inter-war years it was the residence of The Rt. Hon. Sir George Cave KC M P, later Viscount Cave PC GCMG Lord Chancellor of England and subsequently his widow, Countess Cave of Richmond.

SANDAWAY HOUSE
BUR 375 Allen, John #

At this time Sandaway house was part of the brewery complex and was the residence of John Allen who owned the brewery. It was the residence of his successor Richard Shackel and, later, William Holt, the last of the Holts to live there as Thomas Holt, his son took up residence at the Hall.

SANDYWAY FARM
BUR 473 etc Symons, Benjamin Parsons, U.D./Barker, Richard

The name derives from the old name for Burnham Road – Sandy Way, in the same way that Sandaway (or Sandway) House marked the Burnham end. Also known as Hatcher's Farm at the time that it was sold and some of the land re-developed in the mid twentieth century. Described in the register as House Garden and Barton, it was part of the barton, left after the new road was put through that became the site of the bungalows (16-38 Burnham Road).

Huish, also known as Sandyway Farm, on Old Burnham Road.

The name Huish was bestowed on the house by the late 'Sam' Nash a keen local historian, when he lived there. It originates from the Manor of Huish which extended to the coast and included Pillsmouth Farm. It is a name which also lives on in the Huish Rhine.

SEATON HOUSE
BUR 346 Adams, Alice / Keats, Joseph

Seaton House stood on what became the corner of Cross Street and Oxford Street. It was a well built stone house and is probably the building shown on the Tithe map, at which time Alice Adams owned property opposite the Crown and all the land between there and the sea as well as at Worston and Sandyway. The Tithe Apportionment survey gives the plot as

Seaton House on the corner of Cross Street and Oxford Street.

Wallbutton's Garage car showroom, built on the front garden of Seaton House which can be seen top R.

House and Garden with the land being cultivated as a garden. By the time of the **1884** survey Alfred Street had been extended across it as far as South Street as well as Stanley Terrace on the south side of upper Cross Street and the 'garden' had become an orchard. By the time of the **1902** revision the orchard had become a nursery which remained until the mid **1930s** when Charles Wallbutton bought it and built his garage and motor sales showroom on much of the land. Sedgemoor Council acquired the site and built a

Seaton House sheltered accommodation, built on the site of Wallbutton's garage and the original Seaton House.

block of warden-controlled flats on the site although retaining the old name. Unfortunately there were serious flaws in the construction necessitating its demolition. The site was then used as a car park.

SEAVIEW COTTAGE
BUR 8 Daunton, William / Hawkins, George

The only pre-**1838** building not still standing in **2010**. It was demolished to make way for Paxton House which has, itself, been altered many times over the years.

SOMERSET (ARMS / VAULTS)

Sometimes referred to as the Somerset, more often as the Somerset Vaults, and most frequently, as the Top House because it was almost the last building in Newtown Road before the docks, John Bland's sawmill and the Britannia Brickworks – or, put another way, the first that the men came to when they left work.

SOUTHWELL HOUSE
BUR 953 How, Robert / Hancock, Benjamin

Recorded on the Tithe Apportionment Register as House, Garden, and Barton (a farmyard). It was one of more than twenty parcels of land and properties between Worston and East Quay (Market Street) owned by Robert How, and leased by him to Benjamin Hancock who also leased land from an Edward Parfitt, between Worston and Sandyway.

The buildings were demolished during the first half of the twentieth century although the name lives on in a small building used for meetings and minor functions in a corner of the Recreation Field adjoining Southwell Gardens.

STEAM PACKET INN
BUR 351 Rich, Thomas

Although the building was undoubtedly standing at the time of the Peachey Williams survey it is possible to be moderately certain that at that time it was a private residence of some importance as it is one of only two that are listed as 'House and Lawn' in the parish rather than 'House and Garden' suggesting that the occupiers could afford a leisurely lifestyle, buying in all the produce they required or growing it elsewhere.

The first reference to the 'Steam Packet Inn' is in Kelly of **1861** which gives the licensee as John Neck. It was an inn which throughout the **1860s** provided commercial accommodation together with some limited stabling facilities. Being located on the Esplanade separated from the Custom House only by the width of what later became known as South Street,

Steart House, originally the spa bath house.

it was also a popular rendezvous for the local seafaring community. Some time between **1866** when the establishment had been taken over by James Lever and **1871/72**, it was acquired by Miss Millicent Bowley who operated it as an apartment and boarding house and was responsible for renaming it York House, a name and function which was carried forward into the twenty-first century by Mrs Jane Browning until **1914**. It was later acquired by Somerset County Council who have continued to use it as a residential home for people in the Council's care.

STEART HOUSE
BUR 45 Davies, David / John, William

Originally the bath-house for the spa complex, that was run by William John until its sale in **1856**. John also rented other properties from the Rev. Davies **BUR 46** (The Myrtles) and **BUR 47** (The Pump House), as well as three parcels of land between the brewery and Highbridge. Like the Myrtles the front of the property faced the Berrow Road and was approached by a broad carriage sweep (the line of which is now substantially followed by Myrtle Drive). It is now (**2010**) subdivided into flats with a vehicular approach from the Esplanade which did not exist when the spa complex was originally developed.

Whether William John who in **1838** was the tenant of Rev. Davies and was listed in the local directories as a Bath Proprietor had later acquired the freehold, or whether it was being sold from under him, is not clear, as no name appears on the sale particulars dated **1858**. Certainly, after the sale date, his name is replaced in subsequent directories by that of Mrs Margaret Jones.

By **1874**, she appears to have ceased trading as in the memorandum of association of the BURNHAM BATHS AND MINERAL SPA COMPANY LIMITED, dated 19 November of that year, the objects of the company are given as the purchase of the Spa or mineral Springs, Bath House ....etc. and the subsequent building of a new Bath House etc. with a view to reopening the Baths and Spa and carrying on the business on a larger and more efficient scale. With a declared capital of £20,000, the company seems to have been grossly undersubscribed and failed to get off the ground – certainly there are no references to be found regarding its activities in any of the local directories.

STODDENS FARM
Bur 160 Poole, R. J. / Amesbury, Robert

This farmhouse, among the oldest in the district, has the names John Wride and Caleb Jesse with the date **1688** carved in one of the main first floor support beams. The closeness of this date to that of the Monmouth Rebellion which features strongly in local lore gives rise to the supposition that they were in some way involved. In spite of, or perhaps because of, the supposed support for Monmouth in the Burnham area it is alleged that some of the King's men and horses were accommodated at the farm around the time of the battle and may have been responsible for the carving.

Another suggestion for the presence of these carvings is that they are the names of the builders of the farmhouse. It has also been suggested that they are the names of local rebels who have been commemorated in this way as they have no known grave; so far, however neither of these names has been found in connection with Burnham at that time although there was a family of Wrides in Huntspill around a hundred years earlier, and a Rev. Jesse at Wellington, some years later.

Names carved in a beam at Stoddens Farm.

This determination to establish a link with Monmouth ignores the fact that two events of national importance occurred in **1688**. A son and heir was born to the King, which was a subject for rejoicing among royalist supporters. It is beginning to look less likely that either of these men had anything to do with the rebellion and, much more that, there is some connection with the landing of William of Orange which also took place in that year.

SUNSET HOUSE

Built not long after the Reed's Arms (its neighbour) it has been a private house and flats. The ground floor was altered for commercial use with a coach garage

Sunset House, also showing the Custom House and York House.

and workshop being built over the garden and the ground floor front rooms becoming the booking office for trips and tours. The ground floor was subsequently divided into lock-up shops with the rear of the coach garage becoming a vehicle maintenance workshop and the front re-developed as more lock-up shops.

TREGUNTER
BUR 43 Taylor, Rebecca #
(Literally – House of Gunter)

During the time the house was in the ownership of the Emery family, research carried out by the late Arthur Ruscombe Emery makes it quite clear, that on the site of the present building there had previously, for many years, stood an old farmhouse which had for several generations been in the possession of the Roper family one of whose forebears had the misfortune to be on the losing side at the Battle of Sedgemoor, afterwards being transported to America.

Excavations carried out in the vicinity of the present building reveal that the old farmhouse was built on an earlier Roman site, which with the other remains found at Worston and on Brean Down provides further evidence of the existence of a Romano British settlement in this locality.

The Roper family continued to live here until **1760** when the property was bought by John Gunter, who at that time was chef to George III. It was he who had the farm house pulled down, but retained the present front cellar, which dates from the fourteenth century. Much of the stone from the demolished building being reused in the construction of Tregunter. The Gunter family lived in the house for over sixty years followed by which it was unoccupied for some time, eventually becoming the residence of five doctors in succession. In the present house there is a 'secret room' which leads off from what was the library. This is a replica of a room which it is known existed in the old farmhouse, and is assumed to have been used by early eighteenth century smugglers for concealing contraband from the local revenue men, thereby, fulfilling a more prosaic purpose than that of the original room in the farmhouse that had been intended for personal use at a time when safe concealment from one's political or religious adversaries meant the difference between life and almost certain death.

The present house stands above a number of communicating cellars some of which during the period of time that Dr Last lived there were used extensively for the cultivation of mushrooms. Excavations made at this time and also on a number of occasions since have provided tangible evidence which supports the widely held belief that at one time

Tregunter.

Tregunter cellars.

there existed underground passages with secret exits leading to both the sand hills abutting the seashore and to the old vicarage which were used by smugglers after bringing in wine and spirits. More positive evidence of the existence of such passages was provided during the **1920s** when workmen employed by Dr Last discovered a short section of partially collapsed tunnel. This came to light when debris being cleared from a long unused cellar revealed a bricked up arch way which when opened up led into this tunnel.

Tregunter as originally built by John Gunter was entirely destroyed by a disastrous fire and rebuilt in its present form in **1830**.

An intriguing problem is the origin of the old brick built stable adjacent to the church entrance gates from Victoria Street. Exactly when they were built, or for what purpose, is not clear but they were certainly there during the time of Canon Charles Pulsford **1827-1844**. Their position is clearly outside the churchyard boundary although the tithe map shows the boundary wall between the churchyard and Tregunter with a small building on either side. By **1884** both buildings had gone and been replaced by the structure that we know today **(2010)**, set back from the original line of

the front curtilage wall of Tregunter. In the absence of information to the contrary it seems likely that the building was erected for the stabling of worshippers' horses. This supposition being supported by its close proximity to the mounting block beside the churchyard wall. The suggestion that it or the earlier buildings on the site were stables for Tregunter and/or the Vicarage is untenable as a plan of the Tregunter estate when it was offered for sale shows both a coach house and stables behind the cottages on the corner of Victoria Street. This would have been in keeping with the practice of the time of not having stables and coach houses within hearing or smelling distance of the 'Big House'.

That there was also adequate stabling at and adjoining the old vicarage at the time that Canon Pulsford was resident there tends to support this view.

(OLD) VICARAGE
BUR 3 3a Pulsford, Rev Charles Henry #

For very many years the vicars of St Andrew's resided at the old vicarage. The present building although quite old in its present form is the product of extensive additions and alterations to a smaller building of much greater age, little of which remains.

When the Rev. Dupuis entered into occupation the building was in a very dilapidated condition owing to the reduced circumstances of his predecessor who had no money to spare for maintaining the property. The Rev. Dupuis was obliged to borrow £400. 00 from the Commissioners of Queen Anne's Bounty to augment his stipend of £100 in order to pay for improvements. Writing in **1879** he stated, "The study, the dining room and the two rooms over are the oldest parts of the structure and form the nucleus, so to speak, of the present building". There are indications that these rooms are of fourteenth century origin. The west end having been added about **1820**, the Rev. Walker King and his curate The Rev. David Davies cutting a clearing in the sand hills so that this work could be carried out.

According to Joseph R. Churchill B.A., writing in **1903**, there were to his certain knowledge two trap doors in the floor of the study, undoubtedly at one time used by smugglers. He also stated that opposite the great door of the church is an altar tomb, one panel of which used to be loose, and the cell inside not long since utilised as a cache for kegs of contraband.

The Rev. Dupuis was the last vicar to reside at the old vicarage and after his retirement in **1913** the property was offered for sale in December of that year. By this time however, the Great War was now but months off and with no signs of it being 'all over by

Old Vicarage, interior from the time of Rev. Dupuis.

Christmas', large numbers of Belgian refugees had been brought over to this country and until they were able to return to their homeland several families were provided with accommodation within the its walls.

After the war was over the property was purchased by Benjamin Sherrell a local baker and confectioner with premises on the opposite side of Victoria Street, who converted it for use as tea rooms. By **1923** he had closed the tea rooms, re-converted the property for use as a private dwelling house and lived there until **1928/29**, having sold off that part of the front garden on which the Post Office now stands.

VINE COTTAGE
BUR 345 Tutton, John #

There is little that can be said of this property other than, up to the **1884** survey, its shape and floor area at least, appear to be much as they were when it was shown on the Tithe Map. Between then and the present day it has been added to and subtracted from on a number of occasions. Certain details of its appearance such as the ornamental brick course at wall-plate level could date from an occasion when the roof was renewed and possibly raised, with the style of the bay windows, suggesting, if not a later building on the same foundations, then at least some serious make-over work in the early part of the twentieth century.

Vine Cottage. Note the brickwork at roof level and the style of the windows.

WAR MEMORIAL HOSPITAL

Built at a time before the NHS had been dreamed of, when the only hospital facilities available to ordinary people were supported by voluntary public subscription, charitable organisations or part of the workhouse. Fortunately, the population of Burnham was big enough to make it possible to raise sufficient funds to pay for a practical memorial which would benefit the community all year round, rather than a beautifully carved stone which would be visited by the people once a year on Armistice Day. The decision to make the war memorial a hospital benefited the town in two ways. It provided a much needed service

War Memorial Hospital, early 1920s. The granite block R bears the names of the fallen on a bronze plaque. Another, fortunately smaller plaque, was added after The Second World War.

to the community, and ensured that it would remain in the town for as long as it was needed. After all, it would be a very hard nosed politician who would have the nerve to support the closure and demolition of a war memorial.

WATCHFIELD HOUSE
BUR 1093 Payne, William

The back part of the house was old at the time of the survey and has been added to and altered since.

WATCHFIELD WINDMILL
BUR 1125 Blew, Sarah, Hookway, James

This mill, of which its substantial tower remains, ceased working at the beginning of the First World War, at which time it had a steam powered back-up system. At the time of the survey it had been in operation for some twenty years or more. Of the two other mills in the parish at that time, of which no trace remains above ground, one was Allen's Mill *(BUR 374)* which was part of the brewery complex. The second *(BUR 761)*, owned and operated by James Blew, was located on the east side of the Bristol Road in the region of the present motorway junction.

That property known now as 'Rich's Cider Farm', *BUR 1122*, also belonged to Sarah Blew and was lived in by James Hookway.

WELLINGTON HOTEL
BER 168 Simmonds, Henry / Ball, John

It is not clear if the premises were an hotel or inn at the time of the Tithe survey although by the time of the **1883** O.S. survey they certainly were both used and named as such; whether in commemoration of the 'Iron Duke's' victory over Napoleon, or his demise, in **1852**, is not certain. It was between **1902/06**, when Francis Bacon, having taken it over from William Skerrett around **1895**, changed the name to the Berrow Hotel. There was still a Francis Bacon given as the proprietor in **1939** although this was probably a son as from **1927** he is given as Francis E. Bacon, a common practice when differentiating between a father and son having the same first names as with the American presidents, Bush.

YORK HOUSE
(See Steam Packet Inn)

◇

Chapter 8

Ships and Shipping

Although protection was afforded to some extent by Steart Island[112], in the lee of which it had been the practice of shipping to shelter, the relative absence at Burnham of any other natural or artificial facilities for the safe harbouring of ships was always the main factor in limiting the size of vessels owned or sailed by the local seafaring community. For many years such ships as did sail from Burnham were mainly coasters of shallow draught and used solely for the purpose of domestic trade between ports within the confines of the Bristol Channel and to some extent the Irish Sea. A trade which in later years consisted mainly of coal, in-borne, and the products of the local brick and tile works on the outward journeys. Even after the construction of the jetty it was common for vessels to be beached for the loading and off-loading of cargo, a practice that did not finish until the early part of the twentieth century. The last people to do this on a regular basis were the Hodges family who were coal and salt merchants. They beached their own vessel, *The Brothers*, a little to the south of the low lighthouse to unload into wagons on a temporarily rail line that they laid between the dunes to their place of business, Wharf Cottage, situated between Ellen's Cottages and Saint Ann's Drive, on land that later became the south side of Gore Road.

Although there is no obvious physical evidence to prove that the Romans beached their ships on the sands between Burnham and Brean, there is evidence of their presence in the area, and it would be the obvious landfall for access to the mines of Mendip which we know they used. Records of local shipping in medieval times are scarce, but some indication of the kind of ships used in local waters in times past is provided by the following extract from Somerset and Dorset notes and Queries (unverified) – "Since earliest times it has been customary in time of war to reinforce the King's Ships by the arrest of merchant men for both fighting and trooping, and of a total of 238 vessels employed in Henry V's campaign of **1417**, 117 were hired from the Netherlands, the remaining 121 being English and of these a craier,[113] the *George of Burnham*, master Thomas Dewell together with a Bridgwater barge, master Johnes Gelomton were requisitioned." It would appear from this statement that both men and ships from Burnham and Bridgwater played a small part in the war against France at the time of Agincourt. Not only were local ships requisitioned and men shanghaied by the press gangs, but local vessels were, also, fitted out as privateers which in the case of one Bridgwater vessel brought forth this official comment, There is officially no distinction between a privateer and a letter of marque ship although in the eighteenth century the

Hut on Steart Island.

---

112 At the beginning of the twenty-first century Steart Island had been reduced to little more than an overgrown mud-flat, yet only fifty or so years earlier it was an island of sufficient size to be above the level of the highest tides and had a simple hut or shed standing on it.

113 A type of ship described variously as a merchant ship sometimes used for fishing or a royal navy ship. Most descriptions agree that it was small and cumbersome. The name and spelling also varied considerably.

former was accepted as meaning a vessel equipped and fitted out solely for the purpose of engaging enemy shipping and acquiring booty regardless of the consequences while by virtue of holding a letter of marque a ships commander was legally entitled to take as prize any enemy ship, should an opportunity to do so present itself.

The attitude of most English sailors in those days of looking upon all foreign ships as being potential enemies is exemplified in the Calendar of State Papers wherein it is recorded how in April **1591** an English ship fitted out in a warlike manner by Sir Walter Raleigh captured a French ship *The Gray Honde* of Bayonne in the Bristol Channel and took her into Uphill as a prize, Good Queen Bess possibly graciously accepting a handsome portion of the proceeds of this encounter as a welcome contribution toward her current expenses.

It was during the early years of Elizabeth's reign that two enquiries were made by commissioners appointed by the Court of the Exchequer into the state of the ports and harbours of Somerset. Their report contains information concerning the main creeks and anchorages, the number of ships which could be accommodated at each harbour and the principal commodities handled there. Seven places along this coast were listed which were:-

Porlock Bay...anchorage for only 40 or 50 ships.
Minehead...safe anchorage for 50 ships.
A creek called Watchet not fit either for anchor-
    age, loading or unloading.
Kilve was considered to be very dangerous.
Bridgwater a hedd port most mete to charge and
    discharge for merchants.
A creek called Highbridge which is not meet.
Axwater (the River Axe) was considered a suit-
    able Anchorage but without facilities
    for loading and discharging cargo

The first four decades of the nineteenth century saw the number of ships entering the Parrett rising from 600 per annum in the **1790s** to over 2,000 by **1836**, bound, not only for Bridgwater but also for Highbridge which was then developing slowly from an insignificant creek used by only a few local ships to the busy little port it eventually became after the Clyce[114], sometimes referred to as the New Cut was dug out between **1801–06** by French prisoners during the Napoleonic wars, who were brought up from Dartmoor Prison for this purpose. The construction of the Clyce, the foundation stone of which was laid in **1801** was made necessary by the fact that at times so many ships were moored in the river around the town bridge that the outflow of water from the River Brue was much impeded with the result that some flooding was caused in the low lying country around Glastonbury, and later the installation of tidal sluice gates at the end of the channel enabled the outflow of water to be controlled.

At the same time as the prisoners of war were digging the clyce, further down the river, a man named Bailey was building Gun Brigs[115], presumably to sink more French ships.

It is not surprising that with such a large number of vessels entering the river with no beacon or other aid to guide them safely into the only deep water channel, that the number of ships wrecked on the treacherous Gore Sands was very high indeed. Not only was this number alarming but the resultant loss of human life was also very great, the bodies of drowned seamen washed up on the beach being an all too frequent sight. Many coastal churchyards around the country had an area of ground set aside for the burial of such unfortunates. There is no indication of such plots in Burnham or Berrow although they almost certainly existed. Saint Bridget's at Brean is the only one where the area is still marked. The current stove-enamelled marker replaces an earlier plain iron one of about **1870** which had rusted away.

Saint Bridget's, Brean. This grave marker, replacing an earlier one marks the area reserved for the burial of unidentified drowned seamen washed ashore.

---

114 A clyce is a drainage channel with a sluice gate at its outfall.

115 See *A Week's Holiday at Burnham* by FHH published in 1912 by H. G. Mounter who owned a local book shop and library. A brig was a two masted square rigged ship of indeterminate size carrying, from ten to over twenty guns.

Even with the construction and operation of the new lighthouses many sailing ships were lost in the Bristol Channel during severe winter gales, resulting in a great variety of wreckage being washed ashore at Burnham. On such occasions a great many children stayed away from school for the sole purpose of beach combing among the flotsam and jetsam or to attend the sales of special items of wreckage that were commonly held at the Pier head after such tragic events. Wednesday 11 November **1891** was such an occasion. The school log book for the 13th records:-

> On Wednesday we were visited by a fearful storm. Seven vessels were driven ashore here and much other damage done, our premises suffering much. It was impossible to hold school in the afternoon, and since that many children have been about picking up wreckage along the shore. Our school work suffered in consequence.

On 22 October **1866** Burnham got its first R.N.L.I. lifeboat and the National School closed for the whole day to enable the children to see a grand procession parade the town and witness the official launch of the *Cheltenham* lifeboat, named after that Gloucestershire town whose people had paid for it. The lifeboat committee afterwards presenting each child with a two penny bun. Prior to that day, the crew had travelled to Cheltenham to take part in a special launching of the vessel on the lake in Pitville Park so that the local people could see the boat that they had paid for, in the water.

Previously Burnham had been served by two independently funded lifeboats. The first of these earlier craft, presented by Sir Peregrine Acland, at a total cost of £66-12-2d, preceded the *Cheltenham* by some thirty years. It has been suggested that this boat was kept at Maddox Slade from where many locals fishing boats were launched – certainly this has always been a good point for lunching boats, being used by vessels of some goodly size over the years. Another site, near the present jetty has also been suggested but there is no indication of a boathouse in that area on the Tithe Map. Unlike the local fishermen's work boats that were in regular daily use a lifeboat need a boathouse. It is likely that this boat and its immediate successor was would have been kept near to and on land, belonging to the Clarence Hotel – Item **6a** on the Tithe map of **1838** is given as a boathouse, which would have been well situated for a quick launch It is possible that this was the first home of the *Cheltenham*, before her brick built house was constructed in **1875**.

Sadly there were times when the boat could not be launched, whether for lack of available crew or some other reason. On 16 November **1840** a schooner, the *Mary* was wrecked on the Gore[116] with the loss of its crew. This particular event prompted some correspondence in the local press. The *Taunton Courier* of the following week carried a letter from a gentleman Mr. G. P. Dawson who, when the lifeboat was not launched, went out with the Customs House boat in an unsuccessful attempt to save the crew who were clinging to the masts of the stricken vessel. He laid the blame squarely on the shoulders of the Port of Bridgwater Authority and the local merchants who were too mean to subscribe to the running costs of the lifeboat which had been given them, and the training of a crew. On 30 November, in response to Mr Dawson's letter, the paper published one from John Adams of Brunswick Place, in support of the local men stating that they would always do their best for ships in distress but supported him wholly in his castigation of the Bridgwater authorities and merchants.

Original memorial stone at pier head, since replaced by a bronze plaque on the new sea wall.

The *Cheltenham* was followed by the *John Godfrey Morris* in **1887** which remained on station at Burnham until superseded, in **1902** by the *Philip Beach* that was reported at the time as costing about £800. Notwithstanding that all three boats were manually powered by ten oarsmen they managed, by the time that the *Philip Beach* was taken out of service in **1930**, to put to sea and save something like a hundred lives in conditions such that any normal person would have thought twice about standing on the sea front let alone putting to sea in a rowing boat. A sentiment expressed by Florence Grinfield in the *Burnham Gazette* of 7 November **1903** in a poem entitled "Men We Are Proud Of" that makes up for a lack

---

116 The spit of sand and rock which forms the northern line of the Parrett estuary.

The Cheltenham *lifeboat being launched on the lake in Pitville Park, Cheltenham.*

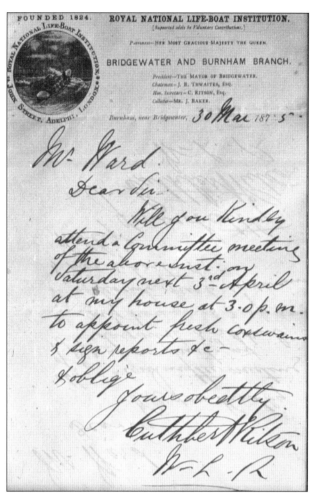

Letter from Cuthbert Ritson, secretary of the lifeboat to the custom officer. 'My house' refers to Ravensworth House where he lived until 1880 when it became a school.

of style with 'oodles' of sincerity:

All three of these boats were housed in a custom built boathouse immediately adjoining the railway station and were launched on a special wagon which ran along the existing railway track from the station to the end of the jetty.

With the departure of the *Philip Beach* Burnham was left without any rescue craft. In **1992** a group of local people decided to go it alone and raise funds for Burnham's own (much needed) rescue boat. When, in **2002**, 5 year old Lelaina Hall died in the mud at Berrow, a major campaign backed by the *Western Daily Press* raised £115,000 which made possible the acquisition of a rescue hovercraft which could reach places inaccessible to a boat or a wheeled vehicle. The *Spirit of Lelaina* Hovercraft which was dedicated in her memory followed in the tradition of the two much earlier craft, by being financed and maintained independently, largely by local effort. The *Spirit of Lelaina* now has a sister craft, the *Light of Elizabeth* named after her sister.

By **1845** the amount of traffic dealt with within the area of the Port of Bridgwater Authority was up to 3340 vessels representing 156,186 tons. And plans were afoot to construct deep water docks at Burnham. A provisional committee was set up consisting of prominent Burnham people and a number of London Ship owners under the chairmanship of Mr J. B. Thwaites of Burnham. Describing the project as The Bristol and English Channels Junction Scheme via Burnham Docks and the Bristol-Exeter Railways advertisements appeared in the *Bridgwater Times* and elsewhere outlining the principal details and stating that the services of a consulting engineer had been engaged and inviting public support.

The John Godfrey Morris *with crew ready to launch for practice.*

Charles Dod one such London merchant and ship-owner recognised the considerable profits that would accrue from the rapidly expanding trade of the Bristol Channel ports was urging the mercantile community of Bridgwater to give their support to this scheme in preference to pursuing some other extraordinary project they had in mind at that time of connecting Minehead with Bridgwater in both a physical and commercial sense. One such scheme was to get rid of the bends in the course of the River Parret by digging a new channel to come out at Steart.

By the very nature of things generally and its geographical situation in particular Burnham has never had the potential to become a port in the accepted meaning of that word. Nevertheless, surveys were made, plans were drawn up and approved, but there appears to have been no immediate or practical developments or further action taken until the Burnham Tidal Harbour and Railway Company, newly formed by Acts of Parliament in **1860** and later in **1866** produced in their turn ambitious plans for carrying out extensive works at Pillsmouth. This scheme called for the altering of the course of the River Brue in the area of its confluence with the Parrett and the construction of deep water docks there, large enough to receive, not only, most ships at that time calling at other Bristol Channel ports, but vessels making trans-Atlantic crossings. The idea behind this scheme was good in theory. The main object being to convey coal and other products from the mines and factories of South Wales as well as passengers by the most direct route across country to ports on the south coast principally Poole and Southampton and from these places across the Channel to France as well as providing a maritime link with Liverpool and the transatlantic trade.

Both Parrett and Brue are tidal rivers and unlike others outside the Bristol Channel are subject to certain effects resulting from a considerable rise and fall of tides with seasonal variations of up to 40 feet or more and this fact alone would have closed the proposed port to ships other than those of shallow draught for most of the time between one high tide and the next. The tidal surge which occurs when the tide rises in the Bristol Channel creates the tidal wave, well known as the Severn Bore. It produces precisely the same effect in the River Parrett where being a lesser river the bore is proportionately smaller, being approximately two feet in height when viewed from the town bridge at Bridgwater where in the days when we had simpler pleasures, schoolboys running through the town and yelling Head-a-tide, Head-a-tide could often be heard when the bore was seen coming up the river from Burnham[117]. Silt, a combination of mud and sand that has always accumulated in vast quantities along the lower reaches of the Parrett and Brue is another major problem when attempting any maritime project in the Burnham area. It has been calculated that in excess of three quarters of a million

tons of silt are held in suspension by the waters of the Bristol Channel at an average height of tide and it is the precipitation of this material in such tremendous quantities that make it necessary for frequent dredging to keep the channels clear for shipping.

Cargoes were unloaded at Highbridge, often directly into freight trains of the Somerset and Dorset Railway drawn up along the quay side and then conveyed in the shortest possible time over that company's rail system to the south coast ports. It was also envisaged that dairy and agricultural produce from the surrounding countryside should be carried by these vessels on their return journeys to South Wales.[118] This was in effect an expansion of what was already happening to some degree. Mr C. Hobson of Wimborne advertised in the *Poole and Dorset Herald* of 29 January **1857** that he was discharging seaborne coals 'ex *Sea Adventurer*' at Wimborne Station and that another consignment was due shortly 'ex *Julia*'.

That part of the scheme involving the construction of a tidal harbour complete with docks and wharves

The Julia. *At some time between the wars she sustained damage to her propeller shaft – a new one, some 20 feet long was turned for her in the machine shop of the locomotive works.*

was bold in conception and although fully authorised by Parliamentary Acts of 6 August **1860** and 29 June **1865** became almost stillborn through lack of sufficient capital, which was, no doubt, a blessing in disguise because the Severn Tunnel constructed some years later and opened for general use in **1886** was able to provide a service for the transport of goods and passengers that did not involve a journey by sea, with the consequent elimination of the extra loading and unloading that the sea crossing made necessary.

---

117 Anyone with sufficient patience and fortitude to stand at the end of the jetty may see it commence its journey up the river.

118 This put a new slant on "Carrying coals to Newcastle" as one of the products loaded at Highbridge was Caerphilly cheese.

At the same time a deep water harbour was mooted in the lee of Brean Down with work starting in **1864**. The *Illustrated London News* is one of a number of papers carrying an illustrated account of the laying of the foundation stone in November of that year.

Brean Down Harbour project, engraving from the Illustrated London News *of 1864.*

Brean Down Harbour project, artist's impression of how the work would look when completed, published by T. Beedle of Weston super Mare.

The railway company having, however, constructed the jetty at Burnham instead of the pier originally planned, made as much use of it as conditions permitted and under the control of the B.T.H. and R Co. inaugurated a ferry service between Burnham and the ports of South Wales which was maintained with some degree of regularity for a periods of almost 30 years.

3 May **1858** was the day when Burnham really was put on the map, with the opening of the jetty to shipping and the opening of the railway station taking place on the same day. The townsfolk rose to the occasion, and the whole place was En fete, with flags and bunting everywhere. Shortly after breakfast

an enormous crowd gathered at the head of the jetty to see the *Iron Duke* come alongside, tie up at the mooring posts and disembark a full compliment of passengers. Later in the morning some seven hundred passengers taking advantage of an excursion specially run for the occasion arrived from Bristol and headed by the railway brass band marched in procession to the pier-head, there to be regaled with speeches from company officials and leading townsmen on the advantages that would accrue to Burnham as a result of this great venture. The management of the newly built Reed's Arms Hotel[119], with its tap the Pier Hotel, both in those days standing in splendid isolation were almost overwhelmed by the capacity crowds requiring much needed refreshments.

Later in May the *Ialiesin* a wooden paddle steamer of some 158 tons owned by the Cardiff Steam Navigation Co was used by the Somerset and Dorset ferry services on charter for the Cardiff-Burnham run. After two years she was taken out of service and replaced by *Ruby* a much superior vessel in both

Poster advertising the steamer Ruby.

---

119 Later to be known as the Queen's before reverting to its original name after over a century and a half.

speed and accommodation. *Ruby* had the distinction of commencing and ending her service on the Burnham-Cardiff run in a dramatic manner. In March **1860** after leaving Burnham her passengers had the exciting experience of witnessing rescue at sea when *Ruby* succeeded in towing free a German ship, *Albert* which had gone aground on the Gore Sands, completing this success by towing the crippled ship into Cardiff where after considerable argument the sum of £200. was paid over by her owners in settlement of their liability in respect of salvage compensation.

Not all ships were as fortunate as the *Albert*. In **1840** the *Mary* was lost with all hands. No trace remains of her nor of many of the other vessels who met their end on the Gore and lie, either at the bottom of the deep water channel or buried beneath the shifting sands that are the Gore. Of the many ships wrecked in the area, only two are recorded on the Admiralty Chart, the others, having sunk in deep water, not being considered as potential hazards to shipping. Of these, the best known is the *Nornen*, the other being the *James and Sarah*, a ketch belonging to the Goodland family of Taunton who were coal merchants. She was carrying a cargo of coal from Lydney to Bridgwater when she was seen to be caught by a squall and disappear from sight in September **1880**. Although the *Cheltenham* lifeboat was launched she could find no survivors. All that could be salvaged on the following day was the ship's boat and some of the smaller sails. The bodies were found a few days later. The *Nornen* fared better when she was successfully beached opposite the church at Berrow in **1897** where she is still a landmark notwithstanding

The Nornen's *figurehead. Removed from the ship and set in the grass bank outside Figurehead Cottage on Coast Road, from whence it was stolen during the 1990s.*

the suggestion of some council officials in **2003** that she should be removed on Health and Safety grounds. Unlike the *James and Sarah*, when the tide went out it was possible for the crew to walk ashore; her cargo being unloaded some days later.

The ferry service was extensively advertised both locally and much further afield. An advertisement for the Burnham Tidal Harbour Co. appearing in the *Cambrian Principality of Wales* 6 February **1863** announced that the fine fast sailing ship *Ruby*, E.L. Baron commanding would be plying between Burnham and Cardiff with passengers and merchandise throughout February. Fares: saloon and after cabin single 3/- return 4/6, fore-cabin 2/- return fare 3/-, 1st class passengers allowed 112 lbs. baggage, 2nd class passengers 56 lbs. baggage.

Certainly for some time after the inauguration of this ferry service the determination of the company to keep it operating on a regular basis was rewarded by the very considerable amount of business that came its way as was reflected in the early balance sheets. In a progress report, shareholders were told that the facilities provided by the company for the rapid two way transport of goods, produce and passengers between the West of England and South Wales had created a great stimulus to trade that was reflected in the considerable increase in the amount of traffic now being handled. The following extract from a report on local shipping matters which appeared in the *Burnham Star and Highbridge Express* for 12 November **1864** amply confirms this: -

> 'Shipping Increase:- The increase in the trade of this company (The Burnham and Tidal Harbour Company) particularly on certain days is beyond all expectations.'
>
> 'Monday last being Highbridge Market day the *Heather Bell* had as much as she could comfortably carry. We have never seen her so heavily laden with cows, sheep, merchandise and passengers.'

The Nornen, *beached at Berrow, from an original photograph taken in 1897.*

Most of the steam packets calling at Burnham were paddle driven and disembarked passengers and discharged cargo after tying up at the specially constructed mooring piles provided for this purpose on the south side of the jetty. To provide the depth of water necessary to enable vessels to come alongside and manoeuvre a channel parallel to the jetty was created, the bed of which at low tide, was some fifteen or so feet below the edge of the landing stage. Referred to locally as the Gut this channel was maintained at the required depth by men employed to stir up the silt deposited by the incoming tide so that it could be carried away as the tide went out. These men were each provided with an implement designed for this particular purpose and similar in appearance to the wooden rakes used by haymakers combined with a squeegee. To provide an additional source of water for flushing away any remaining silt from the mooring channel a reservoir was constructed at the top of the gut near the foot of the sea wall.

This was kept filled by the tide and a manually[120] operated sluice gate enables the men working there to release additional quantities of water when required.

The Ruby, *with her back broken.*

An unfortunate accident involving *Ruby* occurred in **1863** when a particularly violent wind blew her at right angles to the jetty. The ebbing tide left her straddling the mooring channel and finally with insufficient water to support the hull at its centre, she broke her back. There was a somewhat unusual sequel to this misfortune. After being made watertight the fore and aft sections were towed to a Bristol shipyard where after undergoing extensive repairs and overhaul she was sold and after crossing the Atlantic saw service as a blockade runner during the American Civil War.

Although *Ruby* had gone the ferry service was adequately maintained by the employment of the paddle steamers *Defiance* and *Heather Bell*. Captain Barron had transferred to *Defiance* and Captain Densham was in command of *Heather Bell*. The sailing time tables of these two vessels appearing in the *Haverford West and Milford Haven Telegraph* of 18 January **1865** advertised twenty six sailings in each directions between Burnham and Cardiff for that month to connect with four trains a day at Burnham to and from Poole, Southampton and Portsmouth. The tariff indicated that four wheeled carriages would be conveyed in either direction at a charge of 20/- two wheeled ditto for 10/-, horses 6/-, cattle 5/- calves, dogs and pigs 1/- and sheep at 8d each. There were also pleasure trips around the Holmes and to other channel ports as well as the regular ferry service.

Poster advertising trips around the Holmes.

An unusual accident occurred in October **1865** when having spent one Sunday night tied up at Burnham jetty, Captain Barron of *Defiance* on waking up the following morning was greatly surprised to find upwards of 3 ft of water in his cabin. It transpired

---

120 This was constructed of baulks of timber sunk or driven into the beach and presumably lined with mud. A second was added later. They were fitted with a form of sluice which allowed the men working in the gut to adjust the outflow of water according to their needs. The remains of these timbers can be seen projecting from the beach after heavy tides some 20 to 30 metres south of the jetty.

that someone had neglected to close one of the sea cocks used for admitting sea water to the vessel from outside and with the tide rising, the water rushed into the cabins completely flooding all of them. With the valve in question closed the ships pumps cleared away the water and after a very necessary clean up operation she was able to resume her duties without appearing to have suffered any serious damage.

In addition to those vessels engaged on the regular ferry service to Cardiff the railway company's new screw steamer *SS Myrtle* made a successful first trip from Burnham to Swansea in February **1866**, later to be joined by a sister ship then being built for the company. Later in that year, the *George Reed* an iron, screw driven steamer named after Mr George Reed who had a considerable financial stake in the Tidal Harbour and Railway Company was brought into the service but whether for financial or technical reasons remained on the Burnham to Cardiff run for only twelve months when in August **1867** she was sold, and although for a brief period of time she remained on charter to the company she finally left the Bristol Channel for ever, having passed into the ownership of a group of London merchants. Her sailing days ended sadly far away from Burnham in the Indian Ocean where towards the end of **1872** she was wrecked on an island in the Maldives Archipelago.

It was during **1866** that financial difficulties arose causing the company some concern and while it was true that they had been bold enough to invest in the George Reed which had been specially designed and constructed to meet their own particular requirements there can be little doubt that the cost of this acquisition had largely, if not entirely, been met by George Reed himself from his own resources and was the reason for the vessel being so named. The capital of the company was £41,000, divided into a general capital of £37,000 and a special capital of £4,000. The general capital was to be applied to making and maintaining a tidal harbour and other works at Burnham and in promoting a Bill through Parliament. The special capital was to be applied in purchasing a steam vessel to be used for trading between Burnham Harbour, the coastal ports of South Wales and also other places in the Bristol Channel. This £4000 would appear most likely to have been a special loan of that amount made to the company by George Reed as the figure matches exactly the sum raised by him in **1865** by mortgaging the Reed's Arms Hotel the Pier Hotel and his dwelling house (the Manor House) together with various plots of land, to his son in law John Fryer as security for that amount. Whatever criticism, justified or otherwise, that may be levelled at those nineteenth century townsmen it must in fairness be

conceded that they, at least, did their best to get things moving in Burnham and risked quite a lot of their own money in doing so.

A petition to wind up the Tidal Harbour Company was made in **1866** but nothing much appears to have come of this because seven years later in **1873** an agreement was entered into by them to dispose of land owned by the company abutting what is now the South Esplanade. This was in spite of, or perhaps as a result of, a concerted effort being made to restore the ferry service; towards which end two more vessels were brought in: the iron paddler, *Diana*; later the twin funnelled *Avalon*, a much larger vessel, was taken on charter, but before the end of the season both of them for various reasons had departed. In September **1871** the iron paddler *Flora* was chartered by the company, and for some eight years continued to ply between Burnham and Cardiff, maintaining a fairly regular service until, when worn out, she was disposed of and broken up in **1879**.

Although the jetty at Burnham was constructed for the railway company and remained their property until disposed of by them to the Burnham UDC in **1905**, other shipping companies appear on occasions to have made use of its limited facilities, contributing thereby to the strained resources of the Tidal Harbour Company. One such company the Burnham to Cardiff Steam Packet Co was advertising in the *West Country press* during **1872**, and for the brief period of it's existence maintained an office with resident manager in Alfred Street and all the while the B.T.H. and R. Co. continued to advertise a twice daily summer service to Cardiff reducing to a single service, daily during the winter period.

Thereafter, came another bleak period of about three years until **1882** when following vigorous representations made by many prominent local people the *Lady Mary* owned by the Marquis of Bute's family and operated on their behalf by their trustees re-opened the Burnham to Cardiff cross channel ferry. The restoration of this service was again widely advertised, her sailing timetables and other details appearing as a regular feature on the front covers of the St Andrew's church magazines of that time. Other vessels took over the run from time to time as the occasion required until she was withdrawn in **1883** for service elsewhere. The cross channel ferry service had now been operating for almost a quarter of a century in spite of its many vicissitudes and after the withdrawal of the *Lady Mary* one last effort was made by the company to re-establish a measure of stability and regain the support it had received in the early years. Towards that end, the company, in **1884** acquired, out of Government service, the steam yacht *Sherboro* which was converted for use on the Burnham to Cardiff run. *Sherboro* a twin funnelled wood paddler built almost entirely of mahogany was much larger than any of her predecessors. Of some 239 tons gross, 119 T.N. she was built at Cowes in **1870** and until acquired by the S & D Railway Co had seen service off the west coast of Africa where she was mainly used for intercepting ships suspected of being engaged in the still lucrative slave trade which, in spite of the laws passed earlier in the century, was still flourishing, particularly in the Americas and the Caribbean. While so employed she was armed with guns fore and aft, of sufficient calibre to deter opposition from suspected craft. In her more prosaic role she was thus described. "The new fast steamer *Sherboro* Burnham to Cardiff shortest and cheapest route for goods and passengers to and from South Wales, the South and West of England, Somersetshire, Dorsetshire, Southampton, Poole, Portsmouth, Isle of Wight, The Channel Islands and France via Southampton".

Advertisement for the Sherbro.

Although local farmers and market gardeners were able thereby to quickly take across their dairy produce, fruit and vegetables to sell at Cardiff market and return the same day and therefore made much use of the ferry service the dice were heavily loaded against the company's efforts to make it a permanently viable enterprise. The Severn Tunnel was, by

this time, providing a new and strong competition which had not been dreamed of during the early years of the Burnham to Cardiff ferry service. Another debilitating factor was the exposed position of the jetty which during bad weather made loading and unloading a very difficult operation indeed, in addition to which its gradient was such that only railway wagons controlled by cables running over rollers could be safely used on the track way which ran through the centre section of the jetty along its whole length. Some years earlier an attempt to use horse drawn drays for loading and unloading ended in disaster when a cargo of hops for Allen's Brewery together with horses and vehicles were lost in the tide as a result of the animals taking fright.

It is true that from time to time modest profits had been made but enough was enough, and in **1888**, after over 30 years of fluctuating fortunes the service was terminated as far as Burnham was concerned, from then on all commercial cross channel shipping being for all practical purposes accommodated at Highbridge wharf where conditions and facilities were superior in every way.

Although for a time no further attempts were made to re-establish a ferry service various vessels did from time to time call at Burnham jetty. One such occasion being 17 September **1891** when huge crowds attracted to the town by the annual regatta availed themselves of the opportunity to go for trips down the channel in the *Earl of Jersey*, which earlier that day had brought a large number of visitors to Burnham from South Wales especially for the regatta. On another occasion the SS *Scotia* brought a large party of members over from Cardiff early on the morning of 29th September **1895** to attend the public meeting and tea held by the Burnham Adult School, returning to Cardiff later on the same day.

In **1892** after a lapse of four years another attempt to provide a daily ferry service between Burnham and Cardiff was made, this time by Guthrie Heywood and Co of Cardiff with their new Steamship *Clyde*, a vessel which was elegantly fitted up for passengers; fast and with admirable arrangements for the transport of cattle. On her first visit to Burnham she was met by members of the Town Council and other leading townsmen who wished the company every success, before being suitably entertained by the Captain in the saloon. In spite, however, of the initiative of Guthrie's and the undoubted enthusiasm of the public this attempt to revive the cross channel ferry service was short lived and although daily sailings were maintained for a while it was the inherent problems involved in coming alongside at Burnham jetty that in the end brought about the abandonment of this last serious attempt to link Burnham commercially with South Wales by sea.

There then followed a period of three years during which time only isolated visits were made to Burnham by steamers, and these were almost entirely for the purpose of providing one-day excursions to the other Bristol channel ports, and as such were very well supported, not the least by miners from the Rhondda who with their families became familiar and welcome visitors to Burnham, to whose summer trade they made a valuable contribution. Awareness of the support given to these excursions by the people of South Wales undoubtedly contributed to the decision made by the firm of P. & A. Campbell that steamers of their White Funnel fleet should call at Burnham. It was in about **1895** that the first of these vessels called at Burnham for the purposes of both disembarking and taking on passengers. Although for some time after, the visits to Burnham by these paddle steamers were both regular and frequent during the holiday season, as time went by they became less so; until finally, after making a total of only 21 calls during the two preceding years, they ceased all together at the end of summer **1906**. Old inhabitants, reminiscing of those times recalled the regular practice of Campbell's Commanders when approaching the pier at Burnham of ringing the ship's bell which could be heard in all parts of the town and drew the inevitable crowd of onlookers to the jetty. During this period 9,466 passengers were landed at Burnham, but of this total less than 1,500 came during that last year, when only three calls were made, the last being on the afternoon of 15 September **1906** when a full compliment of passengers was brought over from Cardiff.

Whereas vessels used on the old cross channel service were engaged with the transport of passengers, merchandise and livestock on a more or less daily basis the function of Messrs Campbell's steamers was mainly that of providing personal transport for pleasure and business and at no time did they operate on a regular daily schedule as had the original ferry service.

The various cruises that could be taken within the Bristol Channel on occasions as far down as Lundy Island were very popular and supported by both public and press........Item from *Burnham Gazette* 14 September **1895** "Trips from here by sea have been very much enjoyed this week. PSS *Ravenswood* taking passengers to Cardiff, and PSS *Waverley* after picking up at Burnham went on to Weston Super Mare, Clevedon and Chepstow...." Item from *Burnham Gazette* 22 July **1905** "P.&A Campbell's first trip of the season from Burnham was made on Thursday in glorious weather when *Bonnie Doone*

took a large number of passengers to Ilfracombe...". Again, on 9 September **1905** "*Waverley* with 300 passengers from Burnham made a greatly enjoyed Channel cruise on Tuesday last, a large number of visitors having earlier been brought over from Cardiff". *Waverley* had called at Burnham before, her first visit having been made some years earlier in May **1892**, on which occasion she was specially chartered to take about 400 passengers to Swansea where the Bath and West Show was being held that year. This was one of the few occasions which a trip to Swansea had been made from Burnham and hundreds of people assembled on the pier to witness her departure. Interviewed at Swansea her Commander stated that the journey which was enjoyed by all took 8 hours 7 minutes and that he was extremely pleased with the embarking arrangements at Burnham. On the return journey some fifty passengers partook of what was described as a recherché dinner. This sumptuous repast being provided by the company as an additional attraction.

In those 'good old days' of stable prices the tariff in the public restaurant on all Messrs Campbell's steamers offered as alternatives... for breakfast; Fish at 1/6 or cold meat 1/6... for tea, the same; dinner soup, fish, meat vegetables etc at 2/6... Scotch whisky at 4d... gin at 3d brandy at 4d and 6d and rum at 4d. Motor cycles could be conveyed for a return fare of 2/-. For passengers who made frequent use of the services provided by these steamers coupon books were provided in limited numbers enabling the holder to travel at half the ordinary saloon fare. Also, in conjunction with the S & D Railway, excursions were arranged from time to time whereby passengers from as far away as Wimborne in Dorset and all intermediate stations could be brought by rail to Burnham and enjoy a Channel trip to Ilfracombe, calling at Minehead, Lynmouth, and Woolacombe for the moderate return fares of (sea trip) fore cabin 2/6 saloon 3/6, or Minehead only 2/-. At one time or another most of Messrs Campbell's ships called at Burnham including *Ravenswood, Waverley, Cambria, Britannia, Lady Margaret,* and *Bonnie Doone.*

Campbell's decision to cease calling at Burnham served however to bring matters to a head and considerable pressure was brought to bear on the Town Council to take some positive action in the matter. Speaking at the time of his company's decision to terminate the service to and from Burnham, Captain Alex Campbell stated that it was due entirely to the problems created by the silting up of the Gut which made both entering and leaving the mooring channel a most difficult operation. At the same time the Barry Railway Co. also announced their decision to make no further calls at Burnham until either a new pier was constructed or the existing jetty restored and the mooring channel cleared of silt. The situation at Weston super Mare, Clevedon, Minehead and the South Wales ports was very much different from that at Burnham as these places possessed piers as distinct from a solid stone jetty and where at most times the water was deep enough for vessels to come alongside with a minimum of manoeuvring and where the necessity to be continually dredging a mooring channel did not arise.

The 'gut,' with piles on either side, where the steamers moored alongside the jetty. The rowing boat helps to illustrate the width of the channel and the height of the piles.

The timbers projecting from the beach in 2010 are the remains of the reservoirs that stored the sea water used to flush out the silt from the gut.

The exclusion of Burnham from their ports of call by both P.&A. Campbell and the Barry Railway Co. was a sad blow to the town and what course should be taken to encourage their return was a matter that was to exercise the minds of ordinary townsfolk, businessmen, and councillors alike, particularly so, as the jetty now belonged to the town, the Burnham council having been obliged to purchase it together with some adjoining land from the Midland Railway Co. in October **1905** after the railway company had applied for parliamentary powers to sell, lease, or otherwise dispose of it. Being only too well aware of how difficult it had always been for steamers to moor at the

jetty their idea of removing it altogether and constructing a real pier with adequate facilities for pleasure steamers met with a fair measure of support and arising from this in March **1906** an enquiry was held by the Board of Trade to hear the views and opinions of those proposing and apposing the scheme.

The Barry Railway Co. had undertaken to give the proposed scheme financial support to the extent of investing some £16,000 but stated that in consideration of this they would require to have one representative on the board of directors but P. & A. Campbell objected contending that this in effect would mean that the Barry Railway Co. would virtually control the pier. The outcome of the enquiry was that a provisional order was made by the Board of Trade in favour of the new pier scheme following which a private company was set up to act in the capacity of a holding company. It became known as the Burnham Investment Syndicate Ltd and its principal functions were to provide preliminary plans and specifications together with estimated costs for a new pier and to sponsor an Act of Parliament confirming the provisional order made by the Board of Trade and cited as the Burnham Pier and Harbour Order Confirmation (No. 63) Act **1906**, and having achieve this object to supervise the formation of a Pier Company who would be empowered to raise the necessary capital for the construction of the new pier. Almost a year later in February **1907** an article in the local press headed, 'The Burnham Pier Bill', stated, "The progress of this Bill which has now been introduced into Parliament is well assured". Later, in the following March at a special committee meeting of the House of Lords the main objection raised by P. & A. Campbell regarding the Barry Railway Co.'s interest in the new pier scheme was overruled leaving the way clear for the formation of the Burnham Pier Company. The authorised capital of the company was £20,000 of which the Barry Railway Co. had earlier undertaken to provide £16,000. This, however, never materialised because of the objection raised by their shareholders that the directors had exceeded their authority.

The fact that this support was not then forthcoming did not affect the outcome of the issue because Baring Brothers the merchant bankers had expressed their willingness to proved sufficient finance to cover the projected scheme and their offer to do so was provisionally accepted by the Burnham Council as an interested party. After completion of the necessary formalities the company then became owners of the jetty, the council having disposed of it to them for a very low figure.

The preliminary drawings and specifications which had already been drawn up were the work of

Mr Ernest McKaig who had been the resident engineer when the Birnbeck Pier at Weston super Mare was constructed. His illustration of the proposed pier was published in the *Burnham Gazette and Somerset Advertiser* of 5 May **1906**.

In spite of all the apparent enthusiasm and hard work put into the scheme it, sadly, never came to fruition. Tuesday 24 August **1909** was the last occasion on which any steamer called at Burnham jetty for the sole purpose of discharging and taking on passengers when the Barry Railway Co.'s steamer *Gwalia* called on her way to Lynmouth and Ilfracombe, and after landing a large number of passengers from Wales took on a similar number from Burnham. A great deal of excitement was caused in the town and people went in crowds to the esplanade to see this, by then, unusual sight. Being unable to come completely alongside because of silt in the mooring channel she nosed in at the end of the jetty and passengers were obliged to scramble aboard over the bows. It was a rainy day and anything but favourable for a pleasure trip and when returning that evening passengers were brought ashore in boats in the presence of another large crowd.

During the following November all the wood mooring posts on either side of the jetty were cut down to the level of the stonework, but those standing independently some 65 feet to the south were left as originally erected for a further 21 years serving as a relic from and as a reminder of a less sophisticated age when most people took their holidays at home and when they really did 'Love to be beside the sea side'. These piles, used for hauling off vessels from the side of the jetty, were removed in **1930** about the time that the Marine Lake was constructed.

It was not long after this, that the 'Cathedral' was removed. Cathedral was a name bestowed by the locals on a disused railway carriage which stood on a corner of the station field opposite the top of the jetty. It had been given by Mr Salisbury, owner of the Belmont, to provide shelter for a group of local salts, popularly referred to as the 'Pier Head Rangers' who regularly foregathered at the top of the jetty.

Pier Head Rangers in front of the Cathedral.

Although, initially, the maritime traffic from Burnham was mixed, passengers, goods and livestock which tailed off into a sporadic passenger trade, that of Highbridge was only ever commercial. The bulk of the trade being the import of timber, slate, coal and possibly salt; locally made bricks and tiles being the principal outgoing commodity.

Highbridge wharf with ships alongside.

View from Queen's / Reed's Arms looking S (early 1930s) showing new sea front, with Marine Lake on R, and 'Cathedral' L of centre with fairground behind.

Highbridge wharf, number 2 steam crane.

In **1838** Edward Saunders is given as the owner / occupier of property near the junction of Market Street and Church Street although at that time the description would probably have been, more accurately, East Quay Way and the Turnpike. He lived in the house with garden which stood between East Quay Way and the George Hotel. On the other side of the road, on land later occupied by John Tyler's and some of the adjoining properties, was his brick yard, as was most of the land between the clyce and the original river. In Hunt for **1848** Edward Saunders is given as a Timber and Slate Merchant at no specified address until **1866** when he appears to have been succeeded by Cuthbert Ritson who is known to have had the saw mill in Newtown Road in addition to yards at Bridgwater. It is not clear whether Edward Saunders, the timber merchant is the same as the Edward Saunders the brick yard owner, although it is highly likely as many business proprietors at that time had more than one iron in the fire. Neither is it known for certain, where his timber yard was located. It is possible that the site on the corner of East Quay Way, being not particularly large was a sales yard for both bricks and timber sourced from elsewhere: some, if not all coming from his Bridgwater yard and his brick works on the other side of the river along the Clyce.

The rise and fall of the port of Highbridge followed a fairly straightforward course which would have been matched by many similar small ports throughout the country. From a convenient place to moor up for loading and off loading to the establishment of the first fairly basic wharfs, the relatively small east wharf, belonging to the Bristol and Exeter Railway, on the southern side of Walrow, immediately adjoining the station and which was only concerned with the trans-shipment of goods to and from the canal boats. It had been bought by the railway

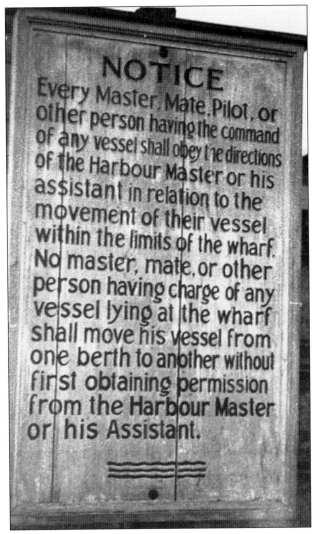

Highbridge wharf, notice board with instructions to masters.

Highbridge wharf, workers on sidings.

company for £7,000 in **1848** when the Glastonbury Canal Company got into serious financial difficulties, due largely to under-funding, faulty engineering and foolishly cut corners, Three years later they sold it on to the proposed Central Somerset Railway company in exchange for £8,000 worth of shares in the new company.

During the early **1860s**, with the formation of the Burnham Tidal Harbour and Railway Company and the extending of the line westwards to Burnham, the expansion of Highbridge was well under way. By **1883,** railway sidings and a wharf, complete with steam cranes had sprung up on the land to the West of the town; Newtown Road and the streets off it had been built to accommodate the workers of Cuthbert Ritson's saw mill and the Britannia Brick Works as well as those who worked for the railway company. Cuthbert Street and its former name, Ritson's Row, both derive from Cuthbert Ritson who was responsible for its construction.

Chapter 9

◇

People

ACLAND, SIR PEREGRINE PALMER, BART.

Sir Peregrine Acland lived at Fairfield House Stogursey. He was well known for his philanthropic works, being responsible for the building of schools in Stogursey and several other villages, as well as many other public works. He was also the prime mover in the establishment of the original West Somerset Railway which, initially, ran from Watchet to the G W R (Bristol and Exeter, as it was then) mainline near

Sir Peregrine Palmer Acland, Bart (by kind permission of Lady Elizabeth Acland Hood Gass).

Norton Fitzwarren West of Taunton. It was he who gave Burnham its first lifeboat in **1836**, prompted by reports of the loss of the *Margaret* with all hands and the partially successful rescue of many of the crew of *Moss Rose* in March of that year in a small boat, ill equipped for the task.

ADAMS, JOHN

John Adams owned the land between George Reed's Manor House and the Berrow Road. On it he built Brunswick Place. At the time of the Tithe Survey only those properties that became 6 & 8 Berrow Road

appear to be completed. It was he who in **1840**, after the loss of the *Mary* with all hands on the Gore Sands, wrote in support of a letter in the Taunton Courier castigating the Corporation and Merchants of Bridgwater for failing to support the maintenance of a life boat at Burnham. In **1846** he also wrote to the *Bridgwater Times* about the appalling level of poverty in Burnham.

ALLEN, JOHN

Owner and possible builder of the brewery. In common with many other employers of his time, he lived on the job, at Sandaway House, being thus able to keep an eye on his employees

BODGER, JOHN

For a time while George Reed and later John Fryer were living in Manor House they had in their employ as gardener one John Bodger by name who was then occupying the Elms Cottage. It was while thus engaged that John Bodger took over some adjoining land where the present Bowling green is now and in doing so took the first steps in a venture that was ulti-mately to take him and his family half way round the world. With his elder sons he worked this land as a market garden and later built greenhouses on it. The principal outlet for the produce from these gardens was a retail shop which he opened in Victoria Street. By **1880** the family were also occupying the living accommodation which formed part of this property remaining there for some years before moving to more commodious premises in College Street adjoin-ing the Railway Hotel. In addition to his ability as a gardener he had a particular aptitude for flower seed production, to the science of which he devoted a great deal of his time and effort.

Although the California Gold Rush of '49 had occurred some thirty years earlier the USA was still very much the land of opportunity to anyone willing to work hard enough, whatever their calling. With his thoughts constantly concerned about a prosperous future for his family in **1889** he sent his eldest son

John Bodger and family at his nursery.

William out to the far west in search of a suitable place for the family to settle. Santa Paula, not far from Los Angeles provided the ideal situation in William's judgement and so in December **1891** John Bodger with his wife and family left Burnham to seek his fortune in far distant California. Some indication of the esteem in which he was held by his fellow townsmen can be gained from the fact that as a founder member and secretary of the Burnham Oddfellows Lodge (The Pride of the West), in **1891** he was guest of honour at a farewell dinner given by members, a few days prior to his departure, when he was presented with an address on vellum and a purse of gold.

His initial hard work, specialist knowledge and integrity maintained by the company he founded have helped it to grow into one of the largest flower seed producers in the USA, with world wide connections. The company, which has been the subject of an illustrated article in the *National Geographic* magazine, still retains its links with Burnham through the local Horticultural Society to which it presented a number of silver cups which are competed for annually by members.

BRAITHWAITE, J. B.

J.B. Braithwaite was a stockbroker and great local benefactor. A man of strict principles, he was a Quaker and was responsible for building the local Adult School in Adam Street (now a carpet shop, **2010**). He subscribed to the temperance movement and was responsible for the construction of the Lifeboat Hotel and Coffee Tavern on the site of the Mason's Arms public house. His house, Blencathra had its own schoolroom for the education of his children. Both buildings were demolished to make way for 'Blencathra Court' in the last few years of the twentieth century. One of his gifts to the town was the

paddling pool on the beach near the church. It was given to the town as a thanks offering for the safe return of their five sons from the First World War and in commemoration of those who had not returned. It has been said that it was opposite the home of a family who had lost all of theirs. A bronze plaque on the sea wall records the occasion although the pool is no more, having been demolished by Sedgemoor Council in **2010** after it had been allowed to decay through lack of proper maintenance.

BUNCOMBE, JOHN

A surveyor and land agent in **1840** he held several official posts, both with the Board of Guardians and Board of Health. One such post was 'Inspector of Nuisances', a job title with intriguing possibilities. He was a member of an old Burnham family with descendants still living in the locality (**2010**) who have, at various times, operated garages as well as a road roller business and continue the family association with the automotive trade.

COX, JAMES (JUMBO)

A local 'character' as well as being a Town Crier of renown, being possessed of the 'Three Mile Voice', which, it was claimed, was the distance out to sea that sailors could hear his cry. A brick layer by trade, he is given as such in the **1901** census, when he was resident at 3 Abingdon Street. He continued crying until the late **1930s**, by which time he had moved to Victoria Street where members of his family had traded as green-grocers and game dealers since **1875** when Thomas Cox moved his business there from College Street. He featured on the front cover of the *Local Government Service* magazine for January **1939**[121].

James (Jumbo) Cox, crying at the opening of the South Esplanade; from a Pathé newsreeel of the event.

---

121 EDITOR'S NOTE:- I can remember him looking exactly like this, when I was a small boy , cycling slowly around the town on an ancient tricycle. His crying days were over by then. Even so, he still had the appearance of someone special and somewhat larger than life.

DAVIES, REV. DAVID

Best remembered for his lighthouse, the Round Tower, now (**2010**) part of Beverley Cottage and his development of the spa complex. He was curate to Dr. Walker King who was also Bishop of Rochester. On the death of the bishop in **1827** his curacy ended and he moved to Hampshire although retaining his connection with Burnham through his property and business interests.

DOD, CHARLES

A London merchant and ship owner who supported the proposals of the Burnham Tidal Harbour and Railway Company. It is possible, although by no means certain, that he may have been related to Henry Dod. Certainly the Charles Dod recorded on the family memorial as having died in Australia in **1865** would have been about the right age.

DOD, HENRY

Builder of the Colony. He is buried in Saint Andrew's churchyard. His memorial stone which carries the name of several other family members stands between the south porch and the west wall of Saint Nicholas's chapel. The names on the stone show him to be a member of an extensive and far-flung family.

DUPUIS, REV. THEODORE CRANE

The son of the rector of Binton in Warwickshire, he was born at Park Lane, London on 7 September **1830**, and at the time of his appointment as vicar of Saint Andrew's Burnham was only 37 years old. His period of service extended from **1867** until just before his death in **1914**. A family man, with his wife and two young daughters he gained and held the trust and esteem of the whole community that he served so faithfully for more than forty six years.

He was a man of considerable intellectual ability and while living at Wells was described by his wife Julia shortly after their first meeting in the following terms;-

> "A very slim man with a large forehead and fine features, marked eyebrows, above keen and restless eyes. No moustache or whiskers and very small hands and feet. A man accustomed to society, satirical, witty, clever and very amusing and observant."

A graduate of Pembroke College Oxford where at the age of twenty four he took his B.A. degree in **1854** and followed this two years later with an M.A. He was made a Prebendary of Wells Cathedral in November **1879**.

Rev. Theodore Crane Dupuis.

Descended from the Huguenot refugee family of Dupuis traditionally of Bordeaux. Although he was born in England he spent so much of his early life in France that he spoke English with a French accent, a trait that remained with him all his life; throughout which, he was blessed with that quality frequently referred to as charisma, radiating his personality to all with whom he came into contact. In those years of the mid nineteenth century young ladies of the upper middle class were obliged by the conventions of the day to lead extremely sheltered lives, which state of affairs undoubtedly contributed to the romantic fantasies that they created in their minds around personable young members of the opposite sex. Miss Julia Salmond, who was some years later to become his wife, was certainly no exception to this, for in the month following their introduction to each other in January **1862** she designed fashioned and composed a most artistic Valentine that is still preserved within the family records. This particular valentine was created in the form of a young Victorian girl wearing a crinoline, the style of dress so fashionable at that time and explains the references made to crinolines in the surprisingly candid 28 lines of verse concealed within its voluminous folds.

His lack of years at the time of his induction in **1867** gave rise to some un-Christian like resentment on the part of the neighbouring clergy by whom he was very coldly received, considering as they did, that the living should have been given to an older man. In spite of the frosty attitude on the part of these pillars of the local establishment, he stood his ground and they were obliged to abandon their prejudices and recognise the worth of the man who was rapidly gaining for himself the love and respect of his parishioners.

He was almost fifty when on 27 August **1879** he married Miss Julia Marie Bolton Salmond, daughter of the Hon. James William Salmond and Mrs Fenella Salmond, at the Old Church Widcombe Bath. The ceremony was performed by the Dean of Wells, the Very Rev. G.H.S. Johnson MA; his brother the Rev. Charles Dupuis being the best man. The honeymoon was spent at Burnham, where he had already spent twelve years as vicar. They were met at the station by a large crown, the more boisterous members of which removed their horses from their carnage and then themselves pulled the newly weds through the streets, thronged with spectators, to the old vicarage where an arch of evergreens had been erected over the drive entrance. To the cheers and the complimentary cries from the crowd, they passed beneath the arch into the old house which was to be their home for the whole of their married life.

He was known to be a kindly man by all who has dealings with him, however at one and the same time quite mindful of the need to maintain order and discipline, which he did but without the harshness which, at that time was so often a feature of Victorian middle class family life. His two young daughters, who, although enjoying a fairly sheltered life and happy childhood had their daily round of tasks and duties set out for them to perform. One entry in Julia's journal dated 4 September **1897** reads;- "My daily duties for week commencing tomorrow Sunday are, 1 waking prayer, 2 learn verses, 3 write verses, 4 wash and dress, 5 clean teeth, 6 prayers, 7 read bible, 8 family prayers, 9 exercise lessons am and pm, 10 breakfast, 11 retire upstairs, 12 lunch and tea, 13 practice on piano, 14 practice singing, 15 lessons, 16 dinner and prayers, 17 read bible portion, 18 go to bed". Idle hands as do mischief was clearly the order of the day in the Dupuis household.

Although in no way ostentatious the Dupuis lifestyle was one that required a substantially greater income than provided by his annual stipend. A coachman Bastin by name was employed full time and doubled up as gardener and general factotum. He was provided with a complete livery outfit for use on Sundays or any special occasion. In addition to women employed on a daily basis, two other women 'lived in'. The younger of these, the parlour maid, hailed from St Mary's, Isles of Scilly, and was often referred to jocularly by the Rev. Dupuis as La fille des Isles Imbecilles.

The enthusiasm with which he involved himself in so many matters concerning the Church for almost half a century and in others concerning the parish generally had steadily taken its toll upon him physically and the closing years of his life were marred by successive bouts of ill health. Writing in the parish magazine of December **1912** he said Three more years must see me retire and a new incumbent here. In the event, however, his time proved to be briefer than he had anticipated, for in May **1913** he was obliged to give up active participation in parochial duties, but this resignation did not become officially effective until 31 December.

At a ceremony held privately at the vicarage on the 7 November **1913** he was presented with a purse of £160. in gold and an album containing the names of over two hundred subscribers, other valuable gifts being later presented to his daughters Julia and Dora at a specially convened meeting of the Mothers Union. Later that same month he published an open letter to his parishioners in which he thanked them for all the love and affection shown him throughout his long vicariate and for the magnificent gift of money, explaining that being crippled and bedridden he was quite unable to attend a public meeting and address them in person. Christmas **1913** was spent quietly at the old Vicarage, it was to be his last. Shortly afterwards in February **1914** his condition worsened and he was removed to Bath where he remained under constant medical care until he died aged 84 years on 19 December **1914**. He lies buried in the churchyard at Brent Knoll in the grave adjoining that of his wife.

He was the last vicar of Burnham to reside at the old Vicarage.

FAY, FREDDY

A professional entertainer who produced summer shows on the beach and elsewhere in the town. His

Freddy Fay.

141

shows were both family entertainment and a family business and included his wife, daughter and son-in-law in the cast. After the war, his daughter, Erin, was the projectionist at the Picture House in Highbridge until its closure when she transferred to the Ritz in Burnham as relief operator. His grand-daughter continued in the family tradition running her own dancing school for a number of years during the latter part of the twentieth century.

FOWNES-LUTTRELL, MARY ANN RUSCOMBE

Married Henry Acland Luttrell in 1857 by whom she had an only daughter, Eva. She was responsible for

Mary Ann (Fownes) Luttrell.

the building and endowing of the church of Saint John the Evangelist at Highbridge in **1859** which led to the establishment of Highbridge as a separate parish in 1860. The foundation stone of Saint John's School which followed in **1863** was laid by her daughter, Eva.

GUNTER, JOHN

One time chef to George III, he retired to Burnham and lived in the house called Tregunter (house of Gunter) with his family. After his death, his widow and daughter continued living there until **1866**.

John Gunter.

HIGGINS, GENERAL E. J. CBE

Edward John Higgins was born on 26 November **1864** at 10 Church Street Highbridge. His father, who was a saddler and became a Salvationist, reaching the rank of Commissioner. In **1929**, after many years travelling over much of the world on his army duties, EJH, as he was known to his friends became the third head of Salvation Army and was the first to be elected to the post, his predecessor having inherited the position from his father who founded the organisation. He died in December **1947**.

HODGES, GUY (ta Guy Hodges & Sons)

A coal and salt merchant with his own ships under the command of his sons. They were probably 'trows', a type of vessel common, if not unique to the Bristol Channel, with flat bottoms which made beaching them for the purpose of loading or discharging cargo both easy and safe. The business was carried on from home at Wharf Cottage, Berrow Road which was located to the West of Ellen's Cottages immediately south of Saint Ann's drive, on land where the houses occupying the south side of Gore Road now stand. His boats were unloaded in to wagons on a temporary narrow gauge railway track which was run out across the beach when needed. He succeeded to the business of Richard Hodges who first appears at Highbridge around **1848**, moving to the Berrow Road site about **1861**, although the Highbridge yard was retained until the business ceased trading during the first decade of the twentieth century.

KER THOMPSON, HERBERT JOHN

In **1893** H.J. Ker Thompson, in partnership with his father the Rev. J. Thompson, purchased the Grove from J.B. Thwaites and transferred Hart House School there from Tregony near Truro, after their original premises had been destroyed by fire. On the retirement of his father he became the principal and remained as such until his retirement in **1906**.

He was a keen and enthusiastic sportsman. For five years **1898-1903** he was honorary secretary of the Somerset County F.A. and for twenty years **1917-1937** its President. In **1884** he took his degree as Master of Arts Cambridge and ten years later became a member of the Burnham Urban District Council, formerly the local Board of Health, and on which he served for 17 years latterly as Chairman retiring therefrom in **1911**, when he became curate at St Andrew's church.

KING, DR WALKER

Bishop Walker King of Rochester was blind. It was a congenital affliction, his grandchildren being likewise affected. Being totally blind it was necessary for a number of his duties to be carried out by his curate, the Rev. David Davies. He was led about by a boy who when an old man told the Rev. Dupuis that he used to get his ears boxed by the Bishop if he led him wrong. He was, in spite of his handicap, quite a colourful character in many ways and for many years while vicar of St Andrew's it was his practice to drive around the countryside in a coach drawn by six horses, which show of magnificence greatly impressed local people.

It was his wife Sarah who in the opening years of the nineteenth century built The Hall in the Berrow Road for many years the residence of the Holt family, the Burnham brewers, but now having a new lease of life as the Community Centre.

LOCKE, RICHARD

Born at Pillsmouth Farm on the 6 June **1757** to Richard Locke Senior., who was the second cousin of the Philosopher John Locke, and Hannah (née Dod). Young Richard was one of seven children, three of whom died in infancy. It was only by a lucky chance that he was not the fourth, for as a baby lying in a wicker work cot, he narrowly escaped death by drowning when during one of the tidal inundations that occurred periodically in those days the farmhouse was flooded to the height of the oven. This implies some negligence on the part of his parents because since the disasters of **1607** and **1703** it had generally become practice in this area to have cradles made of board pitched at the seams like a coffin so that they could float if flooding occurred

Eventually he took over the running of the farm, and throughout the period of time when it was under his control and management he put into effect practical demonstrations of his theories on how best to increase crop yields by making good deficiencies in soil composition; as a result of which the capital and rental values of this and later his other farms increased considerably. This applied not only to his own land but also to that of others who seeing what he had achieved at Pillsmouth and elsewhere had sought his advice and expertise to improve the production of their own farms. So effective in practice were the methods he advocated for restoring the productive capacity of the soil that it was reported that land which had been thus improved was being sold, in some cases, for as much as ten times its original purchase price.

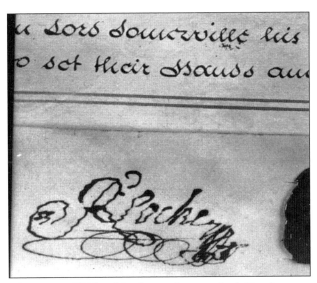

Signature of Richard Locke, on document relating to Pillsmouth Farm.

In **1754** when aged seventeen he took an active part in the affairs of the parish when he was appointed one of the four Overseers of the Poor. He was awarded a diploma in engineering and in **1755** at the age of eighteen, commenced his work as a land surveyor and valuer. In **1758** he accepted the appointment of Chief Constable of the Court Leet of the Hundred of Bempstone which sat, for many years at the Highbridge Inn.

Richard Locke lived to the age of sixty nine and throughout his life maintained a deep and lasting interest in all branches of farming, particularly in regard to studying and devising methods of improving the productivity of the soil.

Although perhaps less well remembered, Locke's work in establishing the 'Burnham Society' was as important to the community as a whole as his agricultural work was to the farming fraternity, not only because a greater number of people benefited from it[122] but it was a forerunner of the local friendly/benefit societies that came into being during the nineteenth century.

LUTTRELL, EVA

See under Fownes-Luttrell.

LYSAGHT, GERALD STUART. JP

The family originated in Ireland but moved to England during the 1850s where they became well established in the iron and steel trade, both in Britain and Australia. He lived at Dorset House on Clifton Downs until moving to Chapel Cleeve around the turn of the century, at about which time he had the Gables built, presumably as a second home.

---

122 See Chapter 4.

MAY, WILLIAM HENRY (PEGGY)

Although he was no entrepreneur nor financial bene-factor of the town, Burnham benefited greatly from his activities as the longest serving and one of the

'Peggy' May at his desk.

most universally respected Head-masters of the local National School, latterly Saint Andrew's. His Headmastership ran from **1880** to **1923** He was also, for many years, organist and choirmaster at Saint Andrew's church.

PARNELL, REV. HUGH

Vicar of Burnham from **1939** to **1970**. A man whose ministry was very much his vocation. Although he was a Prebendary of Wells Cathedral, he seemed content to live a simple life without any of the luxu-ries which are so important to lesser men. As a young man he played a mean game of hockey and was in the

Rev. Hugh Parnell.

county team. During his later years he could only walk with the aid of crutches. One of his great loves was listening to church music, both old and new. Geoffrey Beaumont's twentieth century Folk Mass which was based on the theme music of the 'Dam Busters' film being a favourite modern piece. His name lives on in Parnell Way, just around the corner from where he lived for so many years.

PEARSON, CHAS. D., 'CHARLIE'

Charles D. Pearson was a photographer who specialised in photographic views of Burnham and the locality. His distinctive hand written signature C.P. may be seen on many local post cards. He is known to have been working in **1911** as a card showing Highbridge church with its spire bears his signature although he is not shown as a photographer in any of the local trade directories at that time. His wife (Bertha) is shown as carrying out the business of photographer during the war years at 17 Cross Street, the same address given for Charlie from **1919** to **1935**. The Residents and Visitors list published in the *Burnham Gazette* of January **1911** shows Mr and Mrs Pearson as being resident at that same address although no occupation is given.

PIERSON, C. E.

Charles Emmanuel Pierson lived at 'Flesk', a large house with extensive grounds opposite the high light-house, which has since been split into three, with one end remaining as a house (the Cloisters) and the opposite end being subdivided into flats. He was a shareholder in the company set up to provide an elec-tricity supply to the town. A prime mover in the Burnham Foreshore Dispute heard in the High Court of Justice Chancery Division in which he was the plaintiff and Burnham Urban District Council the defendants.

The case arose after a severe gale in 1903 caused extensive erosion of the dunes between the Retreat and Colony estates and the sea shore, causing the existing boundary fences and the land behind them to collapse into the sea. When a request was made to the council for their surveyor to indicate to the landown-ers the line that a replacement fence should follow at beach level, they were less than cooperative. It was not until the landowners had erected fences on what they considered to be their land that the council acted, and demanded their removal. The fact that Mr Justice Warrington found in favour of the plaintiff was some-thing of a pyrrhic victory in that it established that landowners are responsible for the cost of protecting their land against encroachment by the sea.

REED, GEORGE

According to the **1861** census he was living in 'Church Street' (Manor Road). His household comprised a daughter, Catherine, a granddaughter, Julia(nna). A nephew is also listed as is a visitor. They were looked after by a cook and two maids.

The marble bust of George Reed was removed from the original classroom and now stands in a small courtyard surrounded by the new school buildings.

Bust of George Reed.

He did a great deal in many different ways for the inhabitants and town of Burnham, but this gift of the original school, was, without doubt, the most outstanding service he rendered the community in which he lived. Of him it can be truly said that in St Andrew's Junior School his good works live on long after him. He died in **1865** and lies buried in the churchyard at East Brent wherein may be seen his memorial.

He was considerably involved financially with the Burnham Tidal Harbour and Railway Company and the Burnham-Cardiff ferry services, being personally responsible for meeting the cost of a new vessel the *George Reed*.

RITSON, CUTHBERT

In **1861** Cuthbert Ritson is recorded as having a sawmill and timber business at Somerset Bridge in Bridgwater with a second yard near the docks he had expanded this business into Highbridge by **1866** where his mill and yard was at the top of Newtown Road, off which he built a number of houses to accommodate his workers.

He was the secretary of the Bridgwater and Burnham branch of the Royal National Lifeboat Institute, and lived for a time at Ravensworth House, immediately prior to its becoming a school.

THWAITES, J.B.

John Bolton Thwaites J. P. was a governor of the National School and at one time business colleague and friend of George Reed. He resided for many years at the property known as the Grove, and was one of the prime movers in the formation of the Burnham Tidal Harbour and Railway Company.

TRAVERS, (Major) BENJAMIN, A.F.C.

Better known as Ben Travers, a celebrated playwright in the inter-war years. He lived at Hillam in the Grove, a large house which he made larger. The house was badly damaged by fire after the war the only part remaining **(2010)** is the that which he added on. He is best known for his Aldwych Farces which took their generic name from the Aldwych Theatre where they were performed, in the same way that Brian Rix's

Whitehall Farces acquired theirs after the war. A large rookery in the trees that lined the road outside his home gave him the name for one of his best known plays – *Rookery Nook*.

A great lover of cricket, he wrote a book on the subject.

TRUEMAN DICKEN, WALTER

Local cinema proprietor who moved to Burnham in the **1930s** living at 'Westholm' on the Highbridge Road before moving to a house in Seaview Road. He owned the Majestic (formerly the Burnham Electric Theatre) and the Ritz (which he had built), as well as the Palladium in Midsomer Norton and several other cinemas, in Shepton Mallet, Bridgwater, Taunton and other places further afield. He was born in Buxton at the end of Victoria's reign where he had a high class

Walter Trueman Dicken.

stationers shop although he had been enthusiastically active in the world of cinema from an early age when the prime prerequisite was a degree of expertise in the mechanics of motorcycle engines. He acquired his first cinema at Uttoxeter. He was a founder member of the Cinematograph Exhibitors Association. With the advent of the talkies he embraced the concept with enthusiasm and lost little time in installing the necessary equipment in his cinemas.

Cinemas were the love of his life and he considered the Ritz to be his crowning achievement. He died in 1940, aged 57, a very happy man. Among the letters of condolence was one from his old friend Ben Travers.

Appendix 1

Time Line

For many of us who experience some difficulty in relating to dates in abstract, a number of dates which are of national or international significance, shown in bold italics, thus, ***1066 Battle of Hastings***, have been included to provide points in time relative to local events.

An upper case C suffix = Circa.

Date	Event	Comment
426	**Last Roman troops left Britain.**	
878	**Defeat of the Danes by King Alfred (The Great).**	**There was a sea battle in Bridgwater Bay. When returning their lands to the Abbots of Glastonbury, Alfred retained Burnham for the Crown because of its strategic importance.**
901	**Death of Alfred.**	**Aged 52.**
1066	**Battle of Hastings.**	**Accession of William I by conquest and death of Harold Godwinson.**
1292	Ecclesiastical records show that a church existed in Burnham.	
1314	**Battle of Bannockburn.**	
1314	Church 'rebuilt' by Bishop Brokensford.	
1315	Church dedicated to Saint Andrew by Bishop Brokensford.	
1336	A vicarage was ordained at Burnham.	
1545	**The *Mary Rose* sank in the Solent after a major refit.**	**The extra armament and crew made her top-heavy and seriously unstable.**
1588	**Defeat of the Spanish Armada.**	**With more than a little help from the weather.**
1672	Henry Rogers's Gift.	£2,350 the product of which to be shared unequally between the parishes of Burnham, Cannington, and Porlock. Recorded on a board in the church.
1685	**Battle of Sedgemoor.**	**The last battle on English soil, marking the end of the Monmouth Rebellion. It was followed by the 'Bloody Assize' where 300 people were executed and 800 sold into slavery in the West Indies.**

Date	Event	Comment
1688	**A son born to James II and his 2nd wife, Mary on 20th June.**	**Welcome news to the Catholic and royalist parts of the population.**
1688	**Landing of William Prince of Orange 5/15 November.**	
1688C	Names carved in beam at Stoddens Farm.	The same year as items 1 and 2 above.
1757	Richard Locke was born at Pillsmouth Farm.	6th June.
1773	**Boston Tea Party.**	**Which led to the American War of Independence.**
1780	Saint Andrew's Sunday School established.	
1797	Rev. John Golden's Gift.	£100 (a lot of money then) the interest to be spent on religious books and bread for the poor.
1798	**First successful immunisation against smallpox.**	**By Edward Jenner the local doctor at Berkley in Gloucestershire.**
1801	The Fox and Goose burned down.	Supposedly by the carelessness of a maid burning rubbish.
1801	The Clyce was dug.	A clyce is a drainage channel with a gate to control the outflow of water. The work was carried out by Napoleonic prisoners of war brought up from Princetown (Dartmoor jail).
1805	**Death of Nelson at Trafalgar.**	
1813	Hope Baptist church built.	
1814C	First National School established in Burnham.	
1815	**Battle of Waterloo.**	
1815	First lighthouse.	Built by Rev. David Davies on land near the church. Its lower part remains as the round tower at the back of Beverly Cottage.
1824	The Grinling Gibbons carvings given to Saint Andrew's church.	Dr. Walker King acquired them when they were no longer wanted in 1820, and passed them on to Saint Andrew's.
1829	The remainder of the Rev. Davies lease was bought in by Trinity House.	Arrangements were put in hand to replace his lighthouse with the minimum delay.
1832 1832	Two new lighthouses commissioned by Rev. Davies. Spa complex opened.	Designed and built by Joseph Nelson, an associate of John Smeaton Trinity House, who built the Eddystone Lighthouse. Reported in *Sherbourne Mercury* 16/07 and others.
1837	**Accession of Queen Victoria.**	**Aged eighteen.**
1837	Most of the East side of Victoria Street developed by this time.	
1838	**Tithe apportionment survey.**	**This was carried out across the country.**
1838	Gallery constructed in St Andrew's church.	This involved removing the N. wall and reconstructing it some 14 feet further out.
1840	**Penny Post inaugurated.**	**Because Britain was the first to use postage stamps, it was not necessary to state the country of issue – a practice that persists to this day.**
1841	Bristol and Exeter Railway reached Highbridge.	
1841	Wells Turnpike reached Highbridge.	
1842	Lucerne Cottage, Berrow Rd.	Later known as Puzzle Gardens Inn.
1843	Prew's Terrace, Esplanade.	More recently known as Kinver Terrace.
1843	Burnham Baptist church.	
1844	Custom House.	

Date	Event	Comment
1845	Proposal for deep water docks at Burnham, first mooted.	
1845	**Coca Cola invented.**	
1850	Conditions in Unity Place criticised in Board of Health report.	Its exact location is uncertain but it is believed to have been at the back of Victoria Street.
1850-1860	Catharine and Julia Terraces built by George Reed.	Named after his daughter and Granddaughter.
1851	**Great Exhibition.**	**Held at Crystal Palace in Hyde Park.**
1851	Burnham's first National School.	In a large room at Homebush.
1852	First sewers laid in Burnham.	
1853	Lott's Commercial Inn opened.	John Lott, the owner and first licensee was also a fisherman.
1855	New National School built by George Reed.	On the corner of College Street and the Esplanade.
1858	Somerset Central Railway extended to Burnham.	Later the Somerset & Dorset Joint Railway.
1858	Jetty opened.	The *Iron Duke* was the first ship to disembark passengers.
1859	Highbridge ceased to be part of the parish of Burnham.	
1859	Princess Street laid out.	
1860C	Steam Packet Inn built.	John Neck, given as licensee.
1860	Reed's Arms Hotel opened.	End of April. Pier Hotel opened about the same time.
1860	First Wesleyan Methodist Church built.	Still standing on corner of Adam Street and High Street.
1860-1866	Burnham Tidal Harbour and Railway Company incorporated by Act of Parliament.	Once again, deep water docks were proposed at the confluence of the Brue and the Parret.
1862	Locomotive works built at Highbridge.	
1864	Brean Down Harbour project.	Foundation stone laid by Lady Eardley Wilmot, 5 June.
1866	The *George Reed* and the *Myrtle* went into service on the cross channel run.	Both were screw driven.
1866	Burnham's first RNLI lifeboat came on station.	Called the *Cheltenham* after the town whose people paid for it.
1867	Direct link with Cork established.	Report in *Taunton Courier* 18 August.
1868	Ellen's Cottages built.	
1869	Town / Market Hall built by private enterprise.	16 November was a school holiday for the laying of the foundation stone.
1874	National School extended.	This was the first of many extensions.
1879	New Methodist Church built in College Street.	The old building continued in use as a Sunday School until it was sold in 1906.
1879	Alfred (High) Street extended southwards by this time.	This brought it as far as South Street on the west, and 'Tuppeny Tube' (South Terrace) on the east.
1880	Burnham Coffee and Cocoa House Company formed.	Their premises were at Sutherland House, now 53/53a High Street, on the corner of Cross Street.
1880C	Abingdon Terrace built.	The start of Abingdon Street, built in the first part of the decade.
1881	The old font at Saint Andrew's given to church at Horrington.	The incumbent at the time, Rev. Stephen Peppin was a friend of Rev. Dupuis and like him, a Canon of Wells Cathedral.
1881	The pair of houses later known as Oakover were built.	Originally on the corner of Westfield Road, other houses have since been built in its grounds.
1884	Osborne terrace built.	The second phase of Abingdon Street.
1886	Burnham Coffee and Cocoa House Company wound up.	At a meeting held in the Town Hall.
1887	**Victoria's Golden Jubilee.**	

Date	Event	Comment
1887	Jubilee Terrace built.	This now forms the east side of Jubilee Street.
1889	**Eiffel Tower completed.**	**Designed and built as a *temporary* centrepiece for the Paris Exhibition celebrating the centenary of the French Revolution.**
1890	The National School was further extended.	
1890	Clock installed in Saint Andrew's church tower.	Originally intended for Wells Cathedral, it was found to be under powered.
1890/91	Saint Joseph's School.	Built by the nuns of La Retraite in the convent grounds.
1890/99	Hudson Street built.	
1892	Baptist chapel enlarged.	A schoolroom was added at this time.
1892	The Seamen's Rest (the Cathedral) was given for the use of pilots and seamen.	Donated by Mr G. B. Sully of the Belmont, it was an old S & D railway carriage.
1893	Wilts and Dorset Bank opened.	Originally in Upper College Street, it moved to new premises built on the site of Alfred House in 1911/12.
1893	Hart House School removed to The Grove (Paradise House).	Their original premises at Tregonay near Truro had been destroyed by fire.
1893C	Ravensworth House demolished.	Ravensworth Terrace and Villas were built on the site, as were most of the houses on the N side of lower College Street.
1894	Mason's Arms sold by Holt Brothers.	Bought and demolished by J. B. Braithwaite.
1895	Lifeboat Coffee Tavern and Temperance Hotel opened.	Built by J. B. Braithwaite on the site of the Mason's Arms.
1895-1896	Inauguration of the 'Somerset Lass' horse-drawn brake service.	Operated by the Lifeboat Hotel, it ran between Bridgwater, Burnham and Weston super Mare, with occasional special outings.
1895C	First Campbell's steamer called at Burnham.	
1897	**Victoria's Diamond Jubilee.**	
1897	**First radio transmission over water by Marconi.**	**From Brean Down to Penarth.**
1897	Windsor Terrace.	
1897	Victoria Buildings.	See Appendix Two.
1897	The *Nornen* ran aground.	
1898	Sydenham Terrace built.	With the construction of more houses, opposite, in 1902, it was known as Coronation Street before becoming lower Adam Street.
1898	Cycling Club formed by Edwin Horrell.	Edwin was a fruiterer in Alfred St.. Not to be confused with W. H. Hor*rill*, a grocer in Regent St.
1899	Gardenhurst School established.	In the building to later become Oakover.
1900C	Pageant Society formed.	They performed historical pageants, often in the Manor Gardens or the grounds of Hart House School.
1901/02	Construction and opening of the Lifeboat Pavilion.	An elaborate timber structure on the corner of Victoria Street and Vicarage Street.
1901C	Victoria Terrace built.	This was the beginning of Lynton Road is now 5-13.
1902	**Coronation of Edward VII.**	
1902	The *Philip Beach* superseded the *John Godfrey Morris*.	She was the last lifeboat in Burnham that was 'driven' by oars.
1902	The Coronation bandstand and shelters on Esplanade.	Officially opened on 6 June.
1903	Manor House and grounds bought by F. Lucas.	Ownership was transferred to the local council later that same day.
1903-1904	Two more classrooms added to National School.	There was then, no more space left for further extensions.
1904	Naish House School moved to Burnham from Clevedon.	Like Hart House, its previous premises were destroyed by fire.

Date	Event	Comment
1905	Roads and streets were still, as yet, un-tarred.	A letter to the editor of the *Gazette* complained that the water cart was not visiting Oxford Street.
1905	Manor Gardens officially opened.	By Rev. Dupuis.
1905	Jetty sold by the railway company.	Bought by the Urban District Council.
1906	Electric Light Co. formed.	
1906	A new pier was proposed.	A design was produced by Ernest McKaig.
1906	Old Methodist church and Sunday School offered for sale.	Bought the same day by the local Unionist Club.
1906	The last of Campbell's steamers to call at Burnham.	
1906-1907	The National School was renamed Saint Andrew's.	
1907	The Foreshore Dispute.	Between the local council and various landowners on the seaward side of Berrow Road.
1907	Bowling Club green officially opened.	
1909	Glen Hilda estate developed.	St Ann's, Wharf Cottage etc. – Gore Road created.
1909	Avenue L T C formed.	Originally Croquet and Lawn Tennis Club.
1909	Last steamer berthed at jetty for the transfer of passengers.	The *Gwalia*, owned by the Barry Railway Company.
1910	Manor Gardens enclosure laid out.	This necessitated clearing the Brunswick Cottage site. Bricked up door and window openings may be seen in parts of what is now the boundary wall.
1910	The Grove laid out.	This land was part of the grounds of Hart House School sold off by Rev. Ker Thompson.
1910	The Tin School opened in Princess Street.	Intended as a temporary overspill from Saint Andrew's, it catered for the infant classes.
1910	Mission Church at Edithmead consecrated.	Universally known as the Tin Church.
1911	**Coronation of George V.**	
1911	George Edward Terrace built.	One of two built on Burnham Road.
1912	Burnham Electric Theatre.	Later known as the Majestic.
1912	Overhanging reinforced concrete Esplanade built.	One of the largest reinforced concrete structures in the world, at that time.
1912	Saint Andrew's Church Hall opened.	The last major public engagement of Rev. Dupuis before his retirement and death.
1912	New Wilts & Dorset Bank offices opened	Later Lloyds and then Lloyds TSB, built on the site of Alfred House
1913	Vicarage offered for sale on retirement of Rev. Dupuis.	Used for some time to accommodate Belgian refugees.
1914	**Start of First World War.**	**Also known as the Great War.**
1914	Hart House became a V A D hospital	Lysaght's Hospital also operated during this war at the Gables, later St Margaret's School, in Poplar Rd.
1914	New Infant School opened.	Next door to the Tin School.
1918	**End of the Great War.**	**Armistice signed at the 11th hour of the 11th day of the 11th month.**
1920-1929	Post Office built on part of Vicarage garden.	
1925	Police Station and courts in Jaycroft Road.	Foundation stone dated December 1925.
1927	Marine Cove opened.	
1928	St. Peter's church completed.	
1929	Old Court House demolished.	Shown on O S maps as Court Farm.
1929	Development of 'Board Estate' began.	St Andrew's, St Paul's, St John's. St Mary's and St Michaels were not completed until after WW II. Then came St Mark's etc.

Date	Event	Comment
1930	**R 101 disaster.**	**The airship crashed in October at Beauvais, near Paris.**
1930	'New' sea front started.	Running from the head of the jetty to Pillsmouth, the work included a third bandstand and the Marine Lake.
1930	The Philip Beach taken out of service.	The last RNLI boat that century. The old boathouse later became the local scout HQ.
1932	New Scout HQ opened.	Apart from the removal of the large front doors at that time, the building is little changed today (2010).
1933	Burnham and Highbridge U D councils merged.	Much to the annoyance of many Highbridge people and councillors.
1936	Ritz Cinema opened.	Built for Trueman Dicken Cinemas on the site of the Lifeboat Pavilion.
1939	**End of Spanish Civil War.**	**General Franco became President.**
1939	**Start of WWII.**	
1939C	Tucker's Garage built in Victoria Street.	Built on site of Ivy Lodge.
1943	Homebush bought by St Andrew's PCC.	
1945	**End of WW II.**	**Germany capitulated in May; Japan in September.**
1946	POW camps closed.	The one on Coronation Field was used to provide temporary council housing.
1946	Anti aircraft posts removed from the beach.	These were large concrete or timber posts intended to prevent aircraft from landing safely.
1946	First post war council housing started.	
1946	Burnham Cricket Club moved to new ground.	Gardenhurst playing field. Access was from Charlestone Road.
1946	Burnham Dramatic Society re-formed.	Meetings were held in a single story building that had once been part of St Margaret's School and has since been rebuilt as a bungalow.
1946C	Saint Christopher's School.	Moved from Rectory Rd. to the old Naish House buildings after they were de-requisitioned.
1949	Highbridge docks closed.	
1950/59	**Food rationing ended.**	**It was a gradual process, with bread being the last.**
1951	**Festival of Britain.**	**Apart from being a boost to morale, it was the centenary of the Great Exhibition.**
1952	New telephone exchange opened in Dunstan Road.	This was one of the first fully automatic STD exchanges outside London.
1952	Information Bureau moved from the Town Hall.	New premises were on the site of the old donkey stables adjoining Vicarage Chambers in Victoria Street.
1953	**Coronation of Elizabeth II.**	**2nd June.**
1953	**Hilary and Tensing reached the summit of Everest.**	**Although the feat was achieved at the end of May, the news was not released until Coronation Day.**
1958	King Alfred's School opened.	At that time it was a Secondary modern.
1962	S&D line closed to passenger traffic.	
1963	S&D line closed to goods traffic.	
1965	**Rhodesia (Zimbabwe) broke away from Britain.**	**Prime Minister Ian Smith made a Unilateral Declaration of Independence (U D I).**
1965	RC church of Our Lady and the English Martyrs.	Foundation stone laid.
1965	Holimarine, now Burnham Holiday Village, opened.	Largely on the site of Pillsmouth Farm but also incorporating one of the old clay pits.
1967	RC church officially opened by the Bishop of Clifton.	

Date	Event	Comment
1969	BUDC acquired site of Apex and Colthurst Symons & Co's brick and tile works.	The site then became Apex Leisure Park. The prime reason for this acquisition was control of the lakes to provide an area where local surface water could go when the height of the tide prevented it draining straight into the river.
1970's	Lighthouse Inn opened.	The only custom built hostelry built in the twentieth century.
1970's	Gardenhurst School went into liquidation.	
1973	Saint Andrew's School re-located.	Sited on what remained of the Coronation Field.
1974	Motorway approach road constructed.	Manor Farm was demolished to make way for the roundabout and other road improvements.
1974	Plans for Apex Leisure Park were submitted to the council.	
1980	El Nathan in College Street was demolished.	Work started on extending and improving Baptist chapel facilities.
1980	Marine Drive opened.	
1980	Old Saint Andrew's School demolished.	
1982	Work on Baptist chapel completed.	
1990	**Nelson Mandela released.**	**On the 11th of February. He had been incarcerated for 27 years.**
1994	*Spirit of Lelaina* entered service.	First BARB hovercraft, named in memory of Lelaina Hall a young girl drowned on Berrow beach two years earlier.
2007	Crown Hotel demolished.	
2007	Tucker's Garage demolished.	This included the adjoining shop and flat that had been a newsagent's.
2008	Crown Hotel site re-developed.	A block of fourteen apartments.
2008	A stage of the Round Britain Cycle Race ended on Marine Drive.	

Appendix 2

House and Property Groupings

Subject	Currently	Locale	Tablet reads	Comments
Abingdon Terrace	14/34 Abingdon Street	Burnham	Abingdon Terrace	First part of Abingdon Street to be built.
Alfred's Cottages	John Street N	Burnham		
Bertha Terrace	Off Market Street	Highbridge	Bertha Terrace	Probably built for railway or dock workers.
Brunswick Place	2/8 Berrow Road	Burnham		The name continued in use until the early part of the twentieth century.
Brunswick Terrace	As above	As above		This name replaced the above but not, it appears, as an official postal address.
Catherine Terrace	52/58 Esplanade	Burnham	Catherine Terrace in first floor cornice at ends of building.	Named after the only daughter of George Reed.
Chestnut Terrace	99/107 Berrow Road	Burnham		The name comes from Chestnut Cottage/Farm.
Clyce Place	50/60 Clyce Road	Highbridge	Clyce Place	Probably one of the first buildings in the road.
Daviesville	Church gates up to 51 Esplanade	Burnham		For details see Chapter Seven.
East Terrace	43/50 Huntspill Road	Highbridge	East Terrace 1879	
Ellen's Cottages	59/71 Berrow Road	Burnham	Dedication tablet over gate gives date as 1868	For details see Chapter Seven.
Elm Avenue	Across the end of Hudson Street	Burnham		
Frederick Place	1/13 Adam Street	Burnham		Appears on OS map surveyed in 1884.
Jubilee Terrace	E. side of Jubilee Street	Burnham	Jubilee Terrace	Golden Jubilee 1887.
Julia Terrace	59/69 Esplanade	Burnham		Named after George Reed's grandchild.
Kinver Terrace	Esplanade	Burnham	Kinver Terrace in cast Bronze letters on front.	Originally Prew's Terrace. Renamed when refurbished after WW II. The developer was associated with Kinver, near Birmingham.
Market Terrace	Off Market Street	Highbridge		Probably built for railway and dock workers.
Mayfield Terrace	Off Cuthbert Street	Highbridge		Appears on 1883 OS map. Probably built for brickyard workers. See Victoria Place.
Phoenix Terrace	Off Technical Street	Burnham		Built on part of WJ Pople's builders' yard destroyed by fire.

Subject	Currently	Locale	Tablet reads	Comments
Prew's Terrace	Esplanade	Burnham		Built in 1843. see also Kinver Terrace.
Prospect Place	Newtown Road	Highbridge	Tablet partly obscured by rendering	
Ravensworth Terrace	Off Oxford Street behind R. Villas	Burnham		See below.
Ravensworth Villas	60/62 Oxford Street	Burnham		As with R. Terrace, built on part of the site of R. House.
Richmond Terrace	13/25 Cross Street			
Royal Parade	25/30 Esplanade	Burnham		
South Terrace	Linking High St and Jubilee St	Burnham		Pedestrian access only, at front. Rear access from Ham Lane.
Southend Terrace	1/15 Oxford Street	Burnham	Southend Terrace	
Stanley Terrace	3/7 Cross Street	Burnham		
Summerville Terrace	End of Jubilee Street	Burnham		
Sydenham Terrace	16 / 24 Adam Street	Burnham	Sydenham Terrace 1893	See Coronation St, Appendix Three .
Vicarage Terrace	Esplanade	Burnham		Vicarage Court built on site, corner of Vicarage St.
Victoria Buildings	11/14 Esplanade	Burnham	1897 shared between heads of front doors of 11 and 12	Never finished. Should have been 9/14.
Victoria Cottages	Off Victoria Street	Burnham		Opposite entrance to old Vicarage.
Victoria Terrace	5 /15 Lynton Road Inc. 7a	Burnham		Appears on OS map 1902.
Windsor Terrace	44 / 56 Abingdon Street	Burnham	Windsor Terrace 1897	

Appendix 3

Street and Road Names

Name	*Also known as*	*References*	*Currently*	*Comments*
Alfred Place	Frederick Place Frederick St		1/5 Adam Street	
Alfred Street		Kelly 1861/1910 OS 1886	High Street	Alfred Street was renumbered circa 1900.
Saint Andrew's Street			Vicarage Street	
Berrow Lane	Hale Lane	OS 1902	Brent Road	
Brunswick Street			Berrow Road	Clearly took its name from B. Place. Whether it applied to all of Berrow Rd or merely the town end is not clear.
Bussome Lane	Newton Street	OS 1902/1935	Red Road	
Catherine Street			Seaview Road	Probably an unofficial name when Catherine Terrace was first built.
Church Street (Burnham)			Manor Road, Oxford St. and Highbridge Rd. as far as the Brewery	
Coronation Street (Burnham)		OS 1902	Lower Adam Street	NB. 17 Adam St still has 'Coronation House' carved in the lintel over the front door.
East Wharf Way			Market Street	
Fackerell's Lane			Alstone Road	
Frederick Place	Alfred Place Frederick St		1/5 Adam Street	This short row of houses did not seem to keep any of these names for long.
Frederick Street	See above	Kelly 1868		
Gas House Lane	Springfield Road	Springfield Road		
Gas House Street			Oxford Street	This was probably an unofficial name and may have applied only to the short length of road immediately S. of the Ring o' Bells that led onto the gasworks site.
Hale Lane	Berrow Lane	Tithe App. survey	Brent Road	
Hern('s) Lane		Tithe App. survey	Heron Lane	
Hodge's Cottages			Cottage Row	Like Chapel Street, a footpath linked it at one time with the Esplanade.
Magg's Lane			Pople's Bow	

Name	Also known as	References	Currently	Comments
Newton Street	Bussome Lane	Tithe App. survey	Red Road	
Parliament Row			Exact location uncertain	Referred to as Bug Alley in Board of Health report 1849.
Parsonage Lane		Tithe App. survey	Parsonage Road	
Pitmore Lane	Quaker's Way		Pillmore Lane	Linked Mark Causeway (B3139) with Bristol Road (A 38) until cut by construction of M 5.
Player's Lane		Current OS maps	Player's Lane	Originally the service lane for 62-86c Berrow Road The name comes from a family called Player who lived in a house and ran a nursery on land on the east side of the lane.
Prospect Place		OS 1883	12 – 16 Newtown Road	The name had changed by the 1902 revision.
Quakers Way	Pitmore Lane		Pillmore Lane	
Ritson's Row		OS 1883 1902	Cuthbert Street	Both names derive from Cuthbert Ritson who built the houses for the workers in his sawmill.
Sandyway			Burnham Road	So named for obvious reasons. It ran from the Turnpike to the Brewery and Sandyway House.
Southing		Tithe App. survey	Berrow Road from the Tri angle to Brent Broad, the parish boundary	The name comes from the direction of travel.
Sunnyside		OS 1883 various Kelly	Pier Street, N. side	
Tags Tail Lane			Love Lane	
Vicarage Buildings /Terrace	Daviesville		Vicarage Court	A short terrace between Vicarage St and Marine Cove. During the 1890s the address of the Round Tower and Marina House were given as part of V. Terrace.
Walrow/Walrow Terrace			Walrow/Walrow Terrace	The N side of Walrow is shown as W. Terrace as late as the OS 1902 revision. Until after that date, what is now known as Walrow Terrace was unnamed. An eroded tablet in the wall between 16 / 17 Walrow may have carried the name at one time.

Bibliography/Further Reading

Dumnonia and the valley of the Parrett. Greswell.

Sedgemoor and the Somerset Levels. Hawkings.

Dupuis Diaries.

Methodism in Burnham-on-Sea. Houldin, Arnold.

The Life of Richard Locke. F. Madeline Ward as an appendix to Collinson's *History of Somerset.*

Did Our Lord Visit Britain. Rev C. C. Dobson M.A.

Anglo Saxon Chronicle.

Kirby's Quest for Somerset.

Somerset Pleas.

A History of the Burnham Foreshore Dispute 1907.

Burnham and Berrow Golf Club 1890 – 1990.

Avenue Lawn Tennis Club 1900 – 1984.

Subscribers

Colin Abbotts, Burnham-on-Sea

Reg Barrett, Burnham-on-Sea

Mr and Mrs R. Bayliss, Burnham-on-Sea

Roger Beavis, Solihull

Lee and Katie Berry, Burnham-on-Sea

Jane Elizabeth Bradbeer, Burnham-on-Sea

Clive Brewer, Burnham-on-Sea

Royston J. Broom, Burnham-on-Sea

G. E. Brown MBE, Brent Knoll

John M. Bryant, Burnham-on-Sea

Patrick J. Burge, Burnham-on-Sea

Norman Butt, Burnham-on-Sea

Terry Chandler

Dennis and Kay Chapman, Burnham-on-Sea,
    Somerset

Frank Gordon and Lyn Chick, Highbridge

David Cook, Watchfield, Nr Highbridge

Jeffery Cook, Burnham-on-Sea

Linda Cook (née Turner), Highbridge,
    Burnham-on-Sea

Paul Coombes, Burnham-on-Sea

Julia Copper (née Ham), Burnham-on-Sea

Steve and Hilary Cox, Berrow, Somerset

Nigel S. Craik, Burnham-on-Sea

Royston J. Cummins, West Huntspill

Mr and Mrs D. Derry, Burnham-on-Sea

Alan Dobinson, Burnham-on-Sea

Vernon Draper, Burnham-on-Sea

Ian Dunbavan, Godmanchester

Graham Dunbavan, West Huntspill

Frederick Dyson, Burnham-on-Sea

Ronald Farthing, Weston-super-Mare

Jeff and Jeanette Fisher, Burnham-on-Sea

Forte Family, Burnham-on-Sea

Mary Fox (née Hawkings), Nottingham

Jesse K. E. Freeman, Burnham-on-Sea

The French Family at Electric House

David and Sandra Gifford, Burnham-on-Sea

Stella M. Goldsmith, Hove

Pam Haimes, Yeovil

Peter and Pat Halls, Burnham-on-Sea

Doreen Hauser (née Gould), Burnham-on-Sea

Pirie Hemming, Burnham-on-Sea

Margaret Herbert (Sister-in-Law of
    Bob Thomas), Frogpool, Cornwall

John and Evelyn Herring, Burnham-on-Sea

John and Lindsay Heslop, Burnham-on-Sea

Robin Hewlett, Burnham-on-Sea

Lesley Hewlett, Burnham-on-Sea

Brian Higgs, West Huntspill

A. J. Hill, Brent Knoll

Steve M. J. and Kerrie A. Hobbs, Hobbs,
    Burnham-on-Sea

Peter W. Horsey, Burnham-on-Sea

Trevor Howard, Burnham-on-Sea

Tony Hoyland, Burnham-on-Sea

Eugene A. Hudson, Burnham-on-Sea

Mike Hughes, Burnham-on-Sea

Joyce Hunt, Burnham-on-Sea

R. Hurford, Burnham-on-Sea

Russell Hurling, Burnham-on-Sea

Brenda Inwood, Thatcham, Berkshire

Margaret Janaway, Burnham-on-Sea

Carol Keen, Burnham-on-Sea

Grace Keen, Burnham-on-Sea

P. A. Kilgour, Burnham-on-Sea

Irene J. Klein, Burnham-on-Sea

Rosemary Lavender, Ringwood

Tony Lewis, Burnham-on-Sea

D. and T. Liles, Burnham-on-Sea

Mrs Marie and Mr John Lindsey

Jean Mahon (née Pittey), Berrow

Katharine Manchip (née Stone),
    Burnham-on-Sea

Miss Judith Marchent, Taunton

Bob and Pat Masterman, Burnham-on-Sea

Dale Matthews, Burnham-on-Sea

Shaun Matthews, Burnham-on-Sea

William and Brenda McAlister,
    Burnham-on-Sea

Margaret McLauchlan, Burnham-on-Sea,
    Somerset

Peter R. Merrett, Burnham-on-Sea

Arthur and Betty Miller, Burnham-on-Sea

The Mrs Milner Simonds, Burnham-on-Sea,
    Somerset

Louis H. Moreau, Burnham-on-Sea

Michael Newby, Burnham-on-Sea

Hilary Niblett, Berrow

Peter and Pauline Nicholson, Burnham-on-Sea

John Page, Burnham-on-Sea

Janet and Ron Parker, Berrow

Des Parsons, Burnham-on-Sea

Harold Parsons, Edithmead

Roger and Jacky Pearce, Burnham-on-Sea

David Pearce

Sylvia A. Pedley, Burnham-on-Sea

Marion J. Pittey (née Hawkings), Carnforth,
    Lancs

Robert Poole, Burnham-on-Sea

Mrs Ann Popham, Burnham-on-Sea

Rob Pudner, Burnham-on-Sea

David V. J. Rands, Burnham-on-Sea

Mr Barry S. Read, Burnham-on-Sea

John F. H. Richards, Burnham-on-Sea

John and Betty Roberts, Burnham-on-Sea

Alan and Zoe Ryder, Burnham-on-Sea,
    Somerset

Julian N. Scott, Burnham-on-Sea, Somerset

Basil J. Searle, East Huntspill

Thomas Albert Shellis, Burnham-on-Sea

Douglas A. Smith, Burnham-on-Sea

Timothy John Smith

Dennis A. Smith, Burnham-on-Sea

Mr and Mrs M. J. Smith, Burnham-on-Sea

Jim Spottiswoode, Burnham-on-Sea

Mr Martin Stevens, Burnham-on-Sea

Mr George Stevens, Tregynon, Powys

Stodden Farm Cottages, TA8 2DE

Valerie E. Stone, Burnham-on-Sea

Emma Stradling, Burnham-on-Sea

Terence John Street

John R. Strickland, Burnham-on-Sea

Terry Temlett, Worle, Weston-super-Mare

Paddy Thompson, Street

Sally and Robert Trueman-Dicken

Jenny and Alex Turco, Burnham-on-Sea

Monica Turner, Burnham-on-Sea

Kimberley Wainwright, Burnham-on-Sea

Peta V. H. Wake, Burnham-on-Sea

Colin H. Watts, Burnham-on-Sea

Joseph (Joe) Wignall, South Esplanade,
    Burnham-on-Sea

Mr J. Wilsdon, Birchington, Kent

Malcolm and Ruth Winlow, Wedmore

Rev. Graham Witts, Burnham-on-Sea

Mrs A. R. Wynn, Burnham-on-Sea